German Prisoners of War
AT CAMP COOKE, CALIFORNIA

Personal Accounts of
Fourteen Soldiers, 1944–1946

• SECOND EDITION •

JEFFREY E. GEIGER

Werner Blanck
Hans-Joachim Böttcher
Werner Gilbert
Father Franz Gödde
Klaus Hebel
Rudolf Hinkelmann
Adolf Kelmer
Heinrich Kersting
Georg Kroemer
Leonhard Reul
Herbert Schaffrath
Alfred Schmucker
Heinrich Schünemann
Helmut Wolter

Mechanicsburg, PA USA

Published by Sunbury Press, Inc.
Mechanicsburg, Pennsylvania

www.sunburypress.com

Copyright © 1996, 2018 by Jeffrey E. Geiger.
Cover Copyright © 2018 by Sunbury Press, Inc.

Sunbury Press supports copyright. Copyright fuels creativity, encourages diverse voices, promotes free speech, and creates a vibrant culture. Thank you for buying an authorized edition of this book and for complying with copyright laws by not reproducing, scanning, or distributing any part of it in any form without permission. You are supporting writers and allowing Sunbury Press to continue to publish books for every reader. For information contact Sunbury Press, Inc., Subsidiary Rights Dept., PO Box 548, Boiling Springs, PA 17007 USA or legal@sunburypress.com.

For information about special discounts for bulk purchases, please contact Sunbury Press Orders Dept. at (855) 338-8359 or orders@sunburypress.com.

To request one of our authors for speaking engagements or book signings, please contact Sunbury Press Publicity Dept. at publicity@sunburypress.com.

ISBN: 978-1-62006-750-5 (Trade paperback)
ISBN: 978-1-62006-751-2 (eBook)

Library of Congress Control Number: 2018934831

FIRST SUNBURY PRESS EDITION: February 2018

Product of the United States of America
0 1 1 2 3 5 8 13 21 34 55

Set in Bookman Old Style
Designed by Crystal Devine
Cover by Terry Kennedy
Edited by Catherine Amoriello

Continue the Enlightenment!

Contents

Acknowledgments vii
Introduction to Second Edition 1
Introduction 3

Chapters
   1. From Wehrmacht to Captivity 8
   2. Journey to America 32
   3. The First Weeks as POWs 44
   4. Organization and Management at
      Camp Cooke 62
   5. Prisoner of War Labor Program 83
   6. Everyday Life in the Camp 108
   7. The Branch Camps 176
   8. Auf Wiedersehen 201
   9. Epilogue 222

Appendixes
   A. Biographical Data 228
   B. Survey 229

Notes 234
Abbreviations and Glossary 255
Bibliography 259
Index 263
About the Author 272

Illustrations

1. Werner Gilbert in Derna, Libya, 1942. 9
2. Georg Kroemer with a village girl in France, 1941. 11
3. Helmut Wolter, spring 1945. 14
4. Alfred Schmucker in the driver's seat of his BMW motorcycle, Tunis, Tunisia, 1943. 21
5. The prisoners were thoroughly searched before being shipped to the United States. 30
6. A German prisoner receives water through a barbed-wire enclosure. 30
7. German POWs at an American camp west of Mateur, Tunisia, May 1943. 31
8. German POWs arriving at a port in England under heavy American guard. 34
9. A group of smiling German POWs after showering and delousing. 36
10. Change of address card for POWs, side 1. 45
11. Change of address card for POWs, side 2. 45
12. POW barracks at Camp Cooke. .67
13. Capt. Floyd Smith and Maj. Arthur Wojnowski. 68
14. Lt. John Harris, Capt. John Pellew, and Lt. Harold Wolff. 69
15. Company photo with Rudolf Hinkelmann. 70
16. Rudolf Hinkelmann. 71
17. Werner Blanck. 72
18. Heinrich Kersting. 73
19. Franz Gödde. 75
20. Herbert Schaffrath. 76
21. Hans-Joachim Böttcher. 77
22. Adolf Kelmer. 80
23. Heinrich Schünemann. 81
24. Klaus Hebel. 82
25. Individual Pay Data Record for POWs. 85
26. Instructional booklet cover for picking cotton. 88
27. Instructional booklet illustration showing cotton being weighed. 89
28. Alfred Schmucker. 96
29. Doris Bailey with co-workers Herbie (German POW) and Dora. 109
30. Leonhard Reul. 113
31. Company 2's soccer team at Camp Cooke. 115

32. POW artwork and crafts on display. 116
33. The theatrical group. 117
34. The POW orchestra and chorus. 118
35. Sgt. Manfred Lewinnek. 120
36. Certificate of Achievement. 122
37. Letter from Horst Schneider. 138
38. Canteen coupons. 162
39. POW company mess hall. 165
40. Kitchen crew. 165
41. The German POW cemetery at Camp Cooke. 173
42. Death certificate for POW Walter Mattick. 175
43. Aerial view of Tagus Ranch POW camp. 180
44. Front gate at Tagus Ranch POW camp. 181
45. The POW camp at Edward Ranch. 184
46. POW Nissen huts at Edward Ranch. 185
47. Camp Shafter. 188
48. A farmer and his POW work crew from Camp Shafter. . .189
49. Lieutenants J. D. Mitchell and Franklin De Groodt
    with guards at Camp Shafter. .191
50. A group of guards at Camp Shafter. 191
51. POW medical evacuees file across the deck of a
    harbor boat in New York. 202
52. Processing center for returning German POWs. 205
53. Former POWs board one of the special round-robin
    boxcar trains. 205
54. Earth moving and construction work at the former
    POW camp, Camp Cooke. 223

Tables

1. American Commanding Officers at POW Camp,
   Camp Cooke. 64
2. German POWs initially buried at Camp Cooke 174
3. Camp Cooke's POW Detachments (Branch Camps) 177

Maps

1. The main cantonment area of Camp Cooke and the
   POW camp 65
2. The POW camp at Camp Cooke 66

Acknowledgments

THIS BOOK would not have been possible without the generosity and enthusiasm of the former POWs whose experiences and photographs in the Wehrmacht and as prisoners of war fill these pages. Thank you Werner Blanck, Hans Joachim Böttcher, Werner Gilbert, Father Franz Gödde, Klaus Hebel, Rudolf Hinkelmann, Adolf Kelmer, Heinrich Kersting, Georg Kroemer, Leonhard Reul, Herbert Schaffrath, Alfred Schmucker, Heinrich (Henry) Schünemann, and Helmut Wolter.

Over a period of about three years, I conducted letter interviews with each of these men and compiled their accounts into a narrative. Since most of the participants had written to me in German, I am deeply indebted to my translator, John G. Schmid. He spent countless hours carefully ensuring that everything he translated was precise in meaning and tone.

Special thanks are also due to Mr. Lüdtke of the Deutsche Dienststelle (WASt), the military records center in Berlin, Germany, for his unwavering assistance in locating almost all the former POWs interviewed for this book.

My profound gratitude also goes out to Tony Armas, Ray and Doris Bailey, Helene De Groodt (the widow of Franklin T. De Groodt), Curtis E. Fahnert Jr., Raymond Feinberg, George Foth, Helmut Fritzsche, Anne Hurwitz (the daughter of Manfred Lewinnek), Heinrich Isedor, John T. Pellew, Hans Rosenthal, and Spencer B. Stallings for sharing with me their recollections, documents, and in some instances, photographs of Camp Cooke and its branch camps.

I am also grateful to Mr. C. A. Carlson, former manager at the Johns-Manville plant in Lompoc, for telling me about the POW strike at the facility in December 1944.

The following individuals provided information about the branch camps: Manuel Faria Jr. and his sister Mary Ann Faria Silva, Don Gilkey, Don MacMillan, and Mr. A. E. Panetta for the camps at Corcoran and Tipton; William E. Schneider and Robert E. Steele for the camp at Saticoy; Lisa Gavin, Kern County Museum, and Helen and Carl Sands for the camp at Lamont; Mr. Leslie D. Freeman and Elizabeth E. Hvolboll for the camp at Edwards

Ranch; Tom R. Hennion, Tulare Historical Society, for the camps at Tulare; Phyllis Outhier and Alice Reher, Chino Historical Society, for the camp at Chino; Dave Fraker and Candy Harper, Public Affairs Office, Naval Air Station, Lemoore, for the camp at Lemoore; and William J. Taylor Jr., for the camp at Delano.

Alice Hunter and Wendell A. Fortier of the Veterans Administration were of great help in putting me in touch with American Army veterans from Camp Cooke and in some instances their surviving family members.

The National Archives in Washington, D.C., and its branch at the National Records Center in Suitland, Maryland, were indispensable for official Army records and photographs. Another key information source was the U.S. Army Military History Institute at Carlisle Barracks, Pennsylvania. They made available to me their microfilm copies of the POW camp newspaper from Camp Cooke, *Der Lagerspiegel*, and the American Army newspaper from Camp Shanks, *The Palisades*.

The staffs at the Bakersfield and Tulare libraries were especially accommodating with back issues of the San Joaquin Valley newspapers. Also helpful were the Lompoc and Santa Maria public libraries, and the University of California (Santa Barbara) library. Information about the Army airfields at Lemoore and Rankin was obtained from Richard Gamma, Air Force Historical Research Agency, Maxwell Air Force Base, Alabama. Richard W. Crawford, San Diego Historical Society, helped me with maps to locate the area near the Tijuana River where escaped German prisoners Adolf Kelmer and Horst Stellbrand were apprehended. Finally, I wish to thank the staff at the Golden Gate National Cemetery in San Bruno, California, for identifying the ten German POWs of the twenty-five interred at the cemetery who were originally buried at Camp Cooke.

Introduction to Second Edition

MORE THAN sixteen million Americans served in the military during World War II. The surviving men and women of that war are now mostly in their nineties. Their ranks are rapidly diminishing, and according to the National World War II Museum in New Orleans, Louisiana, it is estimated that by the year 2036 there will be no living veterans of that great generation, which fought to rid the world of fascism and genocide. This sobering demographic shift is also occurring in the far-off lands of the other combatant nations of World War II.

As an example of this vanishing generation, more than twenty years after this book was first published in 1996, almost every person I interviewed for this story has passed on. Each letter that I received from a family member or friend brought the sad news of another death. As the World War II generation approaches their final chapter, I am gratified to have personally known those men and women who whole-heartedly participated in the preparation of this book, and to share with you the gift of their extraordinary wartime experiences.

I am also indebted to my publisher, Lawrence Knorr of Sunbury Press, for making this book available to a new generation of readers.

This second edition of *German Prisoners of War at Camp Cooke, California* smooths out the writing and includes additional information, anecdotes, and photographs. Some of the material came from the interviewees' letters that I received. In rereading their correspondence, I discovered additional anecdotal material that in hindsight is more interesting than my original assessment led me to conclude. The new material required new endnotes, or sometimes enlarging existing ones. In a few instances, I added substantive information to the notes to include the latest scholarship. Among the images added to this edition is a photo showing a relaxed group of POWs standing next to an American farmer and his children. Gustav Thielemann is one of the POWs in the photo. Having heard about my book, he contacted me from his home in Germany in 2008 and generously sent me a copy of the image. Thank you, Mr. Thielemann.

Other changes to this edition involved removing the gazetteer, one of three appendixes in the original book, and two poor-quality images that had been copied from newspaper articles. The gazetteer had become a needless addition. With just a few keystrokes, internet sources offer the same and substantially more geographic data than the gazetteer. Finally, two of the interviewees had occasionally, but incorrectly, referred to the POW camp in Florence, Arizona, as "Camp Hearn." The confusion and misspelling of the camp name originated after the prisoners were instructed to put "Camp Hearne" as the return address on letters they mailed. Camp Hearne, in Texas, was the central postal hub for mail to and from Camp Florence and probably from other small camps within that geographic zone. In this edition, the camp is called by its correct name, Camp Florence.

Courtesy of Heinrich Schünemann

Introduction

THE FIRST great wave of German prisoners of war to arrive in America came after the surrender of the Afrika Korps in North Africa in May 1943. Additional waves of prisoners followed with Allied successes in Italy and France. Out of about 2.5 million German POWs in Western Allied custody shortly before the end of the war, 371,683 were transported to America.

The decision to evacuate prisoners of war to the United States was made by the War Department to ease the burden of American fighting forces guarding and caring for large numbers of POWs. The prisoners were transported on returning ships and then placed aboard trains that delivered them to more than six hundred POW camps constructed across the United States, including Alaska. The camps varied in size from a few hundred POWs to several thousand. The larger camps, known as base camps, served as the administrative headquarters for a string of branch camps. Wherever possible, base camps were located on military installations. They used available housing and were fenced off from the main camp.

Camp Cooke was one of many military reservations to include a prisoner of war camp. The main camp was an armored and infantry training installation established on October 5, 1941. On March 31, 1953, the Army vacated the camp permanently and three years later transferred it to the Air Force. Since 1958, it has operated as a space and missile base known as Vandenberg Air Force Base. It is located about fifty-five miles northwest of Santa Barbara on California's central coast.

The Army activated the prisoner of war camp at Cooke on June 16, 1944. It typically housed about 1,200 prisoners, but occasionally the population expanded for brief periods when captives were shuttled in from other camps. The largest increase occurred a few months before the camp closed on May 18, 1946, when the population jumped to more than two thousand men. Camp Cooke also operated sixteen POW branch camps in six of California's fifty-eight counties. They were set up within a two hundred-mile radius of Cooke at Tulare (three camps), Chino, Goleta, and Corcoran (three camps), Shafter, Lamont, Tipton, Saticoy, Old River, Buttonwillow, Delano, and Lemoore. The

3

maximum number of prisoners recorded at Cooke and its branch camps was 8,700 on January 1, 1946.

Within California, Camp Cooke generally held the largest number of German POWs and operated more branch POW camps than any other base camp in the state.

During its first several months of operation, Camp Cooke housed a sizable number of hardcore Nazis from the Waffen SS and other units. Many of these prisoners, and like-minded troublemakers that arrived later in the camp, were transferred to segregated camps for known Nazi sympathizers. For the most part, the POWs at Cooke were soldiers from infantry, armor, and airborne divisions. Among them were men from Field Marshal Erwin Rommel's Afrika Korps, which had surrendered to American, British, and French forces in May 1943. A small number of naval personnel rounded out the military services represented in the camp. The prisoners were all enlisted men and varied in age from as young as sixteen to men in their fifties. By segregating officers from enlisted men at all the POW camps in the United States, the Office of the Provost Marshal General broke the German officers' grip over the lower ranks and made them more malleable to American control.

The Geneva Convention, signed by the United States in 1929, outlined the specific measures to be followed for the humane treatment of prisoners of war. Seeking to abide by the Convention, the War Department provided the prisoners with not only comfortable accommodations and medical care but also with recreational entertainment and educational opportunities. The "intellectual diversions" mandated by the Geneva treaty became popular pastimes in the camps. The Army broadly interpreted this requirement to fit with its secret reeducation program to "denazify" Hitler's legionnaires.

As authorized by the Geneva Convention, enlisted men were used to fill labor positions left vacant on Army posts by wartime demands. By 1944, the recruitment of American men into the armed forces was causing severe labor shortages in the private sector as well. Despite concerns from organized labor, the Army contracted out much of its prisoner workforce in areas where free labor was unavailable, or was certified in short supply.

There were problems in the camps, to be sure. Nazi groups intimidated fellow prisoners not to work too willingly for their captors and encouraged work stoppages. Other discipline problems included the occasional slacker, the making of moonshine, and escapes.

The Army also addressed the issue of fraternization between Americans and POWs. Although the Army prohibited such interactions, the close working environment between the two groups often led to a mutual rapport in which both captor and captive discreetly ignored Army orders. It's not surprising, then, that shortly after the end of the war when the Army imposed temporary restrictions on certain nonessential foods and canteen items for POWs, discreet bartering between POWs and Americans at Camp Cooke increased.

This book follows the military experiences of fourteen German soldiers who were captured during the campaigns in North Africa and Europe, and then sat out the remainder of the war as POWs at Camp Cooke in California. The story continues through their repatriation and ends with the status of each man. Their personal accounts are presented against a historical backdrop that offers broader context and perspective.

While translating and editing the personal accounts, extreme care was taken to keep the original intent and inflection of their words. With few exceptions, the events described in these accounts are typical of the situation at most other POW camps in the United States. In recounting their experiences as prisoners of war, some of the men relied on diaries they kept and letters they had written home. A few had also retained their official POW records, which often included education certificates, medical records, and job assignment sheets. Collectively, their accounts are significant not only for their historical value, but also for their rich insight into human interaction during an extraordinary period in world history.

When I started my research for this book in 1990, I set out to tell the story through soldiers' personal accounts and written documentation. Using the German camp newspaper, *Der Lagerspiegel*, and the U.S. Army's POW personnel roster from Camp Cooke, I had at my fingertips directories containing the names of six thousand POWs. Together, these documents comprised enough information about each man to develop a system for culling names. The roster was especially useful because it contained each serviceman's POW serial number, date of birth, military rank and organization, date of capture, and a column listing known affiliations with Nazi organizations.

I began selecting names from a cross section of German military units listed in the camp roster. Next, and wherever possible, I chose individuals who participated in POW camp functions or who had achieved notoriety in the camp because of their escape attempts. I reasoned that such veterans must have had strong opinions about the war and captivity, and therefore might also retain vivid memories, documents, and photos. For a slightly different reason, one of the men I selected was Klaus Hebel. Pressed into military service in March 1945, he surrendered two weeks later to American soldiers not far from his hometown. At age sixteen, he was probably the youngest prisoner at Camp Cooke.

In selecting the names that I did, I make no apology for deliberately omitting known Nazi party members, as well as men from the SS or *Schutzstaffel*. Despite the passage of more than seventy years since the end of war, these people have no sense of guilt or remorse for the monstrosities of the Holocaust, or for the unimaginable suffering and death of millions of other victims of Nazi aggression. Given this fact, I felt it would be impossible to trust the historicity of anything these "*Ewig Gestrigen*" (Old order people) might have to say.

The selection of names was made considerably more difficult when a particular individual that I had chosen also served in organizations such as the Hitler Youth (*Hitlerjugend*, HJ) and the National Socialist Motor Corps (*Nationalsozialistisches Kraftfahrkorps*, NSKK), or in the sole and compulsory labor organization permitted in Nazi Germany, the German Labor Front (*Deutsche Arbeitsfront*, DAF). Since many, if not most, German youth were involved in the HJ, disqualification from the book based solely on juvenile organizational membership seemed pointless. In making this statement, I don't want to give the impression that as a group they were mere boy scouts. Among them were fanatical Nazis and some died fighting for their Führer. Apart from their service in the Wehrmacht, two of the fourteen former POWs were reportedly members of the NSKK and DAF. As functional entities of the Nazi government, both organizations existed for the benefit of National Socialism.

After the initial publication of this book in 1996, I traveled to Germany later that year to meet for the first time most of the interviewees and to give each of them a copy of the book. All the men were extremely welcoming and invited me into their homes where I often met with family members eager to practice their English. One encounter, however, was inexplicably strange. While driving through the city with one of the interviewees, he enthusiastically pointed out a couple of landmarks including a Jewish synagogue. Although I smiled and said something like, "Very interesting," I couldn't help wondering why he chose to identify the synagogue. Back at his apartment, and after a couple of beers, he mentioned that between 1940 and 1941 he was a member of the National Socialist German Students' League (*Nationalsozialistischer Deutscher Studentenbund,* USDStB). This organization was a division of the Nazi party and embraced the National Socialist worldview. His information came to light after he gave me a copy of his hearing decision, issued under the March 5, 1946 Law for Liberation from National Socialism and Militarism that every German was subject to in an effort to denazify the country. His certificate, which is dated November 7, 1947, cleared the interviewee of Nazi culpability and was an important document for Germans seeking meaningful employment in postwar Germany. My reason for mentioning this disclosure is to show by example the omnipresence of National Socialism in Germany during the Hitler era. Because the overwhelming majority of the population had enthusiastically embraced and internalized Nazi ideology, it resulted in the setting up of a postwar government apparatus to scrutinize the population and not just the deranged criminal leadership for culpable crimes.

The fourteen former POWs whose experiences appear in this book represent about 10 percent of the total number of individuals I attempted to locate. Many of the others could not be found or had passed away. Some declined to be interviewed for reasons of their own. Others wanted to help, but recollections about internment at Camp Cooke had become too hazy. Still, the narratives that follow give an accurate presentation of life as a German prisoner of war in America, with particular reference to Camp Cooke.

CHAPTER 1

From Wehrmacht to Captivity

ON SEPTEMBER 1, 1939, Germany plunged the world into the Second World War with its invasion of Poland. By October 6, Poland had fallen. During the next seven months, French and British forces kept watch for the second phase of the German onslaught expected to hit the Western Front. But except for occasional border incursions, an uneasy stillness had settled over the front.[1]

The silence ended abruptly on May 10, 1940, with airborne and mechanized German forces smashing through the Netherlands, Belgium, and into France. The defenders were quickly overwhelmed and within weeks had capitulated. France, the last to fall, signed an armistice on June 22. Pushed back to the channel port at Dunkirk, the British evacuated some 338,000 Allied soldiers to Great Britain. The battle for France was over.[2]

Confident of victory in the west, Adolf Hitler turned his attention toward North Africa, where his faltering ally, Italy, was losing to the British. In February 1941, Hitler sent his Afrika Korps to Tunisia, under the command of Erwin Rommel. Then, ignoring the Russo-German Non-Aggression Treaty signed in 1939, Germany invaded Russia on June 22, 1941. At first, the attack proceeded as planned. But by the end of the year, with the harsh winter setting in and the Russian counteroffensive beginning, German troops were fighting for their very lives. The only bright spot in the Nazi battle plan was in North Africa where the Germans and British were continuing a seesaw battle across the Egyptian-Libyan desert.[3]

World War II was already two years old in Europe when the Japanese attacked Pearl Harbor in Hawaii on December 7, 1941. Slow at first to respond, the United States eventually struck back with a vengeance, first at the Imperial Navy and the occupied islands, and later at the Japanese homeland, with bombing raids that culminated in the destruction of Hiroshima and Nagasaki by two atomic bombs in August 1945. But until that time, the bulk of America's industrial might was directed against Nazi Germany. As early as 1942, the United States began planning with its Allies,

Operation Torch, an amphibious assault against Axis forces in North Africa. This operation would net the first massive wave of German prisoners of war and would be followed by similar landings in Europe.⁴

The opening assault came on November 8, 1942, when American and British forces began a series of landings in French North Africa from Casablanca to Oran and Algiers. Despite stubborn resistance, the force moved eastward, ending with the capture of more than 250,000 Axis soldiers in Tunisia on May 13, 1943. The prisoners were put into temporary collection camps before being moved to one of two embarkation points—Casablanca in Morocco, or Oran in Algeria. There they waited in reception centers for the returning Liberty and cargo ships that would take them to America, Canada, or Great Britain.⁵

WERNER GILBERT

I joined the Luftwaffe on November 1, 1938, and was assigned to the 841st Regiment, 2nd Battery, Light Antiaircraft Unit (*Leichte Flakabteilung*). I remained with this unit for my entire military service and was trained in range-finding and motor vehicle driving. When the campaign in the west began on May 10, 1940, I was sent to the Netherlands and then to Belgium. I remember that when we entered Belgium, we were under heavy artillery fire. We discovered that someone using a blinking signal light in a nearby church steeple was revealing our position. We immediately destroyed the signal system and turned the priest over to our military police. Later, my unit was transferred to Dieppe, France, for occupation duty.

On February 2, 1941, we embarked on a twelve-day journey that first took us to Sicily, Italy, by train, and then by airplane to Tripoli, Libya. In North Africa, the battles were always fought fairly and with a certain amount of chivalry. For instance, between the fronts the wounded were cared for and the dead were buried. When we buried our best fighter pilot, Hans-Joachim

Werner Gilbert in Derna, Libya, 1942.

Marseille, the English asked for and received a three-hour truce so they could send three Blenheim bombers overhead to drop a wreath on the grave. The cease-fire ended a half hour later.

While in North Africa, I was stationed at Tripoli, Derna, Tobruk, and El Alamein. When the war turned badly for us, we gradually retired to Cap Bon, Tunisia, and surrendered to the English on May 11, 1943. While in British custody, a group of Moroccan troops attempted to massacre us. Fortunately for us, the British were determined to spare the lives of their prisoners and fired their weapons to disperse the angry crowd that had formed. Probably in part for our own safety, we were taken to Constantine, Algeria, and handed over to the Americans in June 1943.

GEORG KROEMER

I was born in the small Silesian village of Komeise on April 12, 1913. I was just under a year old when my mother became a widow at age twenty-six with two small children, my brother who was two years old, and me. We lived on a small working farm, and sometimes visited with cousins, uncles, aunts, and our grandmother who lived on a beautiful farm estate nearby.

It was a wonderful idyllic life that ended in December 1939 when I was drafted into the Wehrmacht and assigned to the 257th Infantry Regiment, 3rd Battalion. A short time later, I was sent to Normandy, France, and billeted on a farm with six other soldiers in Saint-Germain-des-Vaux, about twenty-five miles from Cherbourg. I developed a good relationship with the farmer who often invited me to dine with his family. In return, I would bring food from our field kitchen, including sweets for the children. We had become very fond of each other, and when it was time for me to leave for the Russian Front in December 1941, the whole family had tears in their eyes.[6]

Early in January 1942, we arrived by rail at a town called Vitebsk in Belorussia. We were assigned to barracks formerly used by Russian troops and had neither heat nor hot water. Everything was frozen solid, including the toilets filled with human excrement. Shortly thereafter we were trucked about fifty miles east to the town of Velizh, which at that time was still untouched by the war. We stayed in a clean, well-managed soldiers' home and were served tea by beautiful Russian women. We reveled in the warm waters of a sauna followed by massages given by young men using bundles of birch twigs.

Orders directing us to the front line cut short our respite at Velizh. Partially by truck, but mostly by very long foot marches,

Georg Kroemer with the farmer's daughter in Saint-Germain-des-Vaux, 1941.

we advanced to Velikiye Luki. Along the way, we were sometimes quartered in farmhouses. Without being ordered to do so, the residents of these dwellings always gave us the warm sleeping place on top of the gigantic tile stove. In addition, they frequently gave us honey. They were simple and generous people who usually had in the corner of their living rooms a crucifix and religious icons. Indeed, this was proof that [Joseph] Stalin with all his oppressive Communism never overcame the influences of religion in Russia. It is awful to think how much these people suffered when the German troops, retreating in 1944, exercised the scorched earth policy.[7]

At Velikiye Luki we replaced a unit of troops that had been at the front since the start of the Russian campaign in June 1941.

Those poor men had absolutely no winter clothing to keep them warm and suffered through temperatures as low as 30 degrees Celsius below zero [or minus 22 degrees Fahrenheit].[8]

Within a short time, we were engaging Russian troops who still occupied part of the town. Without tank or artillery support, we fought in pitched battles that seesawed back and forth. When the pressure from the Russians became too great, we reluctantly pulled back to Velizh and fortified our front by digging foxholes in the snow. The Russians continued to press the attack and encircled our unit. In places where they broke through our defense, bitter hand-to-hand combat ensued. During this time, we had almost nothing to eat. To satiate our hunger, we shot and ate our horses after they had exhausted their food. Although we occasionally received supplies air dropped to us from Ju 52s, everything collected had to be turned in and redistributed. Anyone caught stealing these provisions was ordered shot on the spot.

In February 1942, shrapnel from a Russian grenade ripped into my back. I was taken to a frontline aid station located in the cellar of a building that reeked from the stench of stale air and blood. To escape the pain and misery all around me, I fantasized about peaceful Velizh with its lovely tea-serving Russian women and the sauna.

Later, after our panzers had broken through at Velizh and captured the runway, I was airlifted to Germany. While recovering in the hospital I found out that the Russians later encircled the airstrip and cut my unit to pieces. For my service in Russia, I received the "Cold Cuts Order" (*Medaille Winterschlacht*) and the Infantry Assault Badge (*Infanterie Sturmabzeichen*) in silver.

By early 1943, I had recovered fully from my wound and was sent to Palermo, Italy, and then by plane to Tunis, Tunisia, in North Africa. I was assigned to Assault Battalion A27 (*Sturmbataillon A27*) and remained with this outfit until the Afrika Korps capitulated in May 1943.

Our captors were French Moroccan Berbers, the so-called "Goums" in Tunisia. They confiscated everything, leaving me with only one shirt, shorts, and shoes. I was sent to a triage camp at Constantine, Algeria, and later to a camp at Foum Defla, Morocco, that we POWs dubbed as "Camp Hunger." The guards were again these cruel Berbers, but also black Senegalese troops who in contrast were fair and warm people. Life in the French camps was extremely difficult. Hunger, typhus, dysentery, and jaundice decimated our ranks.

WERNER BLANCK

I enlisted in the German army on November 1, 1939, and was assigned to the 605th Flak Battalion. We participated in the campaign against France in 1940 and were redeployed to the Eastern Front when the war against Russia began in June 1941. During this time, I drove a truck delivering food from our depot to various field kitchens.

The Russian winter of 1941–42 was especially harsh. I tried everything to get away from Russia and to join the Afrika Korps. Happily, for me, my transfer request was approved and in the summer of 1942, I left Naples, Italy, for Tripoli, Libya. Halfway to Libya, British aircraft torpedoed our ship. Fortunately, we transferred from our sinking ship to an escort vessel, an Italian destroyer, without getting wet. We returned to Italy and back to Germany for rest and recuperation before making a second attempt to reach the Afrika Korps. This time we went by airplane and succeeded. We started with a Ju 52 from Athens via Crete and landed at Tobruk in October 1942. To evade enemy planes and radar, our plane skimmed the sea a few feet above the waves.

In North Africa, I was assigned to the 612th Flak Battalion at El Alamein, Egypt. I now drove a half-track with a 20mm antiaircraft gun on top. After an abortive attempt to break through British lines to Alexandria, the Afrika Korps began its retreat on November 3, 1942. In the ensuing months we were pushed back to Tunisia, where I was captured by British troops in May 1943. Along with many other German prisoners, I was taken to Oran, Algeria. After a few weeks, we sailed to Liverpool, England, where we changed ships and went to Halifax, Canada.

HELMUT WOLTER

My job as a commerce clerk at the harbor in Bremen ended with my induction into the Wehrmacht on October 4, 1940. I was sent to Denmark on October 25 for basic training and service as an infantryman. I remember the constant drilling and the long marches that sometimes dragged far into the night.

On June 22, 1941, the war against Russia began. My unit, the 490th Infantry Regiment [269th Infantry Division], was mobilized and sent to the Russian Front as part of the initial strike force. We were assigned to the northern sector and reached the outskirts of Leningrad by the end of September 1941. Throughout this time we were continuously in combat with Russian troops.

Helmut Wolter, spring 1945.

Most of our fighting occurred in open fields and forest regions as opposed to villages. In one particular instance, we encountered strong enemy resistance and sustained heavy casualties when we crossed the Luga River near Tolmachevo on August 27, 1941.

Just in front of Leningrad, we built solid underground bunkers and lived a relatively quiet life until December 6, 1941, when we were ordered into the forest south of Lake Ladoga. Here we experienced brutally cold weather with absolutely no shelter. Adding to the misery were constant attacks from Russian partisans who disrupted our supply lines. It was not long before the combination of partisans and weather were inflicting tremendous losses among our troops.

Suffering from frostbitten feet, I was evacuated to Germany for hospitalization on January 10, 1942. In March, I was sent to Heide, the hometown of my regiment, and placed in a convalescent company for light duty. In January 1943, I was transferred to Hamburg and assigned to the newly formed March Battalion for Special Details (*Marschbataillon z.b.V.* [*zur besonderen Verfügung*]), which became an element of the Afrika Korps. On January 17, we shipped out to Tunisia. While in North Africa, we came under the command of various outfits, depending on where we happened to be at the time. Our unit was designated March Battalion 27.

When our North African campaign ended, I was taken prisoner by French troops thirty miles south of Tunis, near Pont du Fahs, on May 12, 1943. Our treatment was extremely harsh. We were crowded together in unsanitary conditions and received inadequate food and medicine. Soon malnourishment and disease spread rapidly through the camp and claimed the lives of many German POWs. Our deliverance came in June 1944, when we were turned over to American troops at Djelfa, Algeria. The Americans treated us well and always provided sufficient food and drink.

RUDOLF HINKELMANN

As a result of the Munich Agreement of September 1938, my homeland of Sudetenland [today part of the Czech Republic] was annexed to the Third Reich. Although I was eligible for conscription into the Czech army as a Sudeten German, I volunteered instead for the German army. By joining, I was shortening my military commitment by nine months. I intended to get this soldiering time behind me as quickly as possible so I could return to the family farm in Mokrau, near Carlsbad.

At the military exam center, I filled out an eight-page questionnaire that asked everything about me, including my birthday, education level, and past illnesses. I heard here for the first time about my "Aryan status." Since it was standard practice for volunteers to have their pick of the service branches, I chose the artillery.

Stark naked, I stood in front of the inspection commission consisting of staff doctors and other officials. They examined me from head to toe and peered at me as if I were a young bull to be used for stud. I became very self-conscious and irritated by the whole affair. Suddenly there came a unanimous decision from the board: "You are not going to the artillery, but to the Waffen SS." Not knowing the type of unit this was, I declined the offer. They tried to convince me that physically I was the type of individual wanted by the Führer for his elite troops. I realized then the nature of this unit. Despite all their entreaties, I remained committed to the artillery. I even threatened to withdraw my volunteer application.

I was still standing naked in front of the entire recruitment board when a new decision was announced: "You're perfect for the Luftwaffe!" Now I was totally distraught. They wanted to make a pilot out of me. They again flattered me and commented on my nice handwriting. Finally, they offered me the Communications Service (*Nachrichtendienst*) and a promise to be garrisoned in Heidelberg. Since I had always dreamed about visiting that city, it was a heartfelt wish come true. I accepted their offer.

On January 9, 1939, I was assigned to the 33rd Armored Communications Unit (*Panzernachrichten Abteilung 33*) in Heidelberg. Our unit was part of the 33rd Infantry Division and was composed mostly of university candidate students and those with technical trades. When war broke out in September 1939, we were sent to the Western Front. In May 1940, we marched through

Belgium and into France. Shortly after the French campaign had ended, our division was pulled back into Germany and sent to army camp Baumholder/Pfalz. It was then reorganized into the 33rd Panzer Division.[9]

In the winter of 1940–41, we underwent rigorous physical exams to determine our fitness for the tropics. As a result of these tests, many new men were brought into the division to replace those who were weeded out. Outfitted in our new khaki uniforms, we entrained for Naples, Italy, in April 1941. Upon our arrival, we immediately transferred to ships. On Easter Monday, April 14, the convoy of eight ships, including three Italian destroyers, was on the open sea. Our air coverage consisted of two German Me 110s.

Because our convoy was vulnerable to attack from British air and sea forces, we were instructed for safety reasons to sleep on deck. We were on the highest state of alert as we passed near the British garrison at Malta around midnight April 16. By 2:15 a.m., just when the danger seemed to have passed, British ships and aircraft suddenly attacked us. In the calamity that followed, alarms filled the air while spotlights illuminated the skies, and everywhere were the flashes of gun muzzles. All around us large columns of water rose into the air while other bombs and shells more accurately aimed found their targets. Through the raging flames and explosions, we could hear the shrill cries of the wounded as one bomb after another ravaged our ship, the *Adana*. Along the horizon, we could see shooting flames erupting on other ships in our convoy as one transport after another broke apart under the weight of the attack. It was a horrible picture of ships exploding and men dying.

Three British cruisers and several destroyers were visible under a clear moonlit sky. Overhead was the droning sound of enemy aircraft. Although the front of our ship was burning, the enemy continued to press the attack. Finally, our adversary turned away.

By dawn, the ocean around us was filled with debris as well as comrades fighting for their lives. Sadly, we were unable to help them. About one hundred men, including myself, were standing on the back deck of the *Adana* when its boiler exploded and the order was given to abandon ship. The men rushed to get off the stricken ship and flung benches, tables, and wood planks overboard to serve as makeshift rafts. Each soldier was also wearing a life jacket.

At about five a.m., I jumped beside the ship's screw [propeller] into the ocean with two empty 20-liter water canisters held tightly beneath my arms. The disgusting taste of the salt water covered by a thick film of oil slowly sapped my energy. But the sight of numerous dead comrades floating beside me strengthened my determination to survive this ordeal. For a whole day, I drifted alone with my thoughts.

Just before sunset, an Italian ship came by and took us to the Kerkennah Islands near Tunisia. The next morning the few survivors of the 33rd Armored Communications Unit were sorted out and taken to Tripoli by three Italian ships. Almost our entire unit perished in the attack. Only twenty-eight radio operators survived this tragedy.

With us sank the German ships *Arta, Iserlohn, Agina,* and *Samos*. Also lost were an Italian munitions freighter and the three destroyers.[10] After a few days, we were taken to Tripoli where we formed the Fixed Radio Communications Center. We later followed our combat troops to Egypt, but were forced back to Tripoli where I was captured by New Zealand forces in the area of Ariana, near Tunis, on May 8, 1943.

During the campaign in North Africa, we were repeatedly warned never to be taken prisoner by the New Zealanders. We were told they would cut the throat of every POW. You can imagine the terror that I felt when I fell into their hands. My entire body was trembling, and in my mind, I could feel the knife at my throat. Fortunately for me, things turned out differently. When I held up my hands to surrender my jacket sleeve fell back, exposing the wristwatch on my left hand. It was an inexpensive stainless-steel watch, but the New Zealander who took me as prisoner indicated that he wanted it. I held out my left arm and gestured that he should take it off my hand. He wouldn't take it. Instead, he had me remove the watch and hand it to him. The soldier then took me to his jeep, where he rustled through his knapsack and gave me six or eight packs of English "Gold Flake" cigarettes. With that exchange, I was well compensated for my watch. Along with a group of other German POWs, I was handed over to the English and placed in a POW collection camp.

After about two or three weeks, we boarded railroad cars that took us to Camp 210 near Algiers. It was a large camp with more than ten thousand POWs guarded by English troops. Several weeks later we were transported to an American-operated camp at Oran. Guarding us during the train ride were French Foreign Legionnaires.

LEONHARD REUL

I grew up in the small village of Krummennaab, about twenty-five miles southeast of Bayreuth. My career as a bank clerk was only four months old when in 1941, at the age of seventeen, I was called into the National Labor Service (*Reichsarbeitsdienst*). The RAD, as we called it, was a compulsory organization composed mainly of young men who were considered unaccustomed to hard labor, the so-called "pencil sharpeners." At that time the RAD was not a military organization.

Immediately following my service in the RAD, I was drafted into the army in the spring of 1942. The war against the Soviet Union had drained Germany's manpower, and every young recruit was needed to keep up the struggle. I was assigned to Headquarters Company, 9th Antitank Replacement Unit (*Panzerjäger-Ersatz-Abteilung 9*) in Büdingen/Hesse, Germany. After basic training, I was sent a few miles away to Gelnhausen for training as a radio operator. My next assignment was Headquarters Company, 1st Regiment, 999th Infantry Division at Heuberg/Tuttlingen.

The 999th Infantry Division was composed mainly of individuals who did not subscribe to the Nazi cause. It also included German army officers who had been reduced in rank. Among our group was Walter Schubrow, the concert master of the Berlin Symphonic Orchestra. He later often entertained us POWs at Camp Phillips in Kansas. Another busted officer, whose name I can't recall, was a former mayor of a German town. He refused to storm an impregnable Russian strongpoint for a third time after his outfit had been decimated to its last twenty-five men. In North Africa, the 999th included former members of the French Foreign Legion, the Arab Legion, and even Italians. It seemed to me that the German supreme command wanted to hide from the British and Americans its unmotivated, motley woebegones in one single division. By the time we arrived in Tunisia in 1943, the Afrika Korps was already fighting a losing battle. Also known to every ordinary German soldier like myself was the persistent rivalry between Field Marshals [Erwin] Rommel and [Albert] Kesselring of the German Luftwaffe in the North African campaign. My senior in our two-man wireless station in Tunisia was a twenty-four-year-old with heavily frostbitten legs and a bullet-shattered left arm, injuries he had sustained while on the Russian Front.

Without weapons or resistance, we surrendered to troops of the American II Army Corps on May 11, 1943, at exactly 4:00 in the afternoon. I was apprehensive at first because I had no idea what would happen to us, but they treated us fairly well.

After about ten days in a temporary holding camp, we were transferred in freight trains to Constantine, Algeria. The following day we were trucked to Sidi bel Abbès, a well-known training center for the French Foreign Legion. We remained at this town for a few days before going to a camp about sixty miles south of Oran. This camp was a large barbed wire enclosure operated by the Americans. Within the camp two men were assigned to each small tent. Water restrictions were strictly enforced.

Father FRANZ GÖDDE
I was born on July 19, 1922, in Flaesheim, a small community at the edge of the Ruhr, twenty-five miles south of Münster, Germany. After graduating from school, I was drafted into the National Labor Service (*Reichsarbeitsdienst*) on April 2, 1941 for six months of compulsory government service. My induction into the Wehrmacht followed automatically. After basic training in Rhine/Westfalia, I was assigned to a replacement battalion on the Russian Front south of Moscow to reinforce the 16th Motorized Infantry Division in February 1942. (By the way, every unit at the front had a replacement unit at home that was continually training troops to fill losses in personnel.) I was a machine gunner (heavy) and had to carry the weapon, which weighed about thirty pounds, wherever we went. In the winter of 1941–42, temperatures in Russia dropped to 40 degrees Celsius below zero [minus 40 degrees Fahrenheit]. During our summer offensive against Stalingrad, I was in the vicinity of Woronesch, near the Don River, when I was shot in the hip on July 2, 1942. I was evacuated to a hospital in Germany.

After about three months of recuperation, followed by sixteen days of home leave, I volunteered for a new unit that was later designated the 999th Infantry Division. Since I had turned down an offer for a commission in this unit, I was stamped "politically unreliable" ("*politisch nicht zuverlässig*"). For this reason, I was assigned as an instructor for basic training. At the end of March 1943, we were transferred to Tunisia and became part of the famed Afrika Korps. We traveled via train to southern France and Italy, stopping for two weeks in Naples before moving on to Sicily and then by ship to Tunisia. In Tunisia, I became the personal messenger of the battalion commander.

Because of the severe heat in Tunisia, the skin on my feet began to swell and split open. I was hospitalized in Tunis on May 5, 1943. Two days later the British Eighth Army occupied the city, and I became a prisoner of war.

HEINRICH KERSTING

In September 1939, I entered the federal finance school at Neustadt an der Waldnaab in Bavaria, headed for a career as a financial administrator. After passing my exams in April 1940, I received a trainee's position in the federal finance administration. I held this job until August 1941, when I was called into the National Labor Service (*Reichsarbeitsdienst*). Following four weeks of basic training as a worker with a shovel in Achmer/Bramsche, near Osnabrück, I was transferred to France. There I sat watch briefly on the Channel coast. I was later reassigned to the office of our RAD unit at Berck-sur-Mer and worked as a postal clerk, sorting and delivering mail.

On April 15, 1942, two weeks after completing my compulsory service in the RAD, I was drafted directly into the Wehrmacht. Assigned to the 36th Heavy Antiaircraft Replacement Unit (*Schwere Flak-Ersatz-Abteilung 36*) near Wolfenbüttel, I trained as a radio code operator. For additional training the entire unit was sent to Uden, Netherlands, and later to the Air Fleet Communications School at Náchod (today in the Czech Republic). Late in 1942, I was transferred to Caserta, Italy, and on February 25, 1943, to Tunis, Tunisia. As a radioman assigned to the staff of the 135th Regiment, 19th Flak Division, my job was to send and receive encrypted radio messages.

In January 1943, I was promoted automatically to the rank of private first class. A few months later on May 7, 1943, I was promoted to prisoner of war. Captured by the English at Grombalia, Tunisia, we were crowded into a large POW collection camp for a few days before being taken to Medjez el Bab. We later moved west to camps in Algeria at Souk Ahras, Constantine, Chansy (near Sidi bel Abbès), and finally to Oran, where we boarded a ship bound for Liverpool, England. From Liverpool, we went by truck to Moreton-in-Marsh and then briefly to another large transit camp before we were turned over to the Americans.

ALFRED SCHMUCKER

I was drafted into the German army on July 4, 1941, just three months after completing a three-year apprenticeship in commerce/bookkeeping. For basic training I was sent to Utrecht, Netherlands,

Alfred Schmucker in the driver's seat of his BMW motorcycle, Tunis, Tunisia, 1943.

and was assigned to a replacement unit (*Ersatz Abteilung*) of the General Göring Regiment. After completing my training with this unit, which included special training as a motorcycle messenger, I was transferred to the *Führerhauptquartier* in Rastenburg (Görlitz) in East Prussia, where I stayed from December 1941 until May 1942. This was a rather dull assignment that consisted of pulling guard duty on the outer ring of the quarters. This went on around the clock; two hours guard, four hours off, with one day off each week.

In 1942 the General Göring Regiment, which was a pure antiaircraft unit used primarily for parade purposes before the war, was enlarged and redesignated the Herman Göring Division. In June of that year, I was transferred to the 1st Panzer Regiment, an element of the newly organized Herman Göring Division. I served in the Motorcycle Reconnaissance Platoon (*Kraderkunderzug*). In Berlin, we picked up our new sand-colored vehicles and moved to France for training and preparation for action in North Africa. We arrived in Tunisia at the end of March 1943, comparatively late in the campaign that turned out to be a useless undertaking.

All our Panzer III tanks, on which we had trained for eight months, were lost at sea. We had loaded them onto an Italian vessel in Palermo, Sicily, for shipment to Tunisia. The vessel was about two hours out when Allied bombers sank the ship in the Mediterranean Sea.

Meanwhile, we went by air transport with our motorcycles from Trapani, Sicily, and landed in Tunis, Tunisia, where we were supposed to pick up our tanks. Instead, we received from decimated German units Panzer IVs on which none of us had ever been trained.

When the Afrika Korps surrendered on May 12, 1943, a group of about twelve of us decided to head for neutral Spanish Morocco to avoid being captured. To prepare for the long journey, we loaded five motorcycles and sidecars with rations, water, and extra gasoline. Traveling by night and hiding during the daytime, we managed to evade capture for eleven days. After traveling about 580 miles, we were finally caught on May 23, 1943 by French/Algerian desert police. We were about 125 miles south of Constantine, near the small town of Gauhss. The next day we were brought to Sétif, located at a railroad junction. From there we were shipped to French POW camps at Bou Arfa and then to nearby Foum Defla in southern Morocco. With a bare minimum of tools and equipment, we were put to work constructing a railroad embankment for a section of railway that was to link the Mediterranean Sea and the Niger River in Nigeria. We toiled in conditions that were unworthy of a human being until July 1944, when some of us were transferred to American jurisdiction. I consider those thirteen months the worse period of my life. I am grateful to the American troops who moved us out of that hellhole.

HERBERT SCHAFFRATH

I was born in Neustadt in Sachsen on April 3, 1924. I attended public school from 1930 to 1938 and continued my education at the school of commerce until 1941. From July to October 1941, I served in the National Labor Service (*Reichsarbeitsdienst*) at Strasburg in West Prussia. With a wheelbarrow, we moved piles of dirt from one place to another for no apparent reason. Immediately following my service in the RAD, I was inducted into the Wehrmacht and ended up in the 4th Antitank Replacement Unit (*Panzerjäger-Ersatz-Abteilung 4*).

From October 1941 to July 1942, I was stationed at Borna, near Leipzig, Germany, for training, followed by office duty. During this time only soldiers who lived within sixty miles of their station were granted weekend leave to their homes. They were eligible for leave once or twice a month based, of course, on good behavior. Since I lived 112 miles away, I was ineligible for leave. In February 1942, I got the bright idea of traveling home for the weekend without official approval. I filled my suitcase with civilian clothes and went to the train station at Leipzig. There I changed out of my uniform and rode home undisturbed by military police.

On my return to the garrison on Monday morning, we ran into a snowstorm that delayed all the trains. When I finally arrived at the garrison, the master sergeant of my company was standing at the front gate. He promptly escorted me to the office of the chief master sergeant who asked if anyone else had noticed my late return or had spoken with me. When the master sergeant replied, "no," the chief let me go with only a stern warning. Incidentally, the wearing of civilian clothing in the Wehrmacht was strictly forbidden.

To reduce the odds of being sent to the Russian Front, I volunteered for the Afrika Korps. Although the Korps at that time did not require special training, the physical exam for duty in the tropics was still taken very seriously. We spent three days undergoing tests at a medical institute in Leipzig. Finally, in July 1942, along with a group of other men, I was sent to a march battalion at Kaiserslautern, where we were issued new uniforms for the tropics. We then went by train through Yugoslavia to Greece. During the ride, we were instructed about North Africa and its people. We then caught a short flight to Crete and waited a few days before flying out aboard a Ju 52 to Tobruk, Libya.

In Tobruk, the men in our march battalion were distributed to various units as replacement troops. I was assigned to the battle staff of our commander in chief (*Kampfstaffel des Oberbefehlshabers*) as a messenger, but was often given other details including guard duty. Sometimes I traveled by foot and other times I drove a Volkswagen.

Initially, our meals consisted of a few types of canned foods and hard wheat bread, supplemented mostly by provisions captured from the enemy. Fresh bread was a luxury rarely enjoyed by our troops at the front.

In one instance, I was stationed at an advanced observation post at the Qattara Depression in north Egypt. During this time we had to prepare our own meals using rice, corned beef, and tomato paste, plus our survival rations and hard bread. Our drinking water was delivered to us in empty gasoline barrels. Everything that we prepared using this water, including the tea that we drank, tasted like gasoline. Thank God that after about three weeks we were rotated out to the back lines. Compared to my cooking and the stench of gasoline, the warm meals prepared by our field kitchens were good.

Water rationing was the highest priority in the desert. In the mornings we were allowed only a "cat wash"; using a piece of cloth, we moistened our face and hands. The fleas, which had found a home on our bodies, were hunted diligently and squashed. Sometimes the infestation became so bad that we had to wash our clothing in gasoline. Only when we were in a reserve line were we sometimes fortunate to have a shower.

Because of these very poor hygienic conditions, I developed dysentery. Since the military hospitals were overcrowded with casualties, I was treated in a mobile ambulance (*Sanitätskraftwagen*). Back and forth and all over creation we bounced in this vehicle. After a few days I was released to my unit, but the effects of this illness plagued me for a long time thereafter.

In early May 1943, the Afrika Korps capitulated in Tunisia. At that time my outfit was near Hammamet, Tunisia. Since we did not want to fall into French hands—their reputation for fairness was bad and the English were not in the vicinity—our technical sergeant got the adventurous idea of not surrendering. All eight of us agreed that we would try to get back to Italy on our own. Our plan was vague, and whether we would have dared to steal a boat and attempt to cross the Mediterranean Sea is doubtful. Nevertheless, that night we destroyed our weapons and headed for Cap Bon. During the next few weeks, we traveled at night and hid in caverns during the day. Every night just before dawn, we looked for Arab farmhouses to obtain drinking water and flat bread. We knew that the indigenous population sided with us and did not like the French. For that reason the Arabs we met always shared with us what few possessions they had.

Our goal of reaching Italy ended on June 15, 1943, when French soldiers captured us near Bir M'cherga, Tunisia, about twenty-three miles southwest of Tunis. Thank God we were unarmed because otherwise they might have mistaken us for bandits and shot us. We spent the first night of our captivity in a trench under French guard. Shortly thereafter they sent us to a prisoner of war camp at Bizerte, Tunisia, and then to a camp at Djelfa, Algeria, on August 10. Both camps were under French jurisdiction. The guards were ex-Foreign Legionnaires and soldiers from Alsace [France] who openly expressed their hatred of us, sometimes with the use of a whip.

On June 22, 1944, I was transferred to POW Camp 131 near Oran. Operated by the American Army as a transit camp, it looked like a giant tent city. Each POW received his own cot, and meals that were significantly better than anything we received from the French. These simple pleasures meant a great deal to the POW.

HANS-JOACHIM BÖTTCHER

I was born on September 8, 1925, in the village of Lüdersdorf (two rail stations east of Lübeck) in the old Fürnstentum Ratzeburg, then part of Mecklenburg-Strelitz. My father ran the local village store, and I attended school where I studied natural sciences, chemistry, and the English language.

In May 1943, I was inducted into the National Labor Service (*Reichsarbeitsdienst*) and was stationed at Bützow. During our RAD days, the Waffen SS and the Regiment Grossdeutschland used to visit our camps to give propaganda speeches and generally try to recruit soldiers. They were especially looking for people who were taller than five feet seven inches. To avoid being caught by these organizations, one had to either adopt a firm attitude with them, which was obviously difficult to do, or write to the recruiting offices of other units as volunteers, hoping that you wouldn't be turned down. Fortunately, the Luftwaffe accepted my application. Following my service in the RAD, I entered the Luftwaffe in August 1943.

After a short stay at Heiligenhafen/Schleswig-Holstein, I was sent to Toul, France, for basic training. I was then assigned to a regiment that changed names every few months. Its last name was absolutely misleading—Luftwaffe Ground Defense Regiment (*Landesschützen-Regiment der Luftwaffe*). Our regiment was composed mostly of youngsters like myself, earmarked for pilot training, and disabled former crew members. We used to service planes at different air bases, first at Lisieux in Normandy and then around Paris in the Melun area.

After the breakthrough of the Allies in Normandy, France, in 1944, every available soldier was sent toward the front. The only weapons we had were machine guns salvaged from wrecked planes, and we had absolutely no experience in using the guns. During the night of August 8–9, about sixty men and I attempted to pass a village near Le Mans. As we got into the village, U.S. soldiers suddenly opened fire on us from all sides. That was the end. We gave up without a fight. At the age of eighteen and with the rank of private first class, I was now a prisoner of war.

We were put on trucks and taken to a larger village where we spent the night in the yard of a house. Between August 9–13,

1944, we were herded into different compounds on meadows at various places around Rennes and then to a collection camp at Ste. Mère-Église. We received daily two or three U.S. C rations. On the evening of August 13, we were brought to the coast and crossed the English Channel in a tank transport ship. We arrived at what may have been Portsmouth, and then transported by train to a POW camp at Devizes, Wiltshire County. During our processing, all papers, pictures, and similar things that we carried with us were confiscated and never seen again. I was at Devizes from August 14–17. Devizes seemed to be an American-operated camp. During this time we lived on K rations.

From Devizes we moved to Camp Bury, about twelve miles north of Manchester. A former cotton mill, Camp Bury had a "room" capacity of between two and nine hundred POWs. I was in a room with six hundred POWs. At first, the camp was under American control. And I must say the guards were strict. We were not allowed to leave our rooms except in counted groups. When the British took over the camp on September 3, 1944, we could move freely within the grounds, but had to be back in our rooms by sunset. Overall, Camp Bury was not unfriendly, but terribly crowded. The food was reasonably good, and we had occasional sports, mostly playing soccer.

On September 19, we were transferred to Liverpool, arriving at the pier near midnight. It was an unforgettably eerie port in darkness—warm and humid with a storm approaching and St. Elmo's fires everywhere. Here we boarded a ship headed for the United States.

HEINRICH SCHÜNEMANN

As a young boy growing up in Hamburg, Germany, I began building model airplanes. Later, over the objections of my father, I became a trained glider pilot in the Hitler Youth organization. My father had opposed the new regime, believing, and correctly so, that it would end in disaster for Germany.

In March 1938, I left school and entered an apprenticeship as an automotive electrician, specializing in Bosch, Lucas, and Scintilla ignition systems. I worked at this position until March 1941, when I enrolled in a one-year course at a technical college for automotive and airplane engines.

In March 1942, I was drafted into the Luftwaffe and was shipped to Gent, Belgium, for four months of basic training. I was then sent to Abbeville, France, for general service, which included guard duty. Between January and April 1944, I trained as a paratrooper near Cologne, Germany. I was assigned to the 6th Parachute Regiment (*6th Fallschirmjäger Regiment*), under the command of [Colonel Friedrich August Freiherr] von der Heydte.

In May 1944, we were transferred to Normandy, France, north of Carentan and east of Ste. Mère-Église. Here, on June 6–7, I experienced my first military combat. Troops from the 101st U.S. Airborne Division landed by parachute and gliders right into our positions. The following day we moved toward Carentan, where we occupied a farmhouse. To our surprise, we were jumped by a strong American force that inflicted heavy casualties on our troops. The remaining fifteen or twenty of us put down our weapons and surrendered.

Two days later on June 9, our troops counterattacked, hitting the farmhouse with small arms fire and mortars. During the skirmish I was hit in the leg by shrapnel from a German mortar shell. The attack was beaten off with casualties on both sides. The following day both the German and American wounded were brought to the beach (Utah Beach) and evacuated to an American hospital in England. While we were in the hospital, Army medics cut off our hair. We thought this was standard military or medical practice. To our chagrin we later discovered that only the POWs from one barrack, about fifty of us, had their hair cut. We never learned the reason for this action. The other prisoners became intensely suspicious of us because in the German army the only troops to have their hair cropped were those assigned to penal companies.

ADOLF KELMER

I was born in Bremen on May 23, 1925. I attended primary school in the small town of Nordhorn, near the Dutch border. Around 1933 or 1934, I joined a youth group called the German Young People (*Deutsche Jungvolk*). My membership in the *Jungvolk* continued until April 1, 1939, shortly after my fourteenth birthday, when I was automatically admitted into the Hitler Youth (*Hitlerjugend*). I attended the usual meetings and rallies, but after a few weeks I stopped going. I was small for my age, and probably for that reason our leaders ignored my absence. My decision to drop out was not politically inspired, but instead motivated by practical reasons. A few months earlier, I had started work at a textile factory and didn't have time for these extra activities. I spent the next five years working at the factory until enlisting in the Wehrmacht in August 1943. My basic training was very thorough on the handling of many weapons, from rifles to the 20mm caliber rapid-firing cannon. After completing this training, I was assigned to the 84th Infantry Division for heavy weapons training that included the 88mm Panzer cannon. None of this training was exciting or interesting.

My division was stationed in Normandy, France, at the time of the Allied invasion on June 6, 1944. Toward the end of August or early September, Canadian troops captured me near Dieppe.[11] I was with a small group of men who were cut off from our main company and overrun by motorized Allied units. For several days we wandered around searching for our unit, until one night we strayed into a field camp of Canadian soldiers. You can well imagine the astonishment all around when we suddenly appeared in their midst. The Canadians didn't have a guard posted. This was probably better for all because otherwise we might have exchanged gunfire. Instead, we peacefully turned over our weapons and in return received cigarettes.

The next day we were moved to a holding area. Several days later we were placed in a small landing craft and evacuated to England. After brief stopovers in Southampton and London, we boarded a train to a transit camp near Glasgow [Scotland]. Two or three weeks later we embarked on a ship sailing to the United States.

KLAUS HEBEL

I was born on December 5, 1928, in Bernkastel-Kues, Germany. When I was nine, my family moved to the nearby village of Lieser. After graduating from school in 1943, I enrolled in a business apprenticeship program. My training was interrupted for three months beginning in September 1944, when I was inducted into the National Labor Service (*Reichsarbeitsdienst*) and sent to Selters/Westerwald. Instead of working with a shovel doing civil works projects, our tools remained in the closet nicely polished while we were trained on the use of a rifle.

Around March 5, 1945, the townsmen in Lieser were ordered to report for military service at the residence of the town priest. From that moment on, we formed into a *Volkssturm* militia and soon after came under the command of the 189th Infantry Division. Our *Volkssturm* did not have a specific number designation. Rather, it was a motley conglomeration of elderly men and boys like myself. By this time the 189th Infantry Division was itself a gallimaufry of marines [Navy personnel], Luftwaffe, Waffen SS, and ordinary soldiers. We had absolutely no military training while in the *Volkssturm*.

As Allied troops moved closer, our retreat went in the direction of the Rhine and Main regions. To avoid attack from American aircraft that dominated the skies over Germany, our troop movements, using horses and wagons, occurred under the cover of darkness. In many of the villages that we passed through, concrete blocks (*Panzersperren*) had been built to slow the advance of Allied tanks. Our small group of *Volkssturm* were assigned to digging tank traps (*Panzergräben*) near Bitburg, Welschbillig, and Helenenberg in the Eifel area. Young and old men alike, we dug ditches in a ridiculous attempt to slow the advance of the Western Allies.

Gazing west toward Luxembourg, I could see flashes of light from artillery fire illuminate the night skies, and hear the awful thunder of guns growing in intensity. All around us troops were on the move. A few of us quit digging and quietly slipped away to the nearest village in the direction of Lieser. Hiding in this village we discovered other youngsters approximately my age. They were trying to avoid being swept into a *Volkssturm* militia. This was a dangerous undertaking for all of us because the military police, disparagingly known as *Kettenhunde*, were always on the lookout for stragglers. There was also the danger of being picked up by remnants of the Wehrmacht that were falling back to reconstitute a defensive line.

We left the village the next day, and as we passed through a canyon, gunfire suddenly erupted. To this day, I don't know who was shooting. In any case, the fusillade caused widespread panic within our group and sent everyone scattering to find cover. At daybreak, we cautiously walked across the open meadow before us and found protection in a little woods that stood past the open field. The woods were soon filled with several hundred soldiers and their horses. Just beyond these woods was the village of Hoppstädten. From there one could recognize twenty, maybe fifty American tanks. It was a picture to cry about: tanks against soldiers with horses. Since we were already encircled by these armored units, we decided to surrender. But, of course, nobody wanted to venture into the open field with a white flag. I remember that a technical sergeant offered me cigarettes and a few cans of sausage as a bribe if I would go. I did. As I approached the American line with a white flag held above my head, a jeep with American soldiers drove toward me. One of the soldiers signaled me to come closer. After exchanging a few words, I waved to my comrades. An entire mass of people moved toward the American line and into captivity. We walked in one large procession in the

German Prisoners of War at Camp Cooke, California

The prisoners were thoroughly searched before being shipped to the United States. (Courtesy of National Archives)

A young German prisoner receives water through a barbed-wire enclosure at Gafsa, Tunisia, February 1943. (Courtesy of National Archives)

Several thousand German POWs at an American camp west of Mateur, Tunisia, awaiting shipment to camps in Britain, America, and Canada, May 1943. (Courtesy of National Archives)

direction of nearby Fischbach/Weierbach. The date was March 19, 1945.

That night we camped on a large meadow surrounded by tanks. The next day and all night long, American tanks and other military vehicles rolled along the country roads deeper into Germany. Toward the end of the war, we had nothing but chaos in our ranks.

Our route into captivity led us from Trier, Germany, to Cherbourg, France. Here, on a large hill, stood the POW camp. Conditions in this transit camp were deplorable. It rained and stormed every day, flooding our tents and making it impossible to keep dry. Many of my fellow prisoners, already ill and weakened from dysentery, would trudge to the latrine but never made it back to their tents. Our daily food ration included cigarettes, which I traded for more food.

CHAPTER 2

Journey to America

THE POWs who came to America from North Africa and later from Europe arrived at ports of embarkation in New York, Virginia, and Boston. They were then showered and sprayed with disinfectant. Their clothing and personal belongings were deloused and searched. After their military papers had been inspected, the prisoners boarded comfortable passenger trains that carried them to their new homes.[1]

In many respects, the journey across America was an eye-opening experience for the typical POW. Having been indoctrinated by the exaggerated and distorted claims of Nazi propaganda, some POWs expected to see wrecked cities and scorched fields caused by the Luftwaffe. Instead, they saw the richness of American soil and industries rapidly churning out unprecedented amounts of war materials. Equally astonishing to many were the vast distances between cities and the seemingly countless number of automobiles.[2]

Father FRANZ GÖDDE
After my capture by the British I was transported to Camp 210 in Algiers. I stayed at this temporary collection camp for only a short time before being taken to Liverpool, England. We were then moved to Camp Oldham near Manchester for seventeen days. Around the end of June 1943, we returned to Liverpool and boarded the ship *Empress of Japan*, which took us to Norfolk, Virginia. We arrived there on July 2.

During the ocean crossing, we passed the time playing cards and occasionally getting topside to enjoy the ocean view. Since I had not studied English in school, I traded some cigarettes for an English grammar book and began to cram.

Following our showering and delousing at Norfolk, we boarded a waiting train. We were split into groups of four POWs to each compartment. The cushions in our compartment could be pulled out and made into beds, allowing the four of us to sleep side by side. The windows could only be opened about four inches, but it was enough to let in fresh air. At each end of our car was a guard who enforced strict military rule. To go to the toilet, one had to raise his arm and receive permission. Only then were we allowed to go, and only one at a time.

The food onboard the train was like a dream come true. We had ham and eggs for breakfast and heated canned foods for our other meals. Traveling across America in comfortable Pullman cars, I was thrilled by the majestic beauty of the Appalachian Mountains, the enormous fields of the Midwest, and the vast western plains. After a few days, we arrived at a POW camp near Concordia, Kansas, on July 4, 1943.

RUDOLF HINKELMANN
We were turned over to the Americans at Oran in the summer of 1943. Shortly thereafter, we were placed in a large convoy of ships headed across the Atlantic Ocean. Throughout the passage we were treated exceedingly well and received plenty of canned food, tobacco, and cigarettes. During the day we were allowed on deck, and to my knowledge there were no incidents on board the vessel. Circulating among us infantrymen, however, was a rumor that if Germany lost the war it was going to be converted into an agrarian nation and that all German males were to be castrated.[3] Whether this rumor was propagated by Göbbels [Josef Göbbels, Nazi propaganda minister for the Third Reich], I cannot say. In any case, at that time we thought there must be some truth to it.

After arriving at Newport News, Virginia, we showered and deloused, and then boarded a train to Camp Phillips, Kansas. On our arrival we walked about four hundred feet from the station to the camp through a corridor of tanks and soldiers holding submachine guns. I got the impression that we were perceived as being a horde of barbarians. Soon after our arrival, however, that perception changed and a more cordial relationship developed.

LEONHARD REUL
Around the end of June 1943, the Americans transported us by truck to the harbor at Oran. We boarded the ship *Monroe* and sailed in a convoy of about eighty ships. After passing the Straits of Gibraltar, we joined another convoy of forty ships coming from Casablanca. We sailed together in the direction of the United States. We were at sea for nearly three weeks, constantly changing course to evade prowling German U-boats.

When we approached the United States, the convoy divided into two parts; our group went to Norfolk, Virginia. At the reception center, we showered and were disinfected, and our personal

German Prisoners of War at Camp Cooke, California

German POWs arriving at a port in England under American guard, June 1944. Before the end of the war, nearly 400,000 prisoners would be sent to the United States. (Courtesy of National Archives)

belongings and papers were inspected. We departed Norfolk by train and a few days later arrived at Camp Phillips, Kansas. In the spring of 1944, we left Kansas by train for Camp Tooele in Utah. Camp Tooele was a supply base for the American theater of operations in the Pacific. We worked in a warehouse doing all sorts of cleaning and moving of supplies. Around November 1944, we were transferred to Tagus Ranch near Tulare, California.

HEINRICH KERSTING
Shortly after landing in England, we were turned over to American troops who promptly put us aboard a 24,000-ton steamer headed for New York. Upon our arrival, we entered a large reception center for showering, delousing, and the processing of our papers by Army clerks. We were then placed aboard a train that took us to Camp Phillips, Kansas, near Salina. We arrived on August 13, 1943. As we traveled across America, we were all astounded by the great distances between places. Nothing like this existed anywhere in Germany.

WERNER GILBERT
The British handed us over to the Americans at Constantine, Algeria, in June 1943. The Americans moved us to a temporary collection camp at Casablanca, and then on July 5 placed us aboard a ship headed for New York. The guards on this ship were Polish nationals and American GIs. On several occasions fights erupted between some of the POWs and the Poles, who were considerably loose with their batons. The GIs interceded in these disputes and usually sided with the POWs.

We landed in New York in mid-July. Seeing America for the first time, I was deeply impressed by the sight of the Statue of Liberty and the skyscrapers of Manhattan. After showering, delousing, and the processing of our papers, we left by train and arrived at Camp Trinidad in Colorado, on July 25, 1943.

WERNER BLANCK
At Halifax, Canada, we were given over to the U.S. Army. To our astonishment we were put aboard very comfortable Pullman cars and traveled by rail for five days to Trinidad, Colorado. Many of us had never experienced such a comfortable journey nor had we seen such enchanted lands. I strained my eyes so I wouldn't miss a single sign or building.

A group of smiling German POWs after showering and delousing at the Port of Embarkation in New York, 1944. (Courtesy of National Archives)

HEINRICH SCHÜNEMANN

We left England for America on July 1, 1944, and reached our destination, the port in New York, ten days later on July 11. Our ship, the *Argentina*, was the largest vessel in the convoy, having a displacement of about 25,000 tons. On board the ship were about three hundred German POWs and an undetermined number of wounded American soldiers. Most of the POWs were fairly anxious about the crossing and what awaited them on the other side. For many of us though, our immediate concerns were the frequent bouts of seasickness and three U-boat alerts. The possibility that we could be sunk by our own navy was never far from our thoughts. In fact, right after boarding the ship we had to don our life preserver jackets and participate in an exercise to abandon ship. Despite our anxieties, we were treated well throughout the entire journey. Every day during certain hours we were allowed on deck for walks.

As we approached New York, I could see the Statue of Liberty and the skyline of Manhattan. It was near nightfall when the ship stopped in the harbor. While the ship waited to dock, the POWs were invited to join the GIs on deck to watch the movie *Going My*

Way, with Bing Crosby. Only some of the English-speaking POWs and a few curious others accepted the invitation.

When we finally disembarked, we went through the delousing station. Military guards, all armed with machine guns, stood watch over us. POWs coming from hospitals in England like myself were generally clean. We were wearing clean underwear and freshly laundered German or GI uniforms. Some wore a mixture of both uniforms. We then boarded a waiting train, and within a few hours the city was far behind us. We were seated in groups of three with the fourth seat left unoccupied. At night, each area became a three-bed compartment. Guards were posted at each end of the Pullman car, and as a further security measure the windows were kept locked. The meals were Army C and K rations, but for us this was first class compared to what we had in the German army in those days. The food was served to us on stainless steel trays, the first time in my life I had ever seen or used these kinds of trays.

I was overwhelmed by the beautiful landscape of the United States. As we passed Niagara Falls, the train slowed down, giving us an excellent opportunity to view the majestic scenery. We didn't know it at the time, but our train was headed for Camp Custer in Michigan.

Thanks to my father and my boyhood readings of Karl May,[4] my knowledge of the United States was better than that of the average German POW. My father had left Germany in 1908 to become a coffee grower in Guatemala. During the First World War, he was a civilian internee in Florida between 1917 and 1919.

ALFRED SCHMUCKER

The greatest day for some of us was when a convoy of American Army trucks moved in and picked up about 80 percent of the German POWs on July 9, 1944. I was lucky to be in the group that was collected. We were transferred by rail to Oran, Algeria, where we received shelter in an American POW camp. Contrary to what we endured while under French jurisdiction, every stock car was well equipped with several "jerry" cans containing water to quench our thirsty throats and sufficient amounts of canned food. Although we lived in tents while in Oran, we felt as if we were living in heaven. For the first time in fourteen months we could take a shower, receive good food, and were treated like human beings. A physical examination performed by American doctors revealed that my weight had dropped to one hundred pounds.

On August 1, 1944, we were transferred to the harbor of Oran, where we embarked on a U.S. Liberty ship bound for the United States. We were part of a convoy of more than seventy vessels. On board our ship were 497 POWs. We received plenty to eat, could shower daily, and slept in hammocks five tiers high. We reached our port of destination, Newport News, Virginia, on August 18.

After debarkation, we were led to a shower room where each of us received a fine-smelling bar of Life Buoy soap and a brand new white towel. Meanwhile, our clothing was deloused. The final two steps were the processing of our papers and a medical exam. Within two hours everything was done, and we were placed aboard a waiting train. We were all very impressed by this extraordinary organization. On the train we found four seats for every three men. Additionally, we received sufficient food and plenty of ice water. We were guarded by military police during the entire five-day journey to our next destination, Camp Florence, Arizona.

GEORG KROEMER

In July 1944, after more than a year of harsh captivity in French camps, we were transferred to the Americans. We were full of fleas and lice, and our uniforms were in tatters. Our appearance was nothing less than skin and bones. The Americans gave us delicious meals and evacuated us to a POW camp in Oran, Algeria. We were deloused, showered, and received fresh new underwear and POW clothing. Oh, how wonderful that was! Shortly thereafter, we left Oran for America in a convoy of about thirty ships. Our ship was in the middle of the flotilla during the entire voyage. We were allowed to move on deck as much as we wanted, and only when we had U-boat alarms were we obligated to go below deck. Our meals consisted of K and C rations. In exchange for additional food, I volunteered to scrape rust off the sides of the ship and to cover those areas with paint. Throughout the voyage the ship's crew and the guards treated us very decently.

After about fourteen days at sea, we arrived at Norfolk, Virginia. We then went by train to Camp Florence, Arizona.

HERBERT SCHAFFRATH

In the early part of August 1944, the Americans took us by trucks to the harbor at Oran. We then went via Liberty ship to Norfolk, Virginia, where we arrived on August 22. This was my first ocean passage. We were tightly stowed together in the cargo holds and slept in bunks three tiers high. The meals were C rations, three times a day. A few other POWs and I volunteered to work on the ship, knocking and scraping rust off the deck. For this work, we received an extra ration and two cigarettes. As a nonsmoker, I traded the cigarettes for other items. During much of the crossing we passed the time playing skat. At other times, one was more content to stand along the gunwales gazing into the dancing waves.

At the processing station in Norfolk, we were astounded by the clean surroundings and the prompt and perfect organization. Before we realized what was happening, we were standing under a hot shower, were sprayed with delousing powder, and our meager belongings were inspected. We were then marched to a waiting train that took us clear across the United States to Camp Florence in Arizona.

The train ride was very exciting for me. I had never traveled so comfortably with the German Wehrmacht. The total journey was a delightful and eye-opening experience. The countryside went flowing by the window in an unending variety of contrast and vastness. For a person from densely populated Germany, this sight was unimaginable and unforgettable. Our guards on both the ship and the train always behaved properly toward us.

HELMUT WOLTER

In August 1944, the Americans moved us to a transfer point at Oran, Algeria, where we were billeted in tents. We were showered, deloused, issued new clothing, and registered. After a short time, we boarded ships that took us to Norfolk, Virginia. Because of the danger from prowling U-boats, we were not permitted on deck for nearly the entire ocean voyage. Except for a very monotonous journey and bouts of seasickness, conditions on board the ship were fine.

When we arrived at Norfolk, we marched from the harbor to the train station. Written on one of the buildings were the letters "WAC." Not knowing the meaning of this word, we asked our GI guard who gleefully answered: "A WAC is a soldier with a foxhole built in." We needed some time to understand what he meant by that.

We boarded a nice passenger train, not the boxcar type that we soldiers had become accustomed to in Germany. Traveling across America, we were especially impressed by the peace and quiet that typified every town we passed. This was in stark contrast to Germany, where by that time most cities had been devastated by the war. We arrived at the POW camp in Florence, Arizona, about September 1944.

HANS-JOACHIM BÖTTCHER

Between September 20 and 27, 1944, we were zigzagging the Atlantic Ocean escorted by perhaps two corvettes. Aboard our ship were 2,200 POWs as well as American and Canadian soldiers (possibly wounded) sailing under the Red Cross flag. We were placed below in E-Deck and had three- or four-tier bunks that we pulled up during the day. Twice a day, for ninety minutes each time, we were allowed on deck to get some fresh air, watch the dolphins, etc. The sea was a bit rough and some of the POWs became seasick, but fortunately not me. We received three meals daily, and by our standards the food was excellent. Some of us were given kitchen details, peeling potatoes and preparing vegetables. We did this work in turns, and it gave us a chance to get an extra bite. The food was served American cafeteria style.

During the crossing we passed the time by playing chess or checkers. I remember one POW who practiced hypnosis and telepathy. He hypnotized a few POWs and made them eat potato peels thinking it was chocolate.

Our ship arrived near Halifax, but stayed off the coast for a day before heading south to Boston. Hoping to see Canada, our British guards greeted the news with a great deal of disappointment. Awaiting us at the Boston harbor was the usual disinfection process, haircuts, and political screening. We then boarded a train and for the next five days traveled to Florence, Arizona. We passed through New York, Cleveland, Chicago, Topeka, Santa Fe, El Paso, and Tucson. No significant events occurred during the train ride, but all of us were impressed by the size and beauty of America.

Our train consisted of ten cars filled with five hundred POWs, as well as one car for the guards, and two kitchen cars in the middle. It looked like a typical express train. Even though each compartment had room for six passengers, only three POWs were assigned per compartment, thereby giving everyone room to put his feet up for sleeping. Guards were stationed in each rail car, and initially we had to raise our hands if we wanted something. Later on we were allowed to move around more freely. Since I could speak English and our car was coupled to the kitchen, I was appointed interpreter and assigned to help serve the meals. This was my first encounter with Heinz 57 Varieties. I heard many complaints from the guards about "them goddam baked beans."

ADOLF KELMER

In the autumn of 1944, we boarded the Dutch passenger liner, *New Amsterdam*, near Glasgow, Scotland, and sailed to New York. It was a beautiful ship of about 25,000-ton displacement and had several decks. We were divided into groups of about five or six men per cabin. Every day we were permitted to spend an hour on deck. Because of the cold winter weather, I was always happy to return to the warmth and shelter of below deck.

Our reception in New York had been well planned. The debarkation, the processing, the registration, the showering, and the sorting of POWs was all done without a hitch. We then walked to a nearby railway station where we boarded a waiting passenger train with large windows. I was impressed by all this organization. Looking down at my unsightly and ragged uniform, I felt ashamed to be dressed like this on a journey through America. As the train lurched forward, none of us had any idea what to expect on this trip. Personally, I had a good feeling and looked forward to it.

In our coach, a young American soldier of about my age impressed upon us the need to cooperate and to follow the rules. Among other things, he told us that we had to remain in our assigned seats. If we had any questions we were to raise our hands, just like in school. These orders were easily obeyed. Soon into the journey the guards themselves relaxed the strict orders of this young soldier.

Every three men in the car shared a compartment outfitted with six fine, upholstered seats. At first, I didn't understand this generosity. I also didn't realize the enormous number of rail cars on the American railroads. Equally unknown to me was the length of the trip. In exchange for a window seat during the day, I volunteered to sleep on the floor between the benches in our compartment. My two companions happily agreed to this arrangement. I obviously didn't have to worry about ruining my uniform. Besides, the car was heated. The only regrettable part of it all was my occasional sneezing attacks triggered by the dust on the floor.

The next morning, we were able to view this promised land. Out the window we could see a continuously changing landscape with little residences and small towns sometimes reminiscent of European villages. Curious to us were the many cars and trucks on the roads and parked near factories and other large commercial buildings. At first, we thought we were passing automobile plants. But very soon we were also surprised to see large numbers of cars in the fields, orchards, and in parking lots. We knew then that many Americans could afford to own an automobile. Obviously, the distance between the continents was greater than just miles.

Our meals usually began with dessert and ended with bread. The porters, who expected us to wait until everything was on our plates before eating, didn't know that our own military food service had become so terrible and unreliable that by force of habit we immediately ate whatever was given to us whenever we received it.

All of us had a wonderful feeling of contentment—something that we hadn't felt for a long time. After several days, we finally reached our destination: Idaho.

KLAUS HEBEL

At the end of March 1945, we shipped out from Cherbourg, first to the port at Southampton, England, and then to the open sea in the direction of America. Our Liberty ship sailed in a convoy of about twenty-five to thirty ships. We zigzagged across the Atlantic to avoid the few remaining solitary U-boats. Alarm exercises were a matter of course. In addition to our guards, other American servicemen were on board. They, however, were kept separate from us. Our ship was also carrying mail to the United States.

We prisoners were at the bottom of the cargo holds and slept on hammocks fastened to the walls of our compartments. When the sea became rough, we just rolled back and forth. For me this was simply hilarious. Many others were not amused and spent much of the trip visiting our too few toilets. Fortunately, I did not get sick.

A fellow prisoner from Hamburg and I befriended the ship's engineer. Since my comrade spoke a passable English, he arranged for us to work on the ship in return for larger portions of food. We did various odd jobs, but mostly passed the time banging and scraping rust off the side of the ship. The food was good; we even received corned beef. I learned later that not every transport ship had the same food.

I believe we arrived in New York on April 25, 1945. I was very young and curious, and kept my eyes open to see as much as possible of this New World. For a sixteen-year-old boy from a small vineyard village on the Mosel River, which had all of 1,350 inhabitants, the gigantic sight of the skyline, the harbor installations, and the Statue of Liberty were simply overpowering. My eyes grew bigger and bigger with amazement at everything I saw. It was an indelible sight. As we came down the gangplank, American soldiers began shouting at us, "Let's go, let's go." Before we fully realized what was happening, our clothes were stripped off, our hair completely cut off, and we were deloused and showered. We were given khaki clothes with "PW" printed on the backs. Then, in double step, we walked to a waiting train.

I was completely overwhelmed by what I saw crossing this marvelous and vast country, the United States. Words cannot adequately express my feelings of exhilaration and excitement. If I remember correctly, we traveled via Chicago and then headed southwest. The food aboard the train was very satisfying. In fact, American white bread was for us a veritable Sunday treat. For years in Germany, we had nothing but hunger, and this was now behind us.

As prisoners of war, we were all very apprehensive about the final destination of this long journey. With every railroad station we passed, we eagerly struggled to read the station sign and asked, "Where are we now? Where is this place?" I believe that our special train was usually pushed into freight terminals, not passenger railroad stations, and then had to wait for available rail lines. These stops gave us time to orient ourselves in what state we happened to be waiting. We traveled this vast country before arriving in the Arizona desert at the POW camp in Florence.

CHAPTER 3

The First Weeks as POWs

AFTER ARRIVING at their new homes, the prisoners were assembled and greeted by an American camp officer who explained what was expected of them. They were then showered, assigned to quarters, and issued U.S. Army clothing. Their new wardrobe generally consisted of khaki and olive green (sometimes blue denim) U.S. Army class X garments.[1] Except for the hats, all other clothing was conspicuously marked with the letters "PW." Shirts were labeled across the back and on the front of each sleeve and the shoulder. Trousers, shorts, and similar articles were marked across the seat and on the front of each leg. Lettering was usually stenciled in indelible marking ink or paint. At Camp Cooke, prisoners were issued two pairs of shoes, four pairs of socks, four sets of underwear, four pants, four shirts, four work jackets, one pair of gloves, one field or woolen jacket, one overcoat, and one raincoat. Hats were issued to prisoners assigned to agricultural jobs in the field.[2]

Prisoners who kept some articles of their German national uniforms, or later received new ones through the International Red Cross, were restricted from wearing these outside the stockade except during transfer to another POW camp or during special occasions, such as burials of fellow inmates. The prisoners were permitted to wear their insignia of rank and decorations. After the surrender of Germany, however, the wearing of their military uniforms or accouterments was prohibited.[3]

Another matter of importance was the processing of prisoners. When time permitted, this was done in the theater of operations by preparing a Basic Personnel Record (BPR) for each prisoner. At the close of the North African campaign in 1943, soldiers were captured in such large numbers and sent so quickly to the United States that preparation of the BPR was frequently not accomplished until the prisoners either arrived at the ports in this country or, more often, at a POW camp. The BPR contained the individual's name, POW serial number, photograph, fingerprints, physical description, inventory of personal effects, and other personal information. It became part of the prisoner's

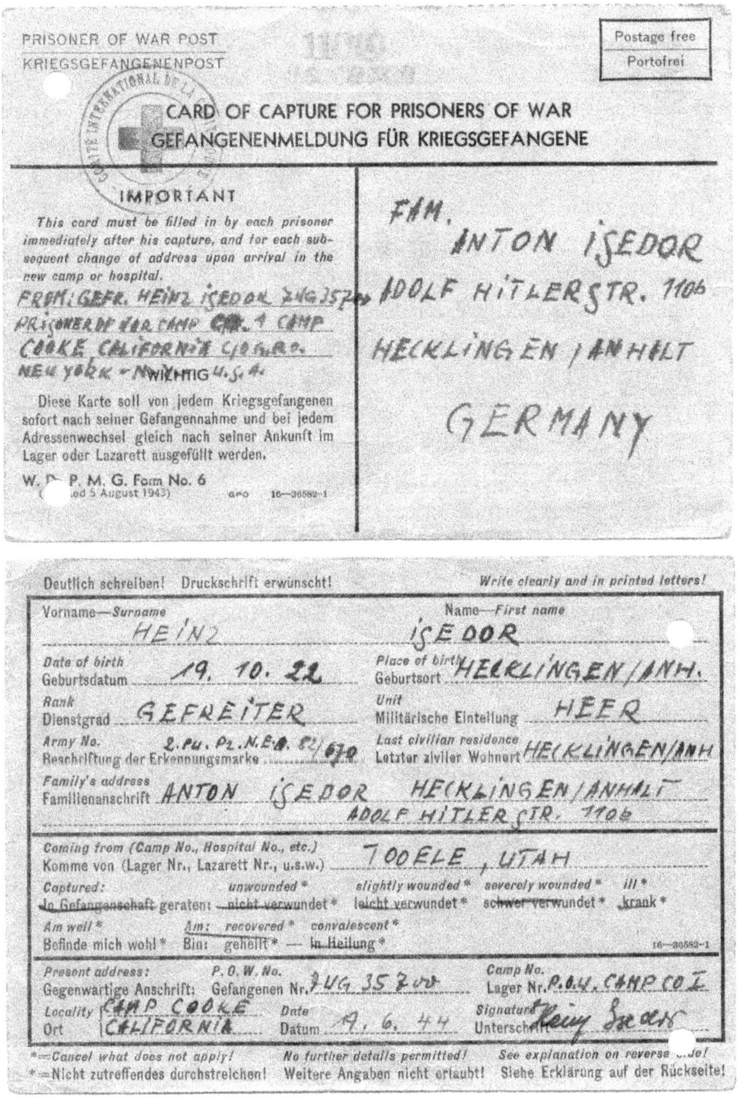
PRISONER OF WAR POST
KRIEGSGEFANGENENPOST
Postage free
Portofrei

CARD OF CAPTURE FOR PRISONERS OF WAR
GEFANGENENMELDUNG FÜR KRIEGSGEFANGENE

IMPORTANT
This card must be filled in by each prisoner immediately after his capture, and for each subsequent change of address upon arrival in the new camp or hospital.

FROM: GEFR. HEINZ ISEDOR 2UG 357
PRISONER OF WAR CAMP No. 1 CAMP
COOKE CALIFORNIA C/O P.M.
NEW YORK - N.Y. U.S.A.

WICHTIG
Diese Karte soll von jedem Kriegsgefangenen sofort nach seiner Gefangennahme und bei jedem Adressenwechsel gleich nach seiner Ankunft im Lager oder Lazarett ausgefüllt werden.

W. D. P. M. G. Form No. 6
(Revised 5 August 1943) GPO 16—30582-1

FAM.
ANTON ISEDOR
ADOLF HITLERSTR. 1106
HECKLINGEN / ANHALT
GERMANY

Deutlich schreiben! Druckschrift erwünscht! *Write clearly and in printed letters!*

Vorname—*Surname*: HEINZ	Name—*First name*: ISEDOR
Date of birth / Geburtsdatum: 19. 10. 22	*Place of birth* / Geburtsort: HECKLINGEN / ANH.
Rank / Dienstgrad: GEFREITER	*Unit* / Militärische Einteilung: HEER
Army No. / Beschriftung der Erkennungsmarke: 2. Pu. Pz. N.E.A. 82/670	*Last civilian residence* / Letzter ziviler Wohnort: HECKLINGEN/ANH
Family's address / Familienanschrift: ANTON ISEDOR HECKLINGEN / ANHALT ADOLF HITLERSTR. 1106	

Coming from (Camp No., Hospital No., etc.) / Komme von (Lager Nr., Lazarett Nr., u.s.w.): TOOELE, UTAH

Captured: / In Gefangenschaft geraten: *unwounded* * / nicht verwundet * — *slightly wounded* * / leicht verwundet * — *severely wounded* * / schwer verwundet * — *ill* * / krank *

Am well * / Befinde mich wohl * — *Am: recovered* * / Bin: geheilt * — *convalescent* * / In Heilung * 16—30582-1

Present address: / Gegenwärtige Anschrift: *P. O. W. No.* / Gefangenen Nr. 2UG 35700 — *Camp No.* / Lager Nr. P.O.W. CAMP CO. I

Locality / Ort: CAMP COOKE CALIFORNIA — *Date* / Datum: 19. 6. 44 — *Signature* / Unterschrift: Heinz Isedor

*=*Cancel what does not apply!* *No further details permitted!* *See explanation on reverse side!*
*=Nicht zutreffendes durchstreichen! Weitere Angaben nicht erlaubt! Siehe Erklärung auf der Rückseite!

The Army issued change of address post cards to each prisoner to mail to his family after his capture and upon arriving at a new POW camp in the United States. (Courtesy of Heinrich Isedor)

201 file that accompanied him throughout his confinement in the United States.[4]

Prisoners who were processed in the theater of operations received serial numbers that consisted of two components separated from each other by a dash. The first component consisted of two digits and a letter, indicating the command in which the prisoner was captured and the name of the enemy country in whose armed forces the prisoner was serving. The second component was the individual number assigned consecutively to each POW processed in the appropriate command. Thus, the first prisoner processed in the Mediterranean theater of operations (North Africa), if a German, would be assigned 81G-1, and the tenth prisoner processed by the same command would be assigned serial number 81G-10. Prisoners captured in the European theater would have first components of 31.[5]

Prisoners transferred to the United States without having been processed by the capturing command were processed by the service command at the prisoner of war camp to which they were first delivered. Serial numbers for prisoners in this category consisted of two components. The first component contained three symbols. The first symbol was the number representing the proper service command, from one to nine. The second symbol was a "W," representing the War Department. The third symbol was the first letter of the name of the country the POW served. The second component consisted of the individual number assigned consecutively to each prisoner processed in the service command irrespective of which country he served or when captured. For example, the first prisoner processed in the Ninth Service Command, if German, was 9WG-1.[6]

With few exceptions, the POWs were treated by their American captors with respect and, in some instances, with admiration. Since the U.S. War Department promised to abide by the Geneva Convention, the prisoners received comfortable quarters, generous portions of food from a varied menu, and a host of other amenities. They were assigned to jobs and were paid for their labor. While most accepted their situation and tried to make the best of it, others were unwilling to tolerate their status as POW and were determined to undermine the American war effort, regardless of how pointless and feeble their actions.[7]

ALFRED SCHMUCKER

At the POW camp in Florence, Arizona, we were housed in two-story military barracks. We slept on cots fitted with white linen. Our worn-out German military uniforms were taken away, and we received blue denim cloth trousers, jackets, and hats with a big "PW" printed on the back of the jacket and on the trousers. In addition, each of us received a pair of GI boots instead of the worn-out shoes or wooden sandals we had until then. For hygienic purposes, our hair was cut off. We used all different sorts of things to make it grow faster with no visible result.

We couldn't believe that we sat at tables, ate from plates, and could have an unlimited amount of food. After four weeks, the American camp commander asked us to go to work. We were more than willing to give something in return for all the hospitality we had received. We organized into work details and were assigned to various jobs that included picking cotton outside the camp, and working in warehouses and the laundry inside the camp.

After breakfast in Florence, the various work details formed discipline marching blocks, heading in various directions to their work sites. Since we used to sing while marching in the German army, we stuck to this custom when marching through the streets of the large U.S. military camp. Within a few days word got around on the installation that a bunch of German POWs were eagerly singing while marching to work each morning and again in the evening on their way back to the camp. Our audience grew bigger every day, and they applauded us. The U.S. camp commander could not tolerate this, for one reason or another. One morning before we were ready to take off for work it was announced that effective immediately we were not allowed to sing outside the compound. After one day of silent marching, we started to whistle our songs on our way to and from work. This, however, lasted only a few days and resulted in a new order: "No singing and no whistling." At this stage there was only one thing left to do and that was to start humming our songs. This too lasted only a few days because we were told: "No singing, no whistling, no humming, and no whatever is allowed from here on."

I think it was October or November 1944, when we were transported by train from Florence, Arizona, to a POW camp known as Camp Ayers near Chino, California. The housing, we were told, was formerly used by Mexican seasonal workers. Within a short time, we made a little jewel out of that place.

We were detailed out in groups that ranged in size from three POWs to about fifty to work on farms nearby. The work included harvesting oranges, lemons, peaches, grapes, walnuts, and tomatoes. I remember that while picking oranges, we had a young GI as our guard who did not like us. Equipped with a shotgun, he would accompany us to the farm where he was supposed to keep an eye on us. Reaching the farm, he would lean his shotgun against a tree and read his *Los Angeles Examiner*. After a while, he would fall asleep until lunchtime. Meanwhile, each POW was expected to fill thirty-five boxes of oranges a day. To do the job we were equipped with a picking bag, a pair of clippers, and a ladder. Sometimes one or two oranges remained way out of reach at the top of the tree. Picking them required frequent moves of the ladder and in some cases artistic and time-consuming movements. Since the farmer never complained, we let these hard-to-reach fruits remain on the treetops. Not so, thought our "guardian angel." In the afternoon, after reading his newspaper and taking a nap, boredom must have overcome him and he wandered through the rows of orange trees to pass the time. If he spotted an orange twinkling on a treetop, he would call the POW assigned to that row of trees and make him go back with his ladder and get that damn orange. Shaking the tree was not allowed.

He played this game with us for about a week before we decided to teach him a lesson. One day while he took his morning nap, we dug a hole in the sand. We then buried his shotgun in the hole. The young GI later went down on his knees, begging for his weapon. We tried to convince him that he had come to the orange grove without a shotgun. To make a long story short, he returned to camp with all of his prisoners, but without a weapon. He was never again assigned to our work detail, and the weapon was never recovered.

During Christmas 1944, our cooks in the mess hall had gone out of their way to prepare an extraordinary Christmas dinner with turkey, cranberry sauce (the latter was unknown to us before this time), and cake for dessert. Since we had not received Christmas decorations from the camp administration, we traded with the farmers those items that we could buy in our canteen such as cigarettes, toothpaste, shampoo, and soap bars for a small Christmas tree and decorations.

A variety of entertainment groups formed within the camp to celebrate Christmas. We had an emcee, a choir, comedians, magicians, and of course our music band to accompany the performers. The Americans, officers and enlisted men alike, enjoyed our show and couldn't believe that within such a short time, we produced so many fine performances. For rehearsals, we only had the evenings after work and Saturdays and Sundays. Another difficulty was the scarcity of American sheet music. Scores for German songs were not available at all. German songs had to be handwritten from memory or played by ear.

As time passed, the camp administration decided that I was not the right man to do farm labor. I was used to office work, and working on a farm was not exactly my cup of tea. One morning in

January 1945, we were ready to leave for work when four names were called out. Mine was among the four. The rest of the POWs were told that the four of us would be transferred to a penal camp because we were considered the poorest workers. I was shocked to hear this because even today I don't think I was that bad. Anyway, after everybody had left for work, we had to pack our few belongings and, under heavy guard, were transported by truck to Camp Cooke.

HERBERT SCHAFFRATH
When we arrived at Camp Florence, we were robbed of our head hair. Not even in the Wehrmacht did we have our hair cut this short. Thank God there were no exceptions among us.

On August 29, 1944, we were inoculated against six different illnesses. Soon afterward, we went to work in the cotton fields. Each person was issued a bag and was expected to pick a certain amount of cotton per day. To achieve our daily weight quota, not only was cotton added to the bag but also a few stones, rocks, and other things. The farmer was probably not very happy with everything that he found in those bags. As soldiers of the Third Reich, however, it was our duty to "damage the enemy in any way possible."

On September 24, 1944, we were transferred to Camp Cooke.

HANS-JOACHIM BÖTTCHER
When we got to Camp Florence, Arizona, we were housed in two-story wooden barracks. We all received fresh bedding, two sets of clothing and underwear, a straw hat and shoes, and $1.50 (in coupons) in advance payment. With a portion of that money, I bought my first beer in the canteen.

Between October 14 and 17, 1944, we formed labor groups to pick cotton. I was put in charge of a detail of some twenty POWs. Nobody had any great inclination to pick cotton. The average daily quantity of cotton picked by each prisoner was twenty pounds. Many just made themselves a pillow and dozed in the sun. On October 18, we packed our bags and were brought to a branch camp, Camp Eloy II. A few days earlier we had been screened once more and given new POW serial numbers. I received number 9WG-7202.

Eloy II was located about fifty miles southwest of Florence. We lived in tents, and many of us were fascinated by the scenery. I was again appointed detail leader, this time to a group of fifty to one hundred POWs. I had to supervise the weight of the cotton bags, which averaged about thirty pounds a day, per prisoner. Each POW received a wage of 80 cents per day regardless of how much cotton he picked. We were unfamiliar with this type of work, and were often distracted by animals, rattlesnakes, vipers, spiders, scorpions, etc. Sometimes we caught as many as five rattlers a day. Fortunately, no one was bitten. I recall that some POWs would kill the snakes and use their skin for making belts. This was done by pulling the skin over leather straps and fastening it with rivets that had been made from silver coins.

Problems started when American officers directed us to pick at least seventy-five pounds of cotton a day, per prisoner. On October 28, the camp commander personally reprimanded a comrade and me because our POWs had not achieved the quota. We knew that according to the Geneva Convention (we called it the Red Cross regulations) we had to work, but could not be forced to do certain quantities. A row developed when the commander refused to show us his copy of the regulations. At that point, my comrade pulled out his copy and presented it to the commander. This ended the conversation, and we were almost kicked out. The next morning two "agitators" and eighteen poor pickers were transferred back to Florence for disciplinary reasons. We were told that we would be sent to Montana for the sugar beet crop.

On November 3, we were put aboard a train at Florence headed for California. Aboard our train were about five hundred POWs. They had all been captured during the campaign in Normandy, France. Approximately half of these men went to Camp Cooke and made up the 4th Company. The remaining men went to the branch camp at Corcoran, California.

GEORG KROEMER

We stayed at Camp Florence in Arizona for about two months, picking cotton. In late September 1944, a rumor began circulating among the POWs that the cotton we picked was being used to manufacture ammunition. For this and other reasons, we decided to pick just enough cotton so that each man could make a pillow. We then napped in a furrow or simply relaxed in idle conversation. This little escapade lasted only a few days. Back at the camp, the Americans fenced us in on the sports field and gave us only bread and water until we would agree to work full-time. I don't recall how long the strike lasted, but toward the end the Americans doused us with fire hoses in one last attempt to persuade us to return to work. When this failed to break our resolve, we were ordered back to our barracks and received dry clothing. Shortly thereafter, we were put on trucks and sent to Camp Cooke.

KLAUS HEBEL
The POW camp at Florence was once part of a lime factory—or so we were told. At this camp, we had to pick cotton. This was very hot work for Europeans. After maybe two weeks, we were transported by truck to Camp Cooke. During the ride, I was amazed by the forest of oil derricks that we passed.

HELMUT WOLTER
At Camp Florence in Arizona, almost every POW was assigned to labor groups that picked cotton. After a few weeks, we were transferred to a camp at Chino, California. Camp Chino was a small branch camp of Camp Cooke. Its wooden barracks, each housing about twenty men, were originally built for Mexican farm laborers. I worked for a farmer by the name of Nando Migletta [or Miglietta]. In addition to producing wine, Mr. Migletta had orchards of walnuts, tomatoes, and southern Mediterranean fruits.

One day a group of us POWs were busy harvesting walnuts when suddenly we realized that our guard was nowhere to be found. We searched the orchards and found his rifle propped up against the tree, but no guard. At the end of the day we took his rifle back to the camp. We handed it to the camp commander who was at the gate to receive us. Since the gun was fully loaded with live ammunition and had not been fired, little was said of the incident. But that night, as if to reward us for our good conduct, we were treated to a cowboy movie in the camp.

In December 1944, a small group of us were sent to work in an orange grove for a Mr. Smith. On December 24, we worked only half a day. At noon, Mr. Smith invited us to his home for a cup of coffee and a piece of cake. Although this was a violation of the Army's anti-fraternization policy, no one ever reported this episode to the camp administration.

Typically, we always brought our lunch with us to the field. It generally consisted of a sandwich with sausage or cheese and a piece of fruit. The farmers provided the drinking water and occasionally gave us tea or coffee.

Shortly before Christmas we informed Captain [Almon F.] Rockwell[8] that we intended to have a Christmas celebration in the mess hall, complete with theatrical skits and songs. The captain had no objection and, in fact, asked that we reserve a few seats for the Americans who would be our guests. Since our whole celebration would be in German, which the guards did not understand, we decided that on behalf of our guests we would sing a Christmas song in English. From my school days, I remembered that included in our textbook, *The New Guide*, was an English Christmas song with many verses. Some of these I was able to piece together for the festival. The song went like this:

> While shepherds watched their flocks by night,
> All seated on the ground,
> The Angel of the Lord came down
> And glory shone around . . .

Although it was a British song and was largely unknown in the United States, the Americans were no less thrilled when we started singing. In fact, we were later asked to repeat the song for those Americans who were unable to attend the first performance.

At Camp Chino we had about thirty older POWs who, like the rest of us, were expected to work the fields and to meet the quota of filling sixty boxes of grapes a day. These men had histories of illnesses or war-related injuries that kept them from achieving the prescribed goal. When they returned in the evening to the camp with far fewer boxes than the required quota, they were immediately taken to jail cells. We thought this was incorrect and unjustified, and decided to make our point by organizing a labor strike the following day. None of the POWs reported for work. The farmers waiting at the gate with their trucks ready to take us to the fields had to return home without their workers. The American camp administration was furious.

The next day an American Army doctor arrived at the camp to examine the older POWs. He determined that they were incapable of meeting the prescribed quota. The doctor then examined everyone else in the camp and set new work quotas that were about 30 to 50 percent less than the original quota of sixty boxes of grapes for each man. After that incident, we had no more problems at work.

Between July 1945 and January 1946, I was transferred to three different labor camps at Pomona, Bakersfield, and Tipton. In Pomona, I worked as a general laborer in a warehouse. At the other two camps, I was assigned to the camp labor offices and worked directly for the American Army. I think that Camp Tipton was built specifically for the POWs—the barracks had a distinct military character. In Tipton, I remember we had a baker who prepared delicious North German butter cakes once a week. Around

January 1946, I was transferred to Camp Cooke and again worked in the labor office until our repatriation three months later.

ADOLF KELMER

I don't remember when we arrived at Camp Rupert, Idaho. I recall, however, that our barracks were generous in size, and that we received new clothing and shoes from military stock. As soon as we had our place in the camp and had our papers processed, most of us were sent to work in the fields. A few men remained in the camp during the day working in the kitchen, in the offices of the American administration, and as general laborers around the compound. I harvested potatoes and sugar beets on farms between Rupert and Burley, Idaho. For me, this was familiar work. From my earliest childhood days, potatoes and sugar beets were part of the yearly harvest on our farm.

After the morning roll call, we walked to the camp front gate where farmers were waiting with their trucks to take us to the fields. The land we worked was good and the climate was mild. The combination of these natural conditions produced an abundance of delectable crops. In fact, they were better and larger than the crops sowed back home. We used a John Deere tractor with front wheels spaced very close together. This design, which was unknown in Europe at that time, gave the tractor a very short turning radius.

It was surprising to me that we were paid for our labor. The money had significant buying power in the camp canteen. We bought cigarettes, sweets, toilet articles, and many other things that for a long time had been unavailable to us in the German army. I would have never thought that one could buy such wonderful things in a POW camp.

Around Christmas 1944, we had completed all the agricultural work near Camp Rupert. Since our labor was needed elsewhere in the country, the Army moved us to a site in central California. Personally, I would have been content to stay the winter at Camp Rupert, but once we were on the train all regrets of leaving this area were left behind.

Heading south, we first passed through Salt Lake City, Utah, and then turned west through Nevada to California. Along this journey we were greeted by beautiful sunrises that illuminated an unspoiled, sparsely populated countryside. Somewhere in either Utah or Nevada, the train crossed a dam and from both sides of the car one could see nothing but water. Since I was just waking up at this time while most of my comrades were still asleep, I could admire undisturbed this extraordinary theater of events. We later crossed a mountain range before entering the flat, rustic plains of central California. Across this region were quaint little villages whose houses and trees appeared different from what I had seen in Idaho. As we rolled past small railway stations, we were greeted by smiling and waving townspeople, some of whom were dressed in colorful Mexican clothing. They obviously did not notice the four-inch letters "PW" stenciled on the backs of our Army shirts, and must have thought we were American soldiers.

Our train ride ended at Bakersfield, where we arrived under a bright afternoon sun. We then boarded trucks that brought us to a tent camp in the middle of a large cotton field.[9] Although built up very smartly, the camp, in our view, was a social descent from the solid barracks of Camp Rupert. Nevertheless, we quickly adapted to our new surroundings.

Our tents at this camp were very spacious. Everyone had a good field cot with the necessary covers and a little cabinet for his possessions. There was also a table with a set of chairs. Placed in the middle of each tent was an oil heater that keep us warm on chilly nights. Everything stood on a double solid wood platform floor.

Other structures in the camp included a day room, a kitchen, a canteen, showers, and a latrine. Everything was mobile, but sufficient for our needs.

After a few days of settling in, we were sent out to pick cotton. Each man was expected to pick one hundred pounds of cotton every working day. During the early hours of the day and with the help of the morning dew, the work was tolerable. Toward noon under a hot sun, however, the harvesting of cotton became a very tedious and difficult regiment. Rumors soon began to circulate among the POWs that the cotton was being used in the manufacture of munitions. This became the motivation—or convenient excuse—for some POWs to ignore the required cotton quota.

Usually, because the work was so monotonous, we eased the burden of picking cotton by thinking of things that were enjoyable to us and scheming of ways to circumvent some of the work. In my particular group we dug a room under our tent and covered it with the wood floor. The soil that we removed was the same color as the top soil outside our tent. This made it easy for us to distribute the excavated soil throughout the camp. When the room was finished we placed a small table and stool inside and would take turns hiding there every workday. Even with much of the ground excavated, the wood floor that covered the hole was still structurally solid.

The First Weeks as POWs

An uneasiness developed between the guards and the POWs at certain times because the morning roll call always came up one short, but in the evening when the roll call was again conducted the count was correct.

One day while harvesting cotton, I foolishly did something without thinking about the consequences. Typically, at the end of the workday, each POW's sack of cotton was weighed and one or two people then climbed up on the side of the cotton wagon and dumped the contents of the sack into the wagon. Loading the wagon was a messy job. On this particular day, I offered to empty into the wagon the cotton bag of one of our hardest working POWs after I had also weighed it for him at the scale. My motive was not entirely honorable. I was actually trying to hide my own meager pickings.

Under the hot afternoon sun, surrounded by fields of white cotton puffs, was a small open square with a scale used to weigh the sacks of cotton. Nearby were many of the high-sided cotton wagons waiting to be filled. Standing around the scale were a group of POWs and guards, and in the center of that assemblage next to the scale was a large man with broad shoulders. Of all the people in that group, he was visibly the grimmest. At that time, I didn't fully understand that the farmer's livelihood depended upon the amount of cotton that was harvested. Several POWs gathered only a few pounds of cotton for whatever reason, but the farmer had to pay the Army full price for each man working on his field regardless of the amount of cotton that was picked.

With my comrade's bag of cotton, I climbed up on the wagon and prepared to unload its contents. Leaning forward, I noticed the guard standing below on the other side of the wagon. In a moment of brazen stupidity, I tossed the entire bag at the guard. It missed him but landed directly at his feet. The guard reacted as one might expect under the circumstances. I was immediately returned to the camp and brought before the camp commander. After some questioning, I was thrown into the clink, a tent near the guard tower, and placed on a diet of bread and water. First, though, I had to give the commander my belt and shoelaces. During the interrogation, I was treated coolly, but properly.

The first night in my new house I was cold and filled with a restless uneasy feeling. The sudden isolation from my comrades and the uncertainty of the extent and duration of my punishment was frazzling my nerves. The next morning I was up early. I couldn't decide whether it was better being in isolation and not picking cotton or in the company of others on the field. As I stood watching the POWs passing by my tent on their way to work, I saw in the faces of many of my comrades their disapproval of what I had done. Some resorted to catcalls and jeering. I was surprised and dismayed by their reaction. After this uncomfortable experience I remained inside my tent whenever the POWs were going to or coming from work.

That first morning after the men had left for work, I asked the guard if I could receive my bed cover from the barrack because it had been cold the night before. The guard spoke with his superior and told me that one of my comrades would bring me the blanket later that evening.

When I received my blanket, it was filled with all sorts of pleasant surprises. Knowing that I was restricted to a diet of bread and water, my friends had cut the cover open and loaded it with Coca-Cola, sausages, tobacco, etc., and then sewed it back together. Nothing was visible, but it had become very heavy. Just as my friends had expected, the guard only visually inspected the cover before it was given to me.

Although isolation causes one to feel lonely, I coped with my punishment by sitting in my tent with the necessary patience and a very well-prepared cover. The smoke from my self-rolled cigarettes wafted out the top of my tent.

During the day it was quiet in the camp, so I usually sat outside. After about eight days in isolation, I was transferred to Camp Cooke along with a few sick POWs. They were moved into the camp hospital. Shortly before my departure the guards returned my shoelaces, belt, barrack bag filled with my property, and handed me a notice of transfer. I was not allowed back into the branch camp. Apparently, I was too much of a troublemaker. I felt the antipathy of the Americans. Had I been an American soldier they probably would have discharged me from the military. No military in the world could tolerate what I did. In Germany, my punishment would have been much different, and even more extreme in other countries. But, of course, I was in America, so the intended punishment was in many respects a turn for the better.

WERNER BLANCK

The POW camp at Trinidad, Colorado, was well equipped down to the last detail. Even our beds had comfortable white cotton sheets. We never expected to receive so much excellent food, and overall it was like being in a first-class hotel. During all my years in the Wehrmacht, we never lived so well.

Camp Trinidad was a large camp with four compounds, each housing about one thousand prisoners. One of these compounds was strictly for officers. One day a German officer asked me to change places with him. I agreed and promptly received my "promotion" and transfer to the officers' quarters. He, on the other hand, became a private first class and was assigned to a labor detail outside the camp. That was exactly what he wanted. While on detail he escaped, but he was returned to the camp a few days later and reclaimed his commission.

During my time in the officers' compound there arrived three new German lieutenant colonels. Their first demand was to have separate toilets for themselves. The younger officers in the compound were astounded by this order, but had little say in the matter. The company barrack had about fifteen or twenty toilets, and each one had a sign painted on it that read: "This One for Lieutenant Colonels," "This One for Majors," "This One for Captains," and finally one large sign that said, "The rest are for the other assholes."

Soon after arriving at this camp I discovered that I could make a lot of money using my professional skills as a barber and hair stylist. I earned 80 cents a day from the American administration plus tips from the other POWs, especially from the German officers. With this money I bought a radio, a wristwatch, and whatever else I wanted from the canteen.

After three or four months, I transferred to Camp Warner at Tooele, Utah, along with about one thousand other POWs. Many of us worked in an Army supply depot doing cleaning work and were later glad to be sent to Camp Cooke.

WERNER GILBERT

The one thing I remember most about Camp Trinidad in Colorado was that some of the POWs dug a tunnel 120 feet long by 4 feet wide and that six men used it to escape. Once outside, they hitched a ride with a farmer who took them some 125 miles away from the camp. The POWs then divided into three groups of two men. Five of the men were captured within fourteen days. The last one, a U-boat crewman, was caught in a bar in Nevada. People there became suspicious of him because he had neither a car nor horse. One of the escaped POWs was an Me 109 fighter pilot. I heard that he was released to his parents, who were living in America because one of them was an American. He had been a student in Germany when the war broke out and went voluntarily into the Luftwaffe.[10] The other five men had their hair cut off and received thirty days detention in the POW stockade. None of the escaped POWs ever revealed the existence of the farmer.

On January 18, 1944, I was transferred to Camp Warner in Utah, and on September 29, 1944, I was moved to Fort Ord in California. While at Fort Ord, an American sergeant brutally beat two POWs. Because of my deposition against him, I was transferred to a POW camp at Tulare, California. Shortly after that incident I developed tonsillitis and was transferred to Camp Cooke for medical treatment on December 17, 1944.

Father FRANZ GÖDDE
In the late summer of 1943, we experienced a sandstorm at Camp Concordia, Kansas, that made night out of day. For days thereafter we worked to remove the sand from our barracks that had blown through every crack in the building. Meanwhile, we sat around in this camp for weeks not doing much of anything. Beginning in October, we were organized into labor groups and assigned jobs on the main Army post. This included working in the kitchens and trash pickup. Sometime in the autumn of 1943, a POW tried to scale the fence and was shot by a guard. The man had become mentally unstable and could not adjust to confinement.

In January 1944, about five hundred of us POWs were relocated to Camp Warner in Utah. Along the way, we passed a fantastic winter panorama of the snow-covered Rocky Mountains. When we got to Camp Warner, the snow was nearly three feet high. Until the end of March, our work at this camp consisted of shoveling snow. With the onset of warmer weather, we received all sorts of assignments, which included working in the various warehouses at the railroad yard in the main Army camp. In June 1944, the whole POW camp, kit and caboodle, was transferred to Camp Cooke. We were allowed to take all our possessions, including dogs and cats. To accommodate our diverse belongings the Americans put two additional freight cars on our train.

HEINRICH KERSTING
Although I was at Camp Phillips for about six months, I only worked at this camp for about thirteen days doing miscellaneous odd jobs on the Army post. Around February 1944, we were transferred to an Army ordnance depot at Camp Warner in Tooele, Utah. My first job at this camp was to help remove the interiors of tanks, especially leather items, and to store these parts in a warehouse already jammed with American equipment.

On one other occasion when I worked in this camp, I was assigned to a labor group as a translator for an American civilian supervisor. We had to pack ballast under the railroad ties, which we did by hammering the rocks in place to the rhythm of the old marching song, "Alte Kameraden." Apparently our pace was too slow for the supervisor, who told us to speed up the work. We simply ignored him and worked to the rhythm of the song. Pretty soon an American officer appeared and asked what was going on. I told him that we were working carefully for the safety of the train and pointed out that where the Americans had laid the ballast the train would wobble along the tracks. With our work, however, the train would travel straight as an arrow. He just smiled and led us back to the camp.

On April 20, 1944 (Hitler's birthday), the entire camp went on strike. The American commander ordered us out of our barracks and sent us marching in columns to a fenced area on the recreation field. At noon we were given dry white bread and buckets of water for our meal. The bread we flung back over the fence and the water we dumped. Placed around the field were American guards, armored vehicles, and jeeps. When evening arrived we were sent back to our barracks. The American commander then directed the German kitchen crews to give us our dinner and the lunch we had missed. That night we feasted with pleasure. Small altercations with the guards during the day didn't amount to much later.

At the end of June 1944, we were transferred to Camp Cooke, California.

RUDOLF HINKELMANN

I stayed at Camp Phillips, receiving the best of care, until January 1944. From there I was moved to Camp Warner at Tooele, Utah. When we arrived at the railway station near Tooele, it was cold, and you could see the snow-covered mountaintops in the distance. Waiting for us at the station were Army buses that took us into the camp. Our barracks were very clean. The beds were fitted with fresh linen. On each bed were two blankets, towels, shaving articles, toiletries, and many other items for our daily use.

The meals were well balanced and always of excellent quality. I was fortunate to be assigned to Company 4 because we had two professional hotel cooks who prepared all our meals. The American soldiers had the same provisions, but our meals were prepared considerably better. If I'm not mistaken, some of the guards ate with us at the first two tables.

The tables in our dining room were always perfectly made up by our kitchen crew. The cups, plates, and the silverware were meticulously aligned. This sense of organization impressed the American camp authorities.

During one of our dinners, an especially hardline POW stood up and tried to encourage the other POWs in the dining hall to break as many dishes and other things as possible and to burn the food supply. This, he said, would hurt the enemy. I refused to participate in this act and asked the other POWs to do the same. "It would be ridiculous," I said, "if we expected to bring the Americans to their knees with this sort of action. Moreover, we would lose all the goodwill that we have earned with them. We had obtained the respect of the Allies by waging a fair war in Africa. We shouldn't resort to acting like spoiled children." My words found approval, and I was applauded. Because I had responded in this way, I was now on the *Schlägertruppen*'s blacklist. Time and again I received written threats through various routes. Fortunately, I was transferred to Camp Cooke before any of these threats were carried out.

I did, however, participate in a celebration of Adolf Hitler's birthday on April 20, 1944. It wasn't so much a matter of conviction as it was a small opportunity to annoy the Americans. Not a single POW was supposed to work that day. Because we refused to work, the Americans fenced us in on the recreation field and gave us only bread and water to eat. The kitchen personnel and their required assistants were kept at their places of work. During the day, they prepared a delicious supper for us. Meanwhile, toward the end of the day we had reconciled our differences with the guards and invited them to join us for dinner later that evening. If I remember correctly, some of them, including the camp commander, who was a major of Polish extraction, accepted our invitation.

HEINRICH SCHÜNEMANN

My first prisoner of war camp in America was Camp Custer in Michigan. I stayed there for five days before going on to Camp Ellis in Illinois, on July 18, 1944. Ten days later I moved to a branch camp called Camp Eureka (west of Peoria). Here we lived in a school gymnasium and worked in Libby's corn factory. Without fences to keep us in, some of the men would slip out at night and later regaled us with stories about romancing American women. Personally, I have my doubts about these claims.

I developed scabies at Camp Eureka and was moved back to the main camp for treatment on September 4, 1944. After my recovery, I worked in the mess hall as a kitchen helper. Our cooks at Camp Ellis developed a fairly lucrative business selling bottles of schnaps for camp money. They had, after all, all the ingredients at their disposal to make the stuff. Another popular method of making an alcoholic drink was to buy two bottles of Canadian

Ace beer and mix in a few drops of Listerine mouthwash. Both items were sold in our canteen.

Probably the richest fellow at Camp Ellis was an elderly Austrian POW. He was a master craftsman of stringed instruments who, for the right price in American dollars and all the raw materials, secretly made custom guitars for U.S. Army personnel.

At Camp Ellis, some POWs wore their German uniforms during national holidays. Others, to make a few dollars, sold parts of their uniform or decorations to guards and civilian employees at warehouses, factories, or farms.

While at Camp Ellis, we received care packages from the German Red Cross. They contained cigarettes and dark bread, apparently made for U-boat crews. With too few packages to distribute to everyone in the camp, we had to draw lots for half a slice of bread and some cigarettes. Later, when German Luftwaffe coats arrived, we again had to draw lots.

The American camp administration offered us many diverse activities to help occupy our free time. Available to us were education courses, frequent showings of American entertainment and instructional films, and even a few German films. Sometimes in the evening we POWs would sing songs. On Sundays, the recreation field was the place to be for both fans and players of soccer matches. Nice weather permitting, it was always a pleasure to take a walk around the camp with friends and to discuss the latest news and rumors of the day.

During my free time, I also played accordion with the camp's "light music band." As I recall, our *Lagersprecher* [camp spokesman] or the band leader obtained the instruments through the U.S. Army officer whom we called the welfare officer. I think this officer had several options of where to obtain the instruments: Army stock, local church donations, the YMCA, the International Red Cross, or from the German Red Cross. The same options probably existed for educational materials, sports equipment, theater props, and costumes. Since the accordion was not my personal property, it stayed behind when I was transferred.

On September 5, 1945, I was relocated to Camp Grant for a week and then to Camp Lodi, twenty-three miles from Madison, Wisconsin. At Lodi, we worked the night shift at the California Packing Corporation in Arlington, canning corn and beans. We also cut cabbage and put it into large wooden barrels together with salt to make sauerkraut.

CHAPTER 4

Organization and Management at Camp Cooke

THE PROVOST Marshal General's Office, which functioned as a staff division of the Army Service Forces, was responsible for all matters pertaining to enemy prisoners of war in the United States. However, by August 1942, a series of Army reorganizations had delegated much of its operational control to nine regional service commands of the ASF. Army posts located within these geographic areas were categorized as Class I installations and were placed under the commanding generals of service commands. Service command units, the local operating arms of each service command, carried out many of the command's functions. For instance, at Camp Cooke, Service Command Unit 1908 of the Ninth Service Command operated the main Army post and its prisoner of war camp. The commanding officer of the POW camp reported directly to the post commander, who, in turn, answered to the Ninth Service Command general. Headquarters for the Ninth Service Command was at Fort Douglas in Salt Lake City, Utah.[1]

In March 1944, Headquarters Army Service Forces in Washington, D.C., directed the commanding general of the Ninth Service Command to begin construction of a prisoner of war camp at Camp Cooke for one thousand German prisoners. The project was to be coordinated with the chief of engineers and the provost marshal general.[2]

According to the initial camp design, six theater of operations (T/O) barracks at Cooke were to be remodeled and used by the prisoners as an infirmary, a chapel, a guardhouse, two laundries, and a post exchange. Four housing barracks, presumably from the main post, were to be moved to the site of the proposed POW camp and eight standard guard towers constructed. (Two of these towers would later be placed around the POW hospital.) The design included installation of an electrical system, security fences, and paved roads. Most of the roads would consist of shale and gravel carved out of the local countryside and covered with a coating of liquid asphalt. The estimated cost for this project was $51,850. Not much later, several more barracks and a large recreation field were added to the stockade as indicated in subsequent diagrams. No construction records of the POW camp remain.[3]

On April 7, 1944, the *Lompoc Record* broke the news to residents that one thousand German prisoners of war were to be confined at Camp Cooke. Based on a press release issued by the Army's Ninth Service Command, the paper indicated that construction of the POW camp was already underway and would be completed by June 10, 1944. The camp opened in time for the arrival of the first German prisoners on June 16, and was officially established ten days later by the Ninth Service Command per General Order 144.[4]

The prisoner of war camp was located at the northwest corner of Cooke at C Street between Idaho and Montana avenues. Its design, which was fairly typical of other POW camps, consisted of a barracks section and a recreation field. The rectangular barracks section measured 450 feet by 860 feet and was slightly more than twice the size of the recreation area. Surrounding the stockade were two 10-foot high chain link fences eight feet apart with barbed wire overhangs and six guard towers outfitted with machine guns. The entire stockade resembled an inverted letter L with the toe portion representing the recreation yard.[5] Despite its formidable appearance, the base camp was functionally comfortable. Inside the stockade were twenty domicile barracks constructed of plasterboard, each measuring 20 feet by 100 feet. There were also four kitchens/mess halls, four lavatories, two laundries, a canteen, an infirmary, a theater, a guardhouse to temporarily segregate recalcitrant or protective custody prisoners, and several barracks used for recreation, classrooms, storage, and administration.[6]

A short distance from the compound between Fire Road and North Hospital Road was the POW hospital. It consisted of two 25-foot by 150-foot wards isolated from the main Army hospital by twin security fences and two guard towers. Staffing the hospital were U.S. military personnel and German Medical Corps soldiers. A German-speaking American Army doctor visited the hospital daily.[7]

Responsibility for the overall operation of the POW camp and the handling of its prisoners rested with the commanding officer of Camp Cooke. With the concurrence of the service commander, he was also authorized to establish and operate branch POW camps. Typically, camp operations and policies were formulated based on War Department and service command regulations and policies, as well as the Geneva Convention.[8]

As indicated in Table 1, Major Earl E. Phillips was the first commanding officer of the POW camp at Cooke. He was officially assigned to the position on June 17, 1944. A headquarters staff of ten officers, thirty enlisted men, and a guard detachment assisted Major Phillips. Heading his staff was Lieutenant (later Captain) Floyd T. Smith, the executive officer, whose duties included supervising the prisoner work program and handling prisoner discipline and punishment.[9]

Table 1. American Commanding Officers at POW Camp, Camp Cooke[10]

Name and Rank	Date Assumed Command
Maj. Earl E. Phillips	June 1944
Col. Charles L. Clifford	Unknown
Maj. Floyd C. Mims	May 1945
Lt. Col. Francis S. Fuller	July 1945
Maj. Arthur J. Wojnowski	November 1945
Lt. Col. E. I. Foster	February 1946

Major Phillips' other staff members were Lieutenant (later Captain) Raymond Wimber, adjutant who supervised all administrative and fiscal matters and ensured that Army regulations were enforced; Lieutenant (later Captain) John T. Pellew, supply officer with additional duty as transportation officer; Lieutenant Alexander G. Makarounis, company commander of POW Co. #1; Lieutenant Lucius D. Remington, company commander of POW Co. #2 with the additional duty as assistant supply officer; Lieutenant Anthony R. Lis-Sette, company commander of POW Co. #3 with additional duty as athletic and recreational officer; Lieutenant George W. Foth, mess supervisor and ration breakdown officer; Lieutenant Harold W. Wolff, purchasing officer with additional duty as POW canteen officer; Lieutenant Theodore Dammel, postal officer with additional duties as work supervision officer, assistant adjutant, and assistant personnel officer; and Lieutenant John H. Ortner, provost marshal with additional duty as intelligence officer. On June 28, 1944, a fourth POW company was added at Cooke.[11]

The final group in the POW camp hierarchy was the guard contingent, which consisted of a detachment of military police.

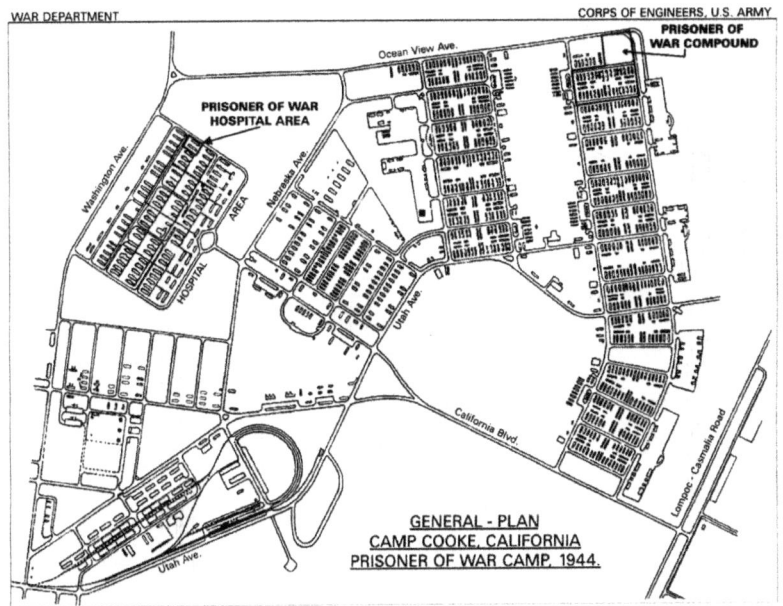

The main cantonment area of Camp Cooke, showing the POW camp at the upper right and the POW hospital barracks adjacent to the U.S. Army Station Hospital, April 1944. (Courtesy of U.S. Army)

In September 1944, the detachment was under the command of Lieutenant Flem W. Sleeth and consisted of about 125 men. Their duties were generally divided into two categories: stockade security, which involved manning the towers and the main gate; and escort duty, which involved escorting prisoners between labor details or for other authorized purposes.[12]

The officer of the day was in charge of the guard detachment. The OD was detailed daily by the camp adjutant from a roster of available officers on the main post. Every day at 6:30 a.m. and at 5 p.m. (except on Sundays when the hours were 7:30 a.m. and 4:30 p.m.), the OD was at the main gate of the POW camp to receive reports from company officers conducting physical counts inside the compound. He was also at the gate when labor details left in the morning and afternoon for work. In the evening, he was at the gate to supervise the searching of prisoners returning from work to the stockade.[13]

Staffing at the POW camp changed frequently and considerably. Many of these reassignments were the result of branch camp activations or deactivations and the Army's standard practice of staff rotations. At the same time, the number of personnel assigned to the camp, particularly guards and medical/dental corps

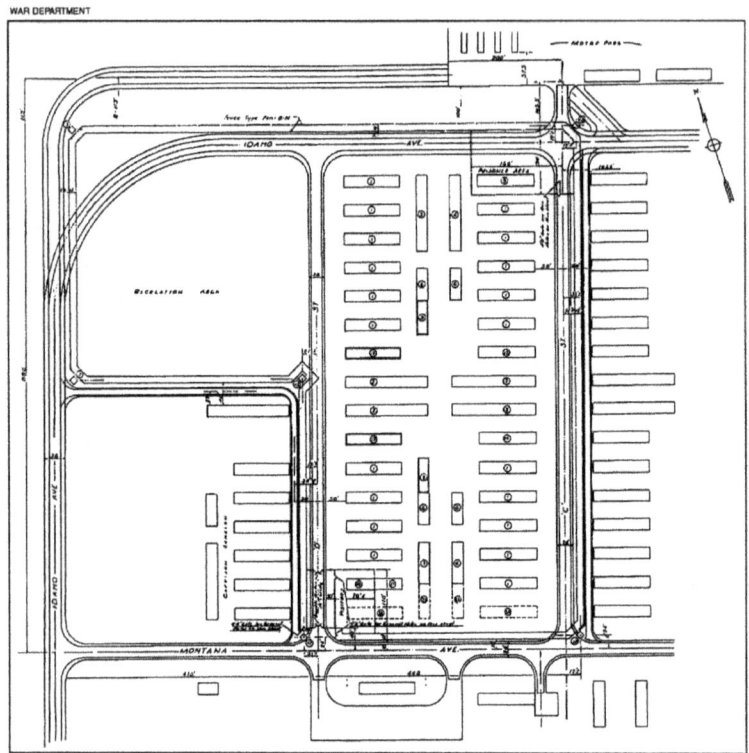

The POW camp, April 1944. (Courtesy of U.S. Army)

personnel, fluctuated with the POW population. Perhaps the two most notable additions to the headquarters staff at Camp Cooke were a POW branch camp inspector, Lieutenant Colonel Frank N. Mallory, and an assistant executive officer, Lieutenant (later Captain) John T. Harris. Holding one of the most important positions in the camp, Lieutenant Harris managed the POW reeducation, athletic, and recreational programs as well as the prisoners' trust fund.[14]

On the evening of June 16, 1944, the first trainload of German prisoners arrived at Camp Cooke. They came from Camp Warner at Tooele, Utah, and had been captured in North Africa. An official record with the exact number of POWs arriving at Cooke that day is unavailable. The earliest surviving document showing POW population numbers is an inspection report prepared by Maurice Perret of the Swiss Legation. Visiting Camp Cooke on September 23, 1944, Perret reported 458 prisoners in the main camp and an additional 211 assigned to the branch camp at Tagus Ranch at Tulare.[15]

The POWs at Camp Cooke transformed their barrack grounds into a beautifully decorated landscape. (Courtesy of Werner Blanck)

Later arrivals to Camp Cooke eventually raised the average number of prisoners held at the main camp to about 1,200. In September 1945, the POW camp newspaper, *Der Lagerspiegel*, reported the number of prisoners in the camp had increased to 2,300. The highest combined number of POWs at Cooke and its branch camps was 8,700, in mid-January 1946. This number undoubtedly included prisoners from other camps, housed briefly at Camp Cooke while en route back to Germany.[16]

The prisoners at Cooke were organized into four companies, each with an initial allotment of about 250 men. Each company occupied five housing barracks.[17] Like every other prisoner of war camp in the United States, Cooke had a POW spokesman. The position was guaranteed by Article 43 of the Geneva Convention, which stated "in every place where there are prisoners of war, they shall be allowed to appoint agents entrusted with representing them directly with military authorities and protecting Powers." Known as the camp spokesman or *Lagersprecher* (sometimes referred to as the *Lagerleitung* or *Lagerführer* by the prisoners), he was the focal point between the prisoners in the camp and the American camp administration. Among a myriad of responsibilities, he was empowered by the Geneva Convention to investigate working conditions and to object to

Capt. Floyd Smith and Maj. Arthur Wojnowski, 1945. (Courtesy of John Pellew)

undesirable situations. He also had access to representatives from the Swiss Legation and with relief organizations such as the International Red Cross and the YMCA. At Camp Cooke, the spokesman was popularly elected and, theoretically, carried out his responsibilities with the approval of the American camp commander. Assisting the camp spokesman were a camp interpreter and camp clerk. In September 1944, the POW camp spokesman at Cooke was Alfred Dahlmann. He was succeeded by Joachim Schermbach.[18]

The next echelon down in the German POW camp administration was the company spokesman, or *Kompaniesprecher*. He

Left to right, Lt. John Harris, Capt. John Pellew, and Lt. Harold Wolff. (Courtesy of John Pellew)

represented the interest of his company to the camp spokesman, and oversaw his company's orderly room and kitchen staffs. Personnel in the orderly room attended to the morning reports, sick calls, the distribution and receipt of mail, and other administrative duties. Most of the barrack chores were carried out by a designated barrack elder. This position was usually filled by an older POW or one with a medical exemption from hard labor because of illness or war-related injuries. A similar arrangement existed at each of the branch camps.[19]

German Prisoners of War at Camp Cooke, California

Seated with Company 2 at Camp Cooke, Rudolf Hinkelmann is ninth from right. (Courtesy of Rudolph Hinkelmann)

RUDOLF HINKELMANN

According to my notes, we left Camp Warner, Utah, on June 15, 1944, and arrived at Camp Cooke the following day. This was a new camp, and everything was done here to make our involuntary stay as comfortable as possible. Fifty prisoners were assigned to each housing barrack. In my company we also had one barrack with enough basins to wash our clothes. We had sanitary toilets and shower facilities, and plenty of hot water day and night. The meals were excellent and plentiful, I would even say overflowing. I would be lying if I said it had been different.

Rudolf Hinkelmann at Camp Cooke.

In accordance with Article 43 of the Geneva Convention, POWs in each camp were authorized to have a spokesman who would represent their interest to the military administration of the camp. The spokesman was also empowered by the Geneva Agreement to represent the POWs at conferences or meetings with members of the Swiss Legation and such humanitarian organizations as the International Red Cross and the YMCA.

From my experiences the spokesman was not always the highest-ranking POW, nor did he have to be fluent in English. Rather, he was elected by the POWs because he was expected to represent their best interest in dealings with the American camp administration.

The Americans were always very sensitive about the periodic inspections of the camp by Swiss and Red Cross representatives. Article 88 of the Geneva Agreement had guaranteed their access to the POWs. Any negative report about German POWs being mistreated would have brought swift retaliation against American POWs in Germany.

Without exaggeration, we POWs were well treated and lacked nothing. For this reason there were no major incidents during my time at Camp Cooke.

Werner Blanck at Camp Cooke.

WERNER BLANCK

I was in the first group of prisoners to arrive at Camp Cooke on June 16, 1944. We were grouped into three companies. Later a fourth company was established. Each company was composed of five housing barracks as well as a bathhouse and a kitchen/dining room barrack. We also had several utility buildings for use by the whole camp. These included an office, a canteen, and a theater. We made the theater by modifying the interior of an existing building.

Heinrich Kersting's official Army photo at Camp Cooke, June 1944.

HEINRICH KERSTING

We left Camp Warner on June 25, 1944, and arrived at Camp Cooke later that night. Although the darkness kept us from getting a good look at the camp, our first impression of Camp Cooke was favorable. For soccer players like myself, we were eager to see the recreation field. The next morning we were disappointed because as far as the eye could see there was nothing but sand. The recreation field was made playable through a joint effort of the Americans and the POWs. The Americans provided the tools and the hardware, and we performed the necessary hand labor. Large earth-handling equipment such as bulldozers were operated by Americans.

In the German Wehrmacht, every unit had an individual responsible for guard and order. He was known as the noncommissioned officer of the day (*Unteroffzier vom Dienst, UvD*). Using a whistle, his primary job was to go from barrack to barrack waking up the troops. Basically, we used the same system at Camp Cooke, where early each workday morning the company was awakened by the UvD. We then got dressed and stood in front of our beds for roll call. The process was conducted jointly by the German spokesman and an American sergeant. The company commander or his representative would verify the number of individuals in each barrack. POWs who were too sick to stand for roll call had to be identified and shown on the roster. Immediately following the count, they were required to report to the infirmary where an American doctor examined them. If the POW was seriously ill, he was transferred to the camp hospital outside the stockade. Once the count had cleared, we rushed to the mess hall for breakfast. After breakfast the men would report to their respective workplaces.

An American doctor conducted monthly physical inspections of each POW. Immediately after waking up, we had to stand naked in front of our beds while the doctor dutifully strolled down the aisle checking for signs of disease or infestation.

Each POW company at Camp Cooke had a spokesman, a translator, a clerk, and a barrack elder. The elder carried out all sorts of mundane but important tasks around the barrack. Our company clerk was Karl Christiansen. He was in charge of entertainment, which included arranging theater performances and movies.

In Company 2 where I was assigned, the company spokesman, translator, clerk, and barrack elder slept in a separate administration room set aside in one barrack. I was the translator. When the Americans decided to consolidate most of these positions, I was also appointed the barrack elder and company spokesman. As the spokesman, I was the intermediate link between the American guards and the POWs of our company. It meant dealing with a lot of men who had vastly different personalities and who were often very homesick. It was not easy to please everyone. I remember holding discussions with both German and American camp representatives about ways to improve the camp and the personal worries and troubles of the POWs. Because of my diverse duties in the camp, I seldom worked outside the compound gates. Nevertheless, I received the standard salary of 80 cents a day or $24.80 per month plus an extra three dollars.

Franz Gödde, back row third from left, on the steps of the contracting office at Camp Cooke.

Father FRANZ GÖDDE

In June 1944, all five hundred POWs at Camp Warner were relocated to Camp Cooke. If I remember correctly, we retained the same POW company structure at Cooke that existed at Warner. Since this was the second or third camp for us in America, and all these camps were similarly organized, we quickly adapted to our new surroundings. After a few days, we were put to work.

Herbert Schaffrath on the right with two companions at Camp Cooke.

HERBERT SCHAFFRATH

When I arrived at Camp Cooke on September 25, 1944, I was pleasantly surprised to find so much green landscape in the camp compared to the desert at Camp Florence.

Our train had stopped inside the Army post at Camp Cooke, and we were then driven by bus to the POW camp. Inside the stockade we were lined up before the *Lagersprecher*, who explained to us the rules, regulations, and policies of the camp. He also handed out written instructions and told us that we would be working outside the camp in agricultural jobs or inside on the main Army post. Everybody eagerly hoped they would be chosen for work inside the main camp and not have to go out into the fields. A few days later, I was given the job of harvesting sugar beets.

Inside the camp, the German *Lagersprecher* was the middleman between the American Army administration and the POWs. On the one hand, he had to convey the orders of the Americans to the POWs. On the other hand, he had to represent the best interest of the POWs to the command section. It was not a comfortable position. Incidentally, the title *Lagersprecher* was the officially recognized term within the camp. Other titles such as *Lagerführer* expressed the same thought. But this name was viewed with disfavor by most POWs who already had had enough of one Führer.

The interior of our barracks was always clean and neatly organized, just as we had become accustomed to in the German army. Each barrack was equipped with two large oil stoves that heated our quarters during the winter months. Our beds were fitted with good mattresses, quilt covers, and pillows. Stowed on shelves along the wall were our meager belongings. And finally, the "pinup girls" of the day decorated our walls.

GEORG KROEMER
It was sometime in late September 1944 when I arrived at Camp Cooke. Cooke was an exemplary camp. We received appetizing meals and clean clothing. The barracks were spotless and our sanitation system excellent.

HANS-JOACHIM BÖTTCHER
We arrived at Camp Cooke on November 4, 1944. The train stopped inside the main Army post, and we were then marched to the POW camp. We lined up inside the compound in front of the German camp spokesman's office, where he greeted us. He told us that Cooke was "*ein ruhiges Lager*" (a quiet camp) and warned us not to start any political activities. He urged us to follow the advice of the 750 or so *"Afrikaners"* who were already in the camp.

My first impression of Camp Cooke was that this could be a place where one could breathe freely. The whole camp was generous in size and style. In contrast to other places such as the camp

Hans-Joachim Böttcher at Camp Cooke.

at Florence, Arizona, where we definitely had *Schlägertruppen*, the individuals at Cooke had no political ambitions, no swastikas, no flags, and did not stage demonstrations.

WERNER GILBERT

I arrived at Camp Cooke on December 17, 1944. Although I was transferred to this camp for medical reasons, I was fortunate to find steady work inside the stockade that kept me here until my repatriation in 1946.

The POWs at Cooke were grouped into four companies. Each company had five barracks, and within each barrack were housed fifty men. I was assigned to Company 2, Barrack 3. Together, we represented a diverse mixture of men from the army, air force, and navy. To my knowledge the highest military rank among the POWs was chief master sergeant. Among the Luftwaffe personnel in the camp was a pilot who flew a Messerschmitt (Me) 109 and another who piloted a Me 262.

ALFRED SCHMUCKER

When the four of us arrived at Camp Cooke in January 1945, we spent the first night in the camp jailhouse. Around ten o'clock the next morning, everything was quiet. We began banging on the doors and barred windows, trying to attract attention. The guards had completely forgotten about us. After apologizing to us, they led us to the U.S. officers' mess hall where we were served a wonderful breakfast. Afterward, we were each assigned to four different barracks within the camp.

Inside the compound there was a POW staff that kept things rolling. We had a camp spokesman, translators, barbers, tailors, shoemakers, cooks, bakers, kitchen helpers, clerks for the orderly rooms of each company, and more. All of these positions were carried as "overhead" on the official labor reports. Individuals assigned to these jobs were selected based on their education or profession.

Elderly and medically unfit POWs, exempt from full-time labor, were carried as "light duty" on the rosters. They were assigned to specific jobs within the stockade such as janitorial duties, helping in the canteen, keeping streets clean within the compound, and miscellaneous other details. In our barrack we had an elderly POW who was limited to light duty. Because of his medical disability, he only received ten cents a day in official Army coupons. To increase his earnings, we all donated a portion of our pay to him. In return, he kept the barrack clean and did our shopping at the canteen during the day so we didn't have to stand in line in the evening during rush hour. He also filled our kerosene stoves and was our handyman.

Our bedsheets were washed by the quartermaster laundry, but all other things such as our clothing and underwear we had to wash ourselves at our own expense. For this purpose we bought Rinso and Lux soap flakes at our canteen. Few POWs at Cooke were professional soldiers. Approximately 98 percent were enlisted soldiers; the rest were noncommissioned officers (sergeants). All types of civilian professions were represented in the camp.

Discipline and morale among the POWs was very good even after almost three years behind barbed wire. The very few negative exceptions were handled by the POWs themselves.

ADOLF KELMER

Much to my satisfaction I was transferred from the tent camp in central California to Camp Cooke sometime in January or February 1945.

The POW compound at Camp Cooke was composed of the same type of barracks that the Americans used on the main post and included all the facilities one might expect to find in a regular army camp. Within the compound each company had its own living quarters, washrooms, toilets, kitchen, and mess hall. The dormitories usually held between thirty and forty people. Each person stored his personal belongings in a small cabinet alongside his bed and in a large duffel bag stowed underneath. Every prisoner also had access to the canteen, the theater, the recreation field, and the library with its large selection of books, many written in German.

An elderly POW handled housekeeping duties within our barrack. In return, we each gave him a small amount of our camp money.

Despite the close living conditions in our barrack, there were no significant altercations among us POWs. There were, however, cliques that sometimes formed based on mutual interests or hometown regions. In my barrack, the Rhinelanders organized their own fraternity. They always sat together in the mess hall and wherever possible acted as a group. Anyone who got too close to them knew by expression or gesture that outsiders were not welcome. We also had a few ruffians in the camp who for whatever reason were always trying to prove their toughness. In general, the social interaction inside the camp and at the work sites was good.

German Prisoners of War at Camp Cooke, California

Adolf Kelmer, front row, third from left, at Camp Cooke.

Overall, we had a colorful group of people at Camp Cooke. Thrown together from the most diverse regions of the Germanic language areas, we represented various sociological and professional levels, and had come from different parts of the Wehrmacht. For those of us willing to learn from this cross section of camp society, it was an excellent school of knowledge.

Morning reveille was early enough so that even the slowest POW could leisurely indulge in his personal grooming and still get to the morning roll call on time. Nobody had to shove or push because our washrooms were amply suited to accommodate more people at one time than we had.

After roll call came breakfast, which for most of us was simply wonderful. In fact, we had plenty of delicious food and an excellent variety available for all our meals. Such bounteous meals were not available at home, not even on high holidays and before the war. After breakfast we had a few minutes to run small errands or to stand around talking with friends while happily awaiting the coming new work day.

HEINRICH SCHÜNEMANN

On October 14, 1945, we boarded a train headed for Bakersfield, California. We arrived at our destination five days later and then went by truck convoy about ten miles to the newly established

Heinrich Schünemann on the far right with his fellow tent-dwellers at Camp Old River.

tent camp at Old River. This camp was a branch camp of Camp Cooke.

When we got to the camp, the captain lined us up and called for cooks, butchers, clerks, interpreters, and other personnel needed to operate the facility. He also asked for two electricians. Only Walter Bankrath stepped forward. Again, the officer shouted, "Are there any electricians here?" I said to myself, "This is my chance." I stepped forward even though I was not qualified. I figured that with a skilled number one man, I would have no difficulty performing the job. As it turned out, I learned a lot from Walter about being an electrician.

We spent our first day in the camp putting up tents for the guards and the POWs. We also attended to various other duties, including organizing supplies and setting up kitchen equipment. At first there was a lot of confusion in the camp. But gradually, as routines were established and all of us settled into our new surroundings, camp operations began to run smoothly.

KLAUS HEBEL

I arrived at Camp Cooke in late May or early June 1945. Our reception at Camp Cooke was typically military—the usual roll call and count. I was at this camp during my first stay for maybe two weeks before being transferred to the branch camp near Goleta.

Klaus Hebel, 1945.

Sometime late one night during these first two weeks came an announcement over the public-address system that everyone should assemble on the sports field for roll call. Lined up in neat rows were about 1,000 to 1,500 men. The Americans counted again and again and each time they came up one prisoner short. This became very comical to me. The counting came to an abrupt end when suddenly a sandstorm kicked up and everybody ran to the safety of the barracks.

CHAPTER 5

Prisoner of War Labor Program

BY 1943, MORE than nine million Americans had been recruited into the armed services, resulting in a critical shortage of civilian workers. To help fill the ranks of its diminishing labor force, the government turned to the POW labor pool. As with other aspects of the POW program, the labor portion was based entirely on the Geneva Convention and Army regulations. Signed by the United States in 1929 and ratified by Congress three years later, the accord stated that prisoners could be required to work for the benefit of their captors, providing that the tasks were consistent with the provisions of the Convention.[1]

Section III, Articles 27-34, of the Geneva Convention became the basis of the POW labor program. Article 27 authorized belligerents the use of POW labor. It exempted the use of officers, however, and limited noncommissioned officers to supervisory duties unless they specifically requested work. Article 28 required the detaining country to ensure that prisoners who were working under contract were properly paid and that their health and well-being were properly maintained. Article 29 required that the POW be physically fit for a particular job. Article 30 stated that the length of a prisoner's workday, including transportation to and from the work site, should not be "excessive," and that in any case, should not exceed the number of hours assigned to civilian workers in the region employed at the same work. Further, every prisoner was entitled to a rest period of twenty-four consecutive hours every week, preferably on Sunday. Article 31 prohibited the use of POW labor in enterprises directly connected with war operations, such as the manufacturing and transporting of arms or munitions or the transporting of materials intended for combat use. Article 32 stated that prisoners were not to be used at "unhealthful or dangerous work." Article 33 entitled POW labor detachments to the same food, sanitary, and medical services available at POW camps. Finally, Article 34 stated that prisoners who performed work connected with the administration, management, and maintenance of the camp would not be paid. All other types of work would be compensated, and the wages fixed by agreements between the belligerents. In addition, a pecuniary savings plan was to be established for the POWs.[2]

Operating within the articles of the Geneva Convention, POW labor eventually moved into nearly every type of job existing inside and outside the stockade at Camp Cooke. This included mechanical and civil engineering positions, heavy equipment jobs, grounds maintenance, laundries, and even food service. At the combined maintenance shops, prisoners repaired and reconditioned virtually all government-issued items, including automobiles, electrical systems, office machines, clothing, and various canvas and webbing articles. They also worked at the Army's rock quarry at Point Sal on the northern edge of Camp Cooke. There they operated the rock crusher and drove many of the dump trucks carrying aggregate to Cooke, where it was used to line ditches and to build roads. To control the mosquito population at Cooke, POW labor was used to build a flush dam at the lower end of two small lakes in May 1945 (excavating four thousand feet of drainage ditch). During that same month, prisoners were used to plant and harvest fruits and vegetables on a plot of land one mile west of the main gate at Cooke along the Lompoc-Casmalia road. The produce ended up on the dining room tables of the camp mess halls. The American camp administration determined the number of POWs needed for these and other assignments at Cooke. The requirements were passed to the POW orderly rooms to make the individual appointments.[3]

Since the United States did not have an agreement with the enemy nations for a minimum labor rate to be paid prisoners of war, the War Department set the rate at 80 cents a day, roughly equivalent to the $21 a month paid the American private in 1941. POWs who did not work or who performed administrative and maintenance details within the stockade received a gratuity of 10 cents a day, which enabled them to purchase certain necessities in the canteen. They could also receive a monthly allowance at the discretion of the camp commander if their tasks were deemed essential, required specialized training, and were full-time. These positions included camp spokesmen, interpreters, clerks, supply men, cooks, assistant cooks, prisoner first sergeants, or infirmary workers in the stockade or within the American camp administration.[4]

Enlisted personnel with a physical disability or permanent battle injury that kept them from performing paid labor for a sufficient number of days to earn $3 in one month, were entitled to a stipend from the camp POW trust fund to make their total income equal to $3 for that month.[5]

Each POW's earnings and personal deductions were recorded on an Individual Pay Data Record that looks like an old-fashioned bank account statement. (Courtesy of Werner Blanck)

Payment in all cases was made in canteen coupons, or credited to the individual's POW trust fund account established in the U.S. Treasury. The balance of a prisoner's monthly allowances, earnings, or pay, after deductions was recorded on their Individual Pay Data Record (WD, PMG Form No. 20, and later WD AGO Form 19-13).[6]

Subject to the approval of the camp commander, a prisoner could make withdrawals from his personal trust fund account to defray personal expenses. Payment was made by a check that was endorsed by the prisoner and addressed to the order of the person or agency for whom it was intended. Upon their repatriation, the prisoners received a check for the balance of their account.[7]

Although by 1942 American industry and agriculture were experiencing the same severe wartime manning shortages as the federal government, bureaucratic bickering and concerns from organized labor delayed the availability of POW labor until late in 1943. To prevent potential competition with the government, prisoners were made available for commercial contract only after the need for "essential" work had been satisfied on military installations.[8]

Meanwhile, in August 1942, the governments of the United States and Mexico implemented the first in a series of bilateral agreements that established a program for the importation of Mexican contract laborers to certain agricultural areas of the United States. Known as the Bracero Program, it was intended as a temporary measure to help alleviate the wartime labor shortage. Before the program officially ended in 1964, it had evolved into an institutionalized employment program for the agricultural industry that attracted both sanctioned and clandestine migration to the United States. During the war years, resident Mexican farmers and Mexican guest workers labored side by side, and often near German POWs working in neighboring fields.[9]

The procedure for obtaining German prisoner labor was complicated, and varied from state to state and even between counties within a state. Typically, prospective employers had to submit a "Certificate of Need for Employment of Prisoners" to the U.S. Department of Agriculture's Extension Service for agricultural projects or to the War Manpower Commission for other types of contract employment. These agencies would determine the eligibility of the request. The employer had to provide the agency with the particulars of employment and a persuasive presentation that POWs would only be used in the absence of free labor. He also had to assure the agency that utilization of POWs would not jeopardize wages or working conditions of civilian employees. Finally, the employer had to assure the government that he would comply with the Geneva Convention and all War Department directives concerning the treatment, security, and safety of the prisoners. Only then would the request be channeled to military authorities, usually the camp commander, who would work with the certifying agency to determine the local manpower needs. If the Army could accommodate the request, a standard War Department contract for prisoner labor would be issued. The contract, modified if necessary for local conditions, would reflect the wages and working conditions established in the certificate.[10]

Labor teams were organized at Cooke and contracted out to local farmers in the neighboring towns of Lompoc and Santa Maria. The demand for POW labor spread to other areas within the region. Typically, employers pooled their labor requirements to form associations. In Fresno, growers formed the San Joaquin Agricultural Labor Bureau. Members of the bureau in that area had first call on the services of prisoners. Other farmers who wished to hire POWs could apply to the bureau for consideration. Further south in the valley, farmers formed the Tulare Procurement

Association and got the Army to establish POW branch camps at the Tulare County Fairgrounds and in Tipton.[11]

Tons of apricots, cabbage, green beans, lemons, lettuce, nectarines, oranges, peaches, potatoes, sugar beets, tomatoes, walnuts, cotton, and guayule were harvested by prisoners.[12] They also chopped wood, worked in dairies, and performed other types of farm labor. Eventually the number of prisoners from Cooke working as contract laborers, overwhelmingly on agricultural projects, exceeded for a time those employed on the main Army post and inside the branch camps. Of the 5,061 POWs reported at Cooke and its branch camps on June 12, 1945, 4,254 were available for work. The remainder were excused for medical and other reasons. The labor status of the employed was as follows:[13]

Unpaid labor inside the stockade. 122
Paid labor inside the stockade 242
Paid post labor 658
Contract labor (chiefly agriculture). 3,206
Idle employable (Shafter branch camp) 26

Prisoners who worked as contract labor received the standard pay of 80 cents a day. Those working in agriculture were often compensated on a piecework basis. The prisoners would still receive at least 80 cents a day, but under this pay plan the productive worker who exceeded the daily work quota could earn up to $1.20 a day. A prisoner supervisor would be paid an amount equal to the average pay earned by the prisoners in the work detail that he supervised. And, as usual, all payments were made in canteen coupons.[14]

For each prisoner assigned to an employer, the federal government collected the full amount of the prevailing wage of free labor. The difference between the amount paid to the Army and what the Army paid the prisoners was deposited into the U.S. Treasury to support the POW program. For instance, at the Tagus Ranch branch camp in November 1944, the contract required the company to pay the government 60 cents an hour for each prisoner to pick nectarines and peaches. As stipulated in the contract, the prisoners received the War Department's minimum wage of 80 cents a day. At the J. G. Boswell Ranch camp in Corcoran, farmers who used prisoner of war labor to pick cotton paid the Army the prevailing wage of $2.25 per hundred pounds of cotton. The prisoners worked on a piecework basis and had a daily picking quota of 150 pounds each. The quota, which varied periodically

and equaled that of free labor, was determined by the Army in cooperation with the state Agricultural Extension Service and the employer.[15]

Between June 1944 and April 1, 1945, farmers in the areas served by Cooke and its branch camps paid the government $555,229.58 for POW labor. From this amount, $133,060.96 was paid to the prisoners.[16]

Although the POW labor program was generally successful in alleviating the domestic labor shortage, a number of problems hampered the efficient use of prisoners. In some cases the prisoners lacked the skill, aptitude, and experience for the type of work that was demanded. To improve their job performance, they received on-the-job training and sometimes instruction booklets printed in German. Another factor was supervision. The Army conducted POW training and education programs that taught farm supervisors to use prisoners effectively. The language barrier between supervisors and prisoners was a persistent problem that was never completely solved. While most of the farmers and the prisoners got along extremely well, instances of anti-German sentiment were not uncommon.[17]

Sometimes prisoners were unwilling to work or to comply with a directive or order. When this occurred, the Army applied Articles 45 and 59 of the Geneva Convention. Article 45 stated that prisoners were subject to the laws, regulations, and orders of the detaining Army. Article 59 authorized camp commanders

Opposite and above: German prisoners were given instructional booklets that explained the intricacies of picking cotton. (Courtesy of Heinrich Schünermann)

to apply to the same extent the same "disciplinary punishment" on prisoners of war as prescribed in the rules governing American soldiers.[18]

For minor infractions, the Provost Marshal General's Office adopted a policy known as "administrative pressure." It authorized camp commanders the following three options for persuading POWs to comply with a legitimate order: (1) admonition and reprimand; (2) withholding of privileges, including imposition of diet restriction; and (3) discontinuance of wages and loss of two-thirds of a prisoner's ten-cent daily allowance, up to $2 a month. Since the policy was not intended to be a punishment, the POW could terminate the pressure at any time simply by complying with the order he had violated. The policy was applied to a host of infractions, but because it was most often used against labor strikes, it became known as the "no work, no eat" policy.[19]

In cases where disciplinary measures were required, the Army imposed military law and Articles 54-58 of the Geneva Convention concerning penalties and punishments. Article 104 of the Articles of War authorized camp commanders to admonish and reprimand a prisoner and to withhold privileges for up to a week. They could also assign extra fatigue (work) during the prisoner's free time or impose hard labor for up to a week without pay. The Convention allowed camp commanders to confine a prisoner for as long as thirty days, fourteen of which could be on a restricted diet of bread and water as prescribed in Army Regulation 600-375.[20]

Prisoners who committed more serious offenses were subject to court-martial. Apart from the summary court-martial, which was largely superseded by disciplinary measures, prisoners were tried under special court-martial for offenses such as willful damage or destruction of government property or contemptuous behavior to a superior officer. General courts-martial were reserved for murder, sabotage, rioting, and so forth, and could, with the approval of the President of the United States, result in the death penalty.[21]

At Cooke and its branch camps the number of disciplinary cases changed frequently. In March 1945, the Army reported fifteen incidents of disciplinary punishment. In June, the number more than doubled to thirty-three. The branch camps accounted for thirty-one of these cases, most of which involved refusals to work. The only known court-martial at Cooke was reported in April 1945 by a representative of the Swiss Legation. In this case, two prisoners were adjudged to eight years' confinement at the U.S. Federal Reformatory at Fort Reno, Oklahoma, for breaking into a facility and stealing Army property. It is unknown whether any portion of the sentence was carried out.[22]

One other option available to camp commanders for maintaining order in the camps was to segregate noncooperative prisoners and to transfer them to penal camps.[23]

In December 1944, Camp Cooke was hit by a rash of POW work stoppages. In one instance, a misunderstanding of the Christmas celebration dates resulted in a strike. Unlike the tradition in the United States, Christmas in Germany then, as today, was celebrated on December 25 and 26. When the prisoners at Cooke refused to show up for work on the morning of December 26, they were promptly assembled on the recreation field and placed on a restricted diet of bread and water until nightfall. The following day they were back at work. A similar strike occurred at the Lamont branch camp and probably at the other branch camps as well.[24]

For considerably different reasons, POWs working at the Johns-Manville mining and processing plant in Lompoc staged a sit-down strike in December 1944. The prisoners worked at the plant daily in three, eight-hour shifts from December 1944 to April 1945. About ten or twelve prisoners were assigned to each shift. They worked as common laborers in the mills, handling diatomaceous earth or diatomite, commonly used in filtration systems.[25]

The trouble started on Thursday evening, December 28, 1944, after a Christmas greeting letter from Admiral Ernest J. King commending the firm for its excellent war work was posted in the plant cafeteria. This, according to the POWs, was proof that their work was contributing to the U.S. war effort, which was a violation of the Geneva Convention. When the prisoners staged a sit-down strike, they were marched into the brick plant at the No. 10 quarry until the end of their work shift. The following day the entire POW camp at Cooke went out on a sympathy strike. Once again, the prisoners were assembled on the recreation field and placed on a diet of bread and water. The prisoners ended the strike that evening and returned to work the following morning. The admiral's letter, incidentally, remained on the bulletin board.[26]

Since the commodities manufactured by the Johns-Manville plant were not specifically for military use, the Army concluded that under the Geneva Convention the prisoners were legally employed at the plant. Despite the Convention's shortcomings in failing to identify specific job prohibitions, one thing was certain: the prisoners who staged this strike had their own motives and interests at heart.[27]

In an unrelated instance of prisoner disobedience, the entire POW population of about six hundred men at the Shafter branch camp invoked a sympathy strike on the morning of December 27, 1944. It started after the Army had segregated twenty POWs from the camp who were protesting an increase in the daily quota of cotton they had to pick. Similar labor-related protests occurred periodically at other branch camps.[28]

Despite instances of unrest, labor strikes by prisoners of war at Camp Cooke and its branch camps were rare when compared with the amount of labor performed by the vast majority of these men. When strikes did occur, they were of short duration and happened mostly at the branch camps. To be sure, many of the strikes were instigated by Nazi groups who pressured other POWs not to work too willingly for their captors. For this and other reasons, work performances by individual POWs varied enormously. Nonetheless, as a labor force, they performed valuable work on military posts and were welcome, though sometimes reluctant, additions as contract workers to areas hardest hit by the manpower shortage.[29]

WERNER BLANCK
Shortly after arriving at Camp Cooke in June 1944, we were all put to work. Because I could speak some English, I was assigned to the post exchange (PX) warehouse as a deliveryman. I distributed merchandise to several PXs on the main installation. To get this job, I first had to pass a road test and receive a U.S. Army driver's license. This wasn't difficult to do. I worked in the warehouse with three American civilians and three or four POWs. Among those I fondly remember are Harry Muldoon, Pete Petersen, Ruben, and Mrs. Alexander, who I think managed PX number 10. The prisoners who worked at Cooke earned a salary of 80 cents a day, which at that time was a princely sum of money. We were paid in coupons that were redeemable at our camp canteen.

The working environment at Camp Cooke was definitely much better than it was at the branch camps. This not only brought prisoners and guards closer, but more importantly for the Americans, it resulted in fewer POW labor problems at the main camp compared to the situation at the branch camps.

HANS-JOACHIM BÖTTCHER
Two days after arriving at Camp Cooke, I was detailed with a group of other POWs to harvest tomatoes about five miles north of Santa Maria and about an hour's drive from the camp by bus.

The tomatoes grew wild and flat on the ground in rows. On November 14, 1944, we were reassigned to picking carrots in fields somewhere north of the tomato fields. The field had been plowed, and all we had to do was pick the carrots up and make bunches for the market. At both sites we never had to meet any harvesting quotas. Everybody did a good job, even if we did eat a lot of the fruit from the orchards nearby. I remember we had nice apricots and watermelons. I stayed with this detail until November 27, 1944.

Two days later, I was ordered to report to the post headquarters together with Lothar Heydel, where we received our new job assignment as janitors for the headquarters building and the finance office. Every morning we reported to Master Sergeant Jack Bear (sometimes to Major David Turpin), who told us what needed to be done, such as cleaning toilets, windows, floors, etc. After a time, Lothar and I had things pretty well organized and knew the routine.

One day after completing our work and feeling bored, we cleaned up the garden in front of the headquarters building. We apparently did such a fine job that gardening then became our main detail. We liked this work and could do more or less as we wanted. Whenever we removed a lot of weeds and other dirt from the garden, we had to call Sergeant Bear. He would send over a few American Army prisoners to carry everything away to the dump.

Because of our gardening activities, we were recommended to the post chapel. Our new bosses were Chaplain Strait, the Protestant clergyman; Chaplain Honeywell, the Catholic chaplain; and Rabbi Nussbaum, the Jewish chaplain. Whatever they needed, we were there to assist them. Our primary duties were to maintain the garden and to set up floral arrangements for services and social functions. We also painted the garden fence. By this time, Rolf Metzler had replaced Lothar Heydel as my partner. On Saturdays, Sergeant Gould, who was Sergeant Bear's assistant, and I (sometimes it was Chaplain Strait) drove to Surf or to other places nearby to buy flowers. Occasionally we went to the swamps of the Santa Ynez River to pick calla lilies. I got to see a lot of the area because of these trips.

While working around the chapel I occasionally had contact with Italian POWs.[30] Their quarters were across from the chapel. We used to communicate with each other by gesturing with hands and feet. They were a friendly lot who sometimes handed me drinks through their barrack windows. Loud music was always coming from their place. On one occasion, when New Orleans jazz was playing on their radio, one of the chaplains, I believe it must have been Chaplain Honeywell, opened the chapel window and joined in with his trombone.

When the NCO Club opened on the post in March 1945, Rolf Metzler and I were sent there to clean up the place, which was literally a mess. We got to know the bartender, Kurt Horn, who was from Vegesack, Germany. Since he spoke *Plattdeutsch* (as I do), we immediately formed a good friendship. He "employed" Metzler and me for Fridays and sometimes for other days of the week to keep the club clean and to serve. On these days we got free drinks. Kurt was one of the nicest guys I met while at Camp Cooke.

In July 1945, the post ordnance shops had requested German mechanics to replace the Italian POWs who were there servicing vehicles and tanks, but were now being repatriated. By a mix up of names—there was a mechanic with my same name in the camp—I was assigned to the maintenance shops on July 15. The shop superintendent, Mr. Davis, realized that I was useless for any technical job and put me in the tool room to assist the keeper, Al Johnson. When Mr. Johnson retired shortly thereafter, his position was filled by several American soldiers including Sergeant Kuster, Sergeant Ronchi, and others, until eventually I was alone. By this time, I had learned most of the names of the tools and had cleaned up the room, so I was put in charge.

We had about ten mechanics, two blacksmiths, two car washers, five precision tool mechanics, five lathe workers, five weapons mechanics, one wireless equipment repairman, and one greaser working in my shop. We were known as Labor Detail 31 of the maintenance shops. I was the interpreter and spokesman for this gang. It was a smooth job, and I don't recall any problems. My immediate supervisor was Mr. Bieber, the shop foreman. On the military side we had Captain [Ralph G.] Boyer of the Labor Office, and Major Rowan, who was in charge of the whole shop. The civilian workers in the shop were especially helpful. I worked in the shop until March 9, 1946. Other POW labor details were assigned to the body shop, chassis shop, and post engineering repair shop.

Communications between the Americans and the POWs in the maintenance shops was a mixture of German and English words. In the blacksmith shop it was basically *Plattdeutsch* that was spoken because Hannes Kusserow, the welder, came from a village near Kiel. The blacksmith shop was also the general meeting place for everybody because there was always a pot of coffee on the forge. A typical sentence from Hannes was "Mr. Smith, will'n ji ook noch 'n beeten coffee hebb'n?" which everybody seemed to understand.

On December 29, 1944, the POWs at Camp Cooke went on a 24-hour labor strike. The strike began as a protest by some of the POWs who were working in quarries owned by Johns-Manville Corporation. Apparently, the company was processing raw materials for military use. When word got around that using prisoners of war to perform war-related activities was a violation of the Geneva Convention, the whole camp went on strike. We were ordered by the Americans to report to the soccer field. There we heard speeches from POWs supporting and opposing the strike. During this time our barracks, the canteen, the kitchens, etc., were searched by American guards for evidence of political activities. Apparently not much was found.

Looking back on the event, most of the Afrika Korps troops seemed to be against any political action. Much of the influence for the strike may have come from the newer POWs, those captured in France. I think that as a result of this strike, the super Nazis and all suspected super Nazis were transferred to Camp Rupert in Idaho. The transfers extended into February 1945. Anyway, since the American commander promised that the work at Manville would be stopped soon, the strike ended the next morning.

ALFRED SCHMUCKER

After about six weeks at Camp Cooke, the clerk from our orderly room asked me if I would like a job. "Absolutely," I said. "It's getting a little boring around here." So, he offered me a job in the tailoring shop on post. When I mentioned that I had no tailoring experience, he told me not to worry because none of the other POWs working in the shop knew anything about tailoring either. So, I got a job.

The tailoring shop was a large room equipped with about forty to fifty sewing machines. American civilian women worked in the shop during the day until five p.m. We picked up the night shift from six p.m. until three a.m. Beginners like myself had a so-called training period of three days. We received a piece of cloth and had to sew back and forth and in circles. After completing the training period, we were to mend holes in thousands of B (barrack)-bags.

We were supervised by a U.S. Army sergeant who was as much of a tailor as we were. But he was good at replacing needles in sewing machines, a task we were not allowed to do. As time went on, we became almost professionals and made German

Alfred Schmucker at his desk in the labor office.

army caps, canvas bags, and even so-called Eisenhower jackets from U.S. Army jackets. In doing so, we made a little extra money selling these articles to other German POWs.

After I had worked for three months in the tailoring shop, my bunk neighbor, who worked as a clerk for the U.S. camp adjutant, Maj. Gerald Murphy, asked me if I would like a job in the American headquarters section. I told him that I didn't speak any English. He assured me that was not problem. He would arrange for an interview with the adjutant and all I would have to say from time to time was "Yes, sir."

This is how I became a clerk in the labor office. The GIs who worked in the office spoke not a word of German, and I in turn at that time did not speak one word of the English language. We got along fine because there was never a word of misunderstanding between us.

The POWs at Camp Cooke were assigned to a great variety of different jobs. If possible, they were given work in their respective profession. Every section within Camp Cooke that had a need for POW labor would have to submit a request to the labor office identifying the requested number of POWs and the required professions. Depending upon the availability of such personnel, we would form the work details and in the morning dispatched them to the various job sites. We also compiled the daily morning reports, which we received from the POW companies at Cooke and from the branch camps such as Edwards Ranch, Tagus Ranch, and Shafter. I always made sure that my morning reports added up. If I was missing a man or two, I had a little entry before my grand total which read: TMIB. Nobody ever asked me what it meant. Otherwise I would have had to say: "To make it balance."

During the afternoon I visited the various POW work sites within Camp Cooke. For this task I was assigned a jeep from the motor pool. I spot checked the people present at work, collected changes of workforce requirements from the American supervisor, and stopped here and there for a cup of coffee and small talk with the fellows. This, of course, was the best part of the day. After I had familiarized myself with the large area of Camp Cooke, I drove several times to the Pacific shore, but I was always afraid of being caught.

Every morning before starting work at the labor office, I had to go to the motor pool to pick up my jeep. I then parked the vehicle in front of the adjutant's office. The adjoining street and parking lot were covered with a heavy layer of gravel. When I returned from the motor pool, I used to make my turn into the parking lot without reducing my speed. Locking the brakes, I swung the vehicle into parking position, spraying gravel all over the place. One day the "Old Man" arrived in the office earlier than expected and caught me. He took away my driver's license for a week. Several months later I was caught a second time, and this time I lost my license for good. My supervisor at the labor office, a very fine man by the name of Corporal Ray A. Bailey, jokingly issued me a driver's license for a bicycle.

ADOLF KELMER

During my time at Camp Cooke, I was often rotated to various jobs, some lasting only a few days and others several weeks. My first job was inside the POW compound tending to a garden. For some unknown and erroneous reason, our *Lagersprecher* appointed me to this job, thinking that I was the gardener type. After about two weeks, I was replaced and was put to work outside the compound scrubbing used bricks. I then worked as a janitor in the large movie house on the main camp, cleaning the hall and scraping chewing gum off the bottom of the folding seats.

Because of the constant arrival and departure of American Army units at Camp Cooke, the barracks used by these soldiers needed to be cleaned and prepared for the next group. Two or three of us POWs were assigned to this task. An American soldier would escort us to each barrack and tell us what needed to be done. For instance, we cleaned the kitchen utensils and replaced whatever was missing. We checked the windows and doors, and cut the dry and sometimes tall grass that had grown around the building.

With a larger group of other POWs, we planted drought-resistant ground cover along the roadsides within the main army installation. This plant had the resiliency to thrive on the barren, dry soil of Camp Cooke.

My next assignment was with a POW road construction/repair crew. We mixed asphalt with gravel brought to the work site by dump trucks. The most surprising part about this job was that the drivers of these heavy vehicles were often women. Seeing women perform this type of work was a novel sight for me. The interaction of these female drivers with the POWs was as relaxed and open as was the case with their male counterparts.

Occasionally, when we were working far away from the main camp, we would finish the job before normal quitting time. When this happened and there wasn't enough time to go to another job site, the POWs, the drivers (the women too), and the group leaders would stand around talking while waiting for the trucks to take us back to the camp.

During one of these interludes we found a piece of gymnastic equipment and made small wagers about who could do the most chin-ups. Two of these attractive, spirited women drivers joined the competition. Of course they lost the bet, which was to be expected. They then invited two of us POWs to a soda fountain for Cokes and hamburgers. We considered this a wonderful gesture, but questioned the possibility and advisability of such a rendezvous. Nevertheless, a few days later the two women, apparently by permission of the American camp administration and our immediate supervisor, quit work a little early and came to pick us up. We all rode to Lompoc and landed in a drugstore with its chrome counter. We were welcomed without hesitation and sat on modern round stools. What does one say to such women who, without hesitation, kept their promise to POWs?

I also worked for some time at a rock quarry where gravel was obtained for paving streets. It was far away from the main camp and directly on the coast.[30] Whenever we finished work early or had a break, we used to explore the area around the quarry. Sometimes we were allowed down to the beach where we swam out to the rocks that peeked through the waves. We also tried our hand at fishing. But with this venture we did not have much experience or luck. We occasionally found small coves where water pockets accumulated after the tide had ebbed. I used to submerge my head under these waters and open my eyes to a beautiful, glittering world of plants and small marine animals all within a rainbow of colors.

For a time, I also worked at a diatomaceous plant owned by the Johns-Manville Corporation in Lompoc. Here, the chalky material that we handled was ground into powder. The mill operated around the clock in three work shifts. We POWs had the early and late shifts. At the end of each workday we received a company meal. Our night crews received sandwiches and coffee. The day shift was served a hot, delicious lunch in the company cafeteria. These lunches always included a large variety of different colored beans, which we thoroughly enjoyed.

We rode to the mill every morning in buses that passed through the small town of Lompoc. Along the route was a military airfield. Every day at the same time we watched as dirigibles were released from their moorings. These airships ascended at a steep angle into the dark morning skies and were probably used to reconnoiter the ocean for submarines.[31]

Sometimes my job would involve unexpected situations, such as the time when I was assigned to sweeping floors and emptying wastepaper baskets in one of the offices on the main post. In this instance, one of the secretaries who was sitting at her desk nonchalantly extended her shapely, nylon-clad legs into the area where I was about to sweep the floor. As I glanced up at her and then quickly at the other women in the room, I saw a mischievous glint in her eye and a pair of waggish smiles. They knew exactly what they were doing while feigning not to notice me. In such situations one decides to leave well enough alone. With broom in hand, I casually moved along to the next room.

Many of the young women who worked at Camp Cooke did not live nearby. During the week they resided in special quarters set aside for women. On weekends they usually went home. Their quarters were off-limits for non-authorized male personnel. Occasionally, POW labor detachments were assigned cleaning and maintenance duties in these buildings. POWs generally sought this assignment until one had worked there for a while. I worked at these quarters for about a month and then asked for a transfer.

All the women in the female quarters were pretty and attractively dressed. They always greeted us with warm smiles and offered us cups of coffee. One day while I was mowing the grass around one of the buildings, I came across a young, gorgeous sun worshiper wearing a bathing suit. She stared at me the whole time and waited to see how I would react. I must admit I was a little nervous. I quickly cut the grass near her and then continued on my way.

One day, the Americans announced that they were looking for volunteers to unload armored vehicles from flatbed rail cars arriving on the main post. Since the work was to be done at night and on weekends, they offered an additional day off from work during the week. I jumped at this opportunity to have an extra free day.

We worked in teams of four or five POWs alongside an American soldier who was our driver. Equipped with the necessary tools, we removed the chocks and other items that held these vehicles in place during their shipment to Camp Cooke. The vehicles were then pulled off the trains and onto an adjacent unloading ramp. By the time several of these vehicles had been removed, a mountain of wooden chocks and other shipping materials began cluttering the unloading area, making it difficult to work. At that point we loaded the scrap into a large three-axle truck, and with our American driver we disposed of the waste at the camp dump. We made several trips back and forth during the night until dawn, when our driver suddenly vanished. Since we still had plenty of wood to dispose of, we decided to drive the truck ourselves.

None of us had the slightest intimation of how to operate this vehicle. In fact, none in our group had even driven a car. This did not seem to matter because each of us had his own theory about the technical principles involved in driving a truck, and an enormous desire to put that belief to the test. We climbed into the cab of the truck and looked, studied, touched, and probed all the controls. After several attempts to start the engine, we finally succeeded.

In the meantime, we had also deciphered the shift pattern. All we needed to do now was to coordinate these activities to drive the truck. The only question was: Who shall drive the truck? Who wanted to be the first to show what he doesn't know? I was excited and felt I could not fail, so I sat behind the wheel. With all of my comrades beside me in the cab, it was more like standing than sitting.

We moved the truck a few feet at a time to the next pile of wood until the truck was full. Each time, the vehicle hopped, and several times I stalled the engine. Gradually, my coordination improved and after about two trips to the dump we finished our work and parked the truck near the unloading dock. We then walked back to the POW camp.

About May or June 1945, I was assigned to the military laundry on the main post. At first I was with a group that loaded and unloaded clothing from the washing machines. I was then reassigned to the steam press and drying areas before I returned to the washing and water extraction station as a supervisor. It was here that I first met Horst Stellbrand. We would later escape together from Camp Cooke.

GEORG KROEMER
I was assigned to harvesting tomatoes, peas, and lettuce in the area around Camp Cooke. I enjoyed the work and had a lot of fun with my fellow workers. Working alongside us were civilian Filipino men and women. We established a good relationship with them and during break times had tomato battles in which everyone got involved, including the guards.

Since the Filipinos were very short on chocolate and cigarettes, we used to buy these items at the POW canteen with script and sell them to the Filipinos for American money. This money later came in handy for me when I escaped from Camp Cooke.

One time, as we were preparing to return to the camp at the end of the day, the guard drove off in the first truck but forgot his rifle. I was about to step aboard the second truck when I noticed the gun and took it with me. I hid the weapon under my jacket until we got to the camp. Standing at the front gate with a worried expression on his face was our guard. I quietly slipped him his weapon, and suddenly a big smile appeared on his face. Whispering through the corner of his mouth, he thanked me again and again.

HERBERT SCHAFFRATH
Shortly after arriving at Camp Cooke, I worked for a few days outside the camp harvesting sugar beets with a group of about twenty other POWs. An American farmer gave us the necessary instructions before turning us loose onto the fields. Mexican laborers were also in the fields, but they were driving the tractor and the pickup trucks. Unlike those assigned to other agricultural jobs, we did not have a work quota to fulfill.

Shortly after the harvest, I was given the job as janitor at the post engineering headquarters building. I had no janitorial experience, but with the help of the women who worked in the adjoining offices I quickly learned the duties of the job. If the windows weren't cleaned or other things didn't meet their satisfaction, they complained to my supervisor, an American sergeant.

After a short time I traded in my mop and bucket for a typewriter, and became a clerk-typist for the same organization. For this worthy cause, I received an assistant, Heinz Jarschky. We worked in the property section making copies of excerpts from Army regulations and preparing inventory lists of camp equipment, utensils, etc. I held this job until leaving Camp Cooke in March 1946.

WERNER GILBERT

At Camp Cooke I was initially put to work in the POW hospital. I was in charge of distributing linen. After four weeks I was reassigned to the shoemaker's shop. Since I was a professional cobbler before coming into the military, I was very happy for the change. In the shoemaker's shop, we were sometimes staffed with up to thirty craftsmen. For my part, I worked exclusively for American officers. It was a good job, and I became very friendly with many of the GIs. I also trained several GIs as shoemakers. Many of them had recently returned from duty overseas in Europe. On one occasion, one of these men boasted of his tour of duty in Germany and showed us an arm full of wristwatches. He pointed to one in particular, whose possessor he allegedly shot dead. One of the POWs grabbed this man by the neck and began choking him. The guards were called out to rescue the GI. When the translators and the officers arrived to sort out the incident, the GI was ordered to apologize to us. He never again returned to the shoemaker's shop.

Father FRANZ GÖDDE

My first job at Camp Cooke was in the tailoring shop, mending GI clothing. During the day this work was performed by American civilians. We began work at five p.m. and worked until about one a.m. We worked only five days a week. I later worked in the contracting office, where we were responsible for billing American farmers who were utilizing German POWs for agricultural work at the branch camps. We compared our labor records with those submitted by the farmers and calculated the payment claims. Captain [Robert P.] Schofield was in charge of the contracting office and was assisted by our immediate supervisor, Sergeant Milton Brooke. After VE-Day, Sergeant Brooke became extremely lazy. He left all the work for us and had only one thing in mind—to get out of the Army as quickly as possible and go home to his family. I don't blame him. If I remember correctly, he intended to take up studies in veterinary medicine.

The Christmas 1944 sit-down strike by POWs at Camp Cooke was allegedly based on the type of work that a small group of prisoners were performing at the Johns-Manville plant in Lompoc.

Since the materials produced by the plant were used in the manufacturing of gas mask filters, some POWs viewed the assignment of German prisoners to this facility as a violation of the Geneva Convention. In actuality, this became a convenient pretext for the real motive to strike. Given the fact that the Ardennes offensive had begun in mid-December and yielded for the Nazis a small, temporary land victory, the episode was worthy enough for certain individuals to celebrate by not going to work.

The general sympathy strike, which began the following morning at Camp Cooke, was unavoidable for the average POW. We had no way of knowing beforehand how many opposed the strike. Since none of the work groups appeared at the main gate that December morning, we were all ordered to line up outside our barracks. We were then marched to the recreation field and placed on a diet of bread and water. As long as it was daylight, we passed the time playing games and eating the food we had stuffed into our pockets before being called out of our barracks.

But boredom set in when it got dark. Also, it got noticeably colder, and by this time we were getting very hungry. Some of our comrades were getting upset and began questioning the motivation behind the strike. There were acrimonious altercations and a call for a democratic vote to see who was in favor of going back to work. From the leaders of the strike came the resolution: "We are not Democrats, we are National Socialist. There is no voting with us." After a messy brawl between the two groups, a delegation of POWs went to the main gate to tell the American commander that all the POWs were going back to work the next morning. With that, the strike was finished, and we got something to eat around ten p.m.

The next morning as we passed through the main gate, Lieutenant [Harold W.] Wolff pulled several men out of line. He had in his hand the picture files of the POWs he wanted. By noon that day these men were on their way to Camp Rupert, Idaho, where, we were told, a camp for Nazis had been established.

Lieutenant Wolff was responsible for security within the entire compound. Although he spoke the German language fluently, he never used his skill to try to sound us out about occurrences within the compound. I found this a noble gesture on his part.

HEINRICH KERSTING

In addition to my duties working in the camp administration, I volunteered to write the sports column for our camp newspaper, *Der Lagerspiegel*. The paper was available free of charge at our canteen. I took this task because I was an avid soccer player and had sufficient time during the day to write these firsthand reports. The articles were fairly long and reflected the considerable amount of leisure time occupied by athletics in the camp. Those not participating in the games were usually fans and wanted to be at the match whenever their company team was playing. Of course, it was painful for them when their team lost.

RUDOLF HINKELMANN

According to the Geneva Convention, and as a noncommissioned officer with the army rank of *Feldwebel*, I was not obligated to work in the American POW camps. Occasionally, however, I was assigned to supervise work details at Camp Cooke. The jobs were outside the stockade and involved teams of five to ten prisoners. I remember once working on a flower field in the nearby town of Lompoc. Most other times, however, I worked on the main military installation. None of the labor performed by the prisoners was very strenuous. In fact, they were happy to work because it helped to overcome the monotony of camp life.

On August 1, 1944, a large group of us POWs were transported from Camp Cooke to Tagus Ranch, near Tulare, to harvest peaches. We were sheltered in spacious Quonset huts. Each hut usually housed ten to fifteen prisoners. Except for the plague of mosquitoes, we lived comfortably at this camp. The guarding by the Americans became very superficial.

I often had occasion to go out with work details as a supervisor. Because of the summer heat, we began work early in the morning picking peaches. Every prisoner had, if I remember correctly, nine baskets to be used for picking, which, if they hurried, they could fill in a short time. Afterward, we played cards in a tree house that we built for this purpose.

Other prisoners walked across the asphalt road to the various plantations staffed by Mexican field workers. They used to help the Mexicans increase their pickings and by doing so became friends with them.

At the end of the workday all prisoners were to gather at a pre-designated pickup point, even if they had been distributed during the day over a wide area. Occasionally, one of the men would get lost and arrive late. There was an unwritten law among us prisoners: Fool around as much as you wish, but don't make difficulties for the guards. After returning from the peach plantation between one and two p.m., we had a small lunch, showered, and then had dinner at five p.m.

LEONHARD REUL

About November 1944, I was transferred to Tagus Ranch where I remained until February or March 1946. At Tagus Ranch, I was made the group leader for a detail of POWs working in the cotton plantations and later in the orchards harvesting peaches, olives, walnuts, and grapes. We never had any labor problems except during the cotton season. Each POW was required to pick eighty pounds of cotton per day. The quota was later raised to more than one hundred pounds. This was grueling work, especially under a scorching sun. Some of the men deliberately ignored their picking quota and only harvested a few pounds. As the group labor leader, I was the responsible person between the farmer and the POWs.

The farmers would get into a rage whenever something went wrong. For instance, on one occasion, one of the POWs sent a watermelon crashing into the bottom of a cotton wagon. It made an awful mess. I continually tried to make the farmers understand that my fellow prisoners and I, a former bank clerk, had been drafted into the army and were not accustomed to such exhausting work. When I told them that some of these prisoners were still recovering from their war wounds in battles against the Russians, the farmers seemed to become intrigued and were much more sympathetic. They would give us cigarettes, and we would again become friends.

As the war in Europe neared its end, we received at Tagus Ranch prisoners captured in France and Germany. Among them were members of the Waffen SS. Despite direction from our camp commander, Captain [Claude L.] Curtis, these men were averse to picking cotton. This situation resulted in a lot of angry farmers calling us wiseacres and brakemen.

Sometimes the farmers were unreasonable. On one occasion, after we had reached our daily quota of eighty pounds of cotton, the majority of my group sat down. An angry and gesticulating group of farmers came over and wanted us to continue working. None of the men, including myself, made a move. After about thirty minutes the guards appeared, and I was brought back to the camp and placed in a small tent below the watch tower. For arranging this "wildcat strike," I spent five days in the tent, receiving only bread and water. When I was freed, this act of rebellion got me more friends and sympathizers than I ever had before among my fellow POWs.

HEINRICH SCHÜNEMANN

Most of the POWs at the Old River tent camp were assigned to pick cotton in the nearby fields. They worked six days a week, eight hours a day. The top picker was a university professor from Berlin. Even though he was about forty years old, he apparently had quick fingers and could easily reach the required weight quota for cotton. I heard that he would fill a second linen bag with cotton and then lie down on it between the bushes and read a book or fall asleep. Some of the other POWs who were also good pickers would fill an extra bag of cotton and then try to sell it to the neighboring Mexican workers for American dollars.

Since my job as an electrician was not a full-time assignment (I was on call 24 hours a day), I did all kinds of other work around the camp, including chopping wood for our little tent stoves and repairing electrical appliances and cars for American officers and the guards. Sometimes the guards would slip me American money. With this cash I would ask them to buy for me books and various electrical tools not available in the POW canteen.

KLAUS HEBEL

From Camp Cooke, I was sent to a very nice branch camp at Edwards Ranch, just north of Goleta, in late May or early June 1945. The camp housed about 250 men in several half-round, corrugated tin barracks [Nissen huts] and occasionally in tents, which we otherwise used for recreation such as ping-pong and reading. Inside our barracks, between the beds, were tables or footlockers on which we placed pictures of our loved ones. The campgrounds we decorated with flower boxes and bushes.

At the canteen we could buy all sorts of personal care items as well as candy and soda. On a small sports field, we played soccer every Sunday. And almost daily we were allowed to go swimming in the Pacific Ocean. A guard would escort us on this short walk to the beach. We were like one big, friendly family. I befriended one of the guards, and occasionally we would go swimming together. In return for cleaning his rifle, he would give me ping-pong balls. That was wonderful. In general, we had a homelike atmosphere at this camp. I honestly did not have the feeling of being in captivity. Additionally, the view out into the Pacific and the sunsets during those warm summer months are unforgettable even today.

We worked at this camp harvesting oranges, lemons, tomatoes, and peas. Typically, we received boxed lunches from our kitchen before going to work in the morning. One day, however, a farmer and his attractive wife drove up to where we were working and brought us a delicious lunch of stew and sausages. After that thoughtful gesture, we worked even harder in the fields.

During my time at Goleta, I developed a large sore on my hip. Additionally, on my left hand I had warts that bothered me whenever I put on a work glove to harvest fruits. I talked with the American medic and he arranged to have me transferred back to the main camp for an operation to remove the warts. Following a successful surgery, I remained at Cooke recuperating for a few weeks.

About November or December 1945, I was transferred to the branch camp at Delano. Here we picked cotton. This work was much more difficult than harvesting produce at Goleta. On Christmas Eve we were out in the fields picking cotton. By quitting time, my group had not yet achieved its daily quota of cotton. At that point the American guards brought in floodlights and we were ordered back into the fields until we reached our quota. I believe it was around midnight when we finally finished our work.

Exhausted and dejected, we climbed aboard the farmer's wagon for our ride back to the camp. We hadn't gone three-hundred feet when the trailer bed tipped over, and the box on which we POWs were standing in slid off the trailer, dumping us into a ditch. The police were summoned, and after a brief investigation they upbraided the farmer for causing the accident. Some of the POWs were taken to the hospital with injuries that included teeth knocked out. Fortunately, I had a soft landing, falling on top of other POWs. When we got back to the camp, some of us joined the Christmas festivities, but by this time the holiday spirit had slipped away.

CHAPTER 6

Everyday Life in the Camp

• American Camp Personnel and Relations with the POWs •

WHEN THE United States entered World War II, it sent most of its able-bodied officers and soldiers overseas to win the war. Left behind, in many instances, were men ineligible for combat service because of their age (some were World War I veterans) or men who were assigned to dead-end jobs. Many staff members and guards at prisoner of war camps were drawn from these ranks. Guard duty at a POW camp was not a job sought by most GIs. Restricted to a small range of routine duties, these guards worked long hours, received limited passes and furloughs, and more importantly, had little opportunity for promotion or hope of transfer to fields more clearly related to winning the war.[1]

In April 1945, the Army's Labor and Liaison Branch of the Provost Marshal General's Office reported that the officers and enlisted men operating the POW camp at Camp Cooke were qualified, but exhibited "unusually low" morale. The report offered no specific details. Nevertheless, in part to improve the guard situation, by May 1945, the Army had replaced 50 percent of the original camp cadre with oversees returnees. Fresh from the battlefields, these combat veterans were finishing out their service before being discharged. Under these circumstances, it was highly unlikely that assigning these men to guard duty was in the best interest of all concerned.[2]

Despite occasional excesses by a few guards, defiant behavior or mischievous antics by some prisoners, and Army prohibitions against all forms of fraternization with POWs, workplace friendships between captives and captors flourished. Prisoners working alongside American GIs or civilian employees were able to circumvent many of the Army's restrictions on food and canteen items. A few POWs enjoyed the ultimate form of fraternization with willing American women. Doris Bailey, who supervised nine civilian female employees and six German POWs at the post motor pool warehouse, recalls that one of her female workers shared

Doris Bailey (left) with co-workers Herbie (German POW) and Dora, 1946. (Courtesy of Ray and Doris Bailey)

affections with a POW bus driver. "She would meet her POW friend on one of the back roads of the main camp. He would pick her up, hide her in the back of the bus and together go off to some secluded area. They were very fond of each other and it was difficult for them when he had to return to Germany in 1946."[3]

In one other reported case, Leah Pereira, a forty-two-year-old mother of nine children, admitted to having sexual relations with a twenty-five-year-old German prisoner of war at Camp Cooke. The couple, both employed in one of the mess halls at Cooke, were caught in Pereira's car parked south of the station hospital in a clump of trees. Appearing before Justice Marion Smith in Santa Maria in June 1945, Mrs. Pereira was charged with vagrancy and sentenced to thirty days in the county jail. Because of her large family, the judge suspended the sentence on condition of good behavior for two years.[4]

ALFRED SCHMUCKER

The average POW did not have contact with American officers at Cooke. The officers transmitted their rules, regulations, and wishes to the German camp spokesman, who in turn passed along the information to the individual POWs through the company spokesmen. Any requests or complaints from the POWs went back through the same channel. I, on the other hand, had direct contact with American officers because of my job in the U.S. camp headquarters. I maintained good relations with them and cannot say anything negative about their behavior. Quite a number of them went out of their way to help us and to make life easier for us.

The guards were given an assignment to accompany the work details to their respective work sites. I don't think they had a choice, and I can't imagine that any of them liked their job very much. First, there was a language barrier, which prevented the exchange of a meaningful conversation. Second, during their eight-hour shift they had nothing to do but stand around, sometimes in other people's way. I would say that most of our guards were fair-minded individuals and treated us well.

Compared with what we had been used to in the German army, I think the discipline of some of the GIs was low. In the labor office where I worked we had a private first class who used to read the newspaper with both feet propped up on the desk while smoking a big cigar. One day the captain entered the office and asked him a question. The private did not move from his position. He just asked, "What's up, Captain?" And the captain tolerated his behavior.

Many times we noticed that a GI did not take his hands out of his pockets while talking to an officer. We are all human beings; there are good ones and bad ones, there are intelligent ones and there are dummies. That applied to the prisoners as well as to the guards.

In the German army, discipline and respect toward an officer was very high and expected from every lower grade. A soldier addressed an officer only in the third person. He always used the title "Herr" (Mr.) and never asked a direct question but instead always prefaced it with the word "may." You would say, "May I ask Herr Hauptmann (Mr. Captain) for permission to go to the canteen?" You would never say, "Can I go to the canteen?" If you were sitting in a restaurant and an officer entered and passed your table you were expected to jump up and salute him.

HEINRICH KERSTING
We had an exceptionally good relationship with our American sergeants and other guards, with whom we spent many evenings partying. For instance, we played ping-pong with our guards for

candy bars and other inexpensive items. Shortly before Christmas and other important holidays, the American company commanders gave us flour, sugar, and other ingredients to bake cakes. Of course, we obtained additional items as well from our labor groups who worked in the appropriate GI sections like the bakery and the canteen.

Sergeant James Wolff supervised our company. A sergeant with the nickname "Blacky" supervised our neighboring company. These two men were always attempting to make their respective company better than the other. For us POWs it was a good-natured competition. And there were others, like Mickey Rosenbaum and Captain [Robert L.] Everett, whom I also remember with fond memories. Captain Everett was always accommodating to us POWs.

During the few times that I worked outside the stockade with a labor group, I became friendly with an American civilian supervisor named Elmar Ruehling. I told him that I met my future wife when we were eleven years old and that we had planned to marry on her twenty-first birthday in 1944. For a carton of cigarettes, he got me a 14-karat gold wedding ring. From that ring we made two rings. Later, my fiancée and I put these rings on our fingers when we married. We wore them until her death in February 1986. Today the rings are worn by my daughter and the wife of my eldest son.

RUDOLF HINKELMANN

The American soldiers who were guarding us were mostly older people. I would say they were home guard troops and that the young healthy men were at the front, just as it was in Germany.

All the guards at Camp Cooke were exceedingly humane, fair, and had an almost friendly attitude toward us. To illustrate this point, I recall one incident that happened while I was supervising a detail of eight or ten POWs who were repairing a section of railroad track on the main post. When the guard who was watching us had to let down his pants behind a nearby bush, he gave me his loaded rifle and told me to watch it. He could have given it to any other prisoner because nobody would have threatened or harmed anyone with it. Why should we have? Secretly we were glad to be in captivity and in safe hands.

HANS-JOACHIM BÖTTCHER

I remember most of the American camp commanders. Colonel [Charles L.] Clifford, who was in charge until April 1945, was well liked. He was followed by Major [Floyd C.] Mims, who stayed for only about six weeks and seemed somewhat mentally disturbed. I had direct contact with the American boys from the post headquarters, where I worked for a time. I have pleasant memories of Sergeant Bishop, who worked in the mimeograph office, as well as Rudy Miller, Jim Arnold, and Frank Sullivan, all of whom worked in the finance office. They and others used to secretly slip coins or chocolate into my jacket pockets. The same thing later happened at the ordnance shops, though more openly. By that time the war was over, and the anti-fraternization policy had been relaxed. Almost every day I would receive Hershey chocolates or ice cream from Sergeant John Ronchi.

I exchanged home addresses with Rudy, who lived in Kansas City, Missouri. After the war, he worked for Procter & Gamble and used to send parcels containing soap, detergents, etc. to my parents' house—valuable items in those days.

From the medical side I remember two individuals: Major [George] Schatz, a German-speaking emigrant who was a pleasant fellow, and the camp dentist, whose name I can't recall. One day while working on my teeth, the dentist complained that he had just completed school and learned how to make money and now he had to look after POWs. Schatz had a very direct approach with people. One day there was a wedding at the post chapel, and I guess he was the best man. He saw me working in the gardens around the chapel, and after the service he complimented me for the floral arrangements that I made. He then took me around to meet some of the guests. This was somewhat unusual and maybe even somewhat embarrassing, but he didn't care.

HERBERT SCHAFFRATH

Several lovely young women worked beside us POWs in the post engineering headquarters. They were always friendly and even offered us candies. For Christmas they gave me a nicely wrapped package containing perfumed soap. Regrettably, that was as far as our relationship went. We had to be careful not to violate American Army regulations that prohibited fraternization.

WERNER GILBERT

We were forbidden by the American authorities to establish personal relationships that might lead to romance with American women who were working at Camp Cooke. Most POWs, myself included, abided by this restriction. Some of us established good friendships, however. One coworker from the shoemaker's shop went a little further and was caught with a woman. Instead of reporting the POW, the GI who caught the couple simply borrowed the woman for three days. In another instance, one of the kitchen helpers had an affair with an American woman. The couple were in a car when unexpectedly a second love pair showed up wanting to get inside the same car. It turned out that the second girl was the daughter of the one already in the car.

LEONHARD REUL
We always got along well with our American guards. Our first guard at Tagus Ranch was a colorful character who used to say, "Fuck the army" or "You damn Germans make me sick. Instead of watching you sons of bitches, I could be at home making a lot of money." I used to cool him down by telling him at least he didn't have to go to the battlefront. We Germans were never offended by his crude remarks because we too were very familiar with a trooper's tongue.

Leonhard Reul.

• *Recreation and Reeducation Programs* •

Two of the most important components of the POW program vigorously applied by the War Department in all the camps were the recreation and reeducation programs. The recreation program was intended to occupy the prisoners' free time with constructive activities designed to overcome the monotony of confinement. The reeducation program attempted to break the grip of Nazi indoctrination by exposing the prisoners to democratic ethos. Reeducation was not without complications. For one thing, it could be perceived as subjecting prisoners of war to propaganda, which was prohibited by the Geneva Convention. Conducting a propaganda program would also have invited retribution against American captives held in enemy hands. The War Department circumvented these obstacles by basing the reeducation program on Article 17 of the Convention, which stated: "So far as possible, belligerents shall encourage intellectual diversions and sports organized by prisoners of war."[5]

With this information in hand, the War Department gave the Provost Marshal General's Office the task of setting up a reeducation program to encourage "intellectual diversion" within the camps. The PMGO, in turn, promptly created the Prisoner of War Special Projects Division, and placed it in charge of operating the program, which officially began in September 1944. U.S. Army personnel, highly competent civilians, and specially screened German POWs who were dedicated anti-Nazis staffed the division. During the next year and a half, they developed an extensive reeducation program that included publishing a national newspaper, *Der Ruf* (The Call), which was sold in all the camps.[6]

The Special Projects Division trained a select passel of American officers and enlisted men and assigned them to service command headquarters and to prisoner of war camps. Using classrooms, films, and other media, they encouraged prisoners to recognize the character of National Socialism and to openly embrace democratic ideals. To avoid complaints of propagandizing, the Army very often used these resources in subtle psychological ways to convey a sense of moral rectitude. This technique might include the showing of Hollywood films that promoted this message, and establishing mandatory classes in American history and civics alongside other courses of popular interest.[7]

In many respects, the reeducation and recreation programs were deftly intertwined and became not only important pastimes in the camps but also well-attended forums for self-improvement. Athletics were encouraged in all the camps and became a popular form of recreation, with soccer by far the favorite sporting event. Soccer matches were held every Sunday at Camp Cooke and at its branch camps. Teams were formed, and championship tournaments were held for soccer, fist ball, handball, tennis, ping-pong, billiards, chess, and cards.[8]

Painting and sculpture were less rollicking diversions among the POWs. Talented prisoners fashioned ornate chess sets, figurines, and other articles from scrap wood. One enterprising POW built a knee-high castle using stone chips and cement. Contests were held and a panel of POW judges awarded prizes for the best paintings and handicrafts. Many of the finished products were available for purchase by other prisoners and American personnel through the POW camp canteen. Artwork also adorned the POW barracks and even the American civilian mess hall.[9]

Nearly all the prisoners enjoyed a POW theatrical group, a twenty-piece orchestra, and a chorus. For most of the prisoners, it was their first opportunity to play an instrument or to perform

Everyday Life in the Camp

Company 2's soccer team at Camp Cooke. Heinrich Kersting is second from the right.

POW artwork and crafts on display at Camp Cooke. (Courtesy of Heinrich Kersting)

on stage. The first theater performance at Camp Cooke was entitled *Der Bibliothekar* (*The Librarian*), and was given on September 16, 1944. Comedies were particularly popular and undoubtedly reverberated with the unabashed bantering of those cast members costumed as women.[10]

The orchestra played a wide selection of music to accommodate all levels of taste that ranged from German classics and operettas to contemporary hits by American composers such as Cole Porter, Irving Berlin, and Glenn Miller. In addition to playing concerts, the orchestra accompanied other theatrical productions in the camp.[11]

Performances by all three groups were often held in a barrack that American camp authorities had intended as a chapel. With American concurrence, however, the POWs modified the building into a theater during one week in August 1944. They slanted the barrack floor toward the stage and installed a piano, gas pipe chimes, and a music stand in a six-foot deep orchestra pit. Using scrap lumber, they constructed wooden seats for an audience of up to two hundred people.[12]

Musical performances and stage shows quickly became much appreciated entertainment sources at Camp Cooke. POWs jammed the former chapel to soak up musical and stage presentations. Outdoor concerts attracted still larger audiences. Within

Everyday Life in the Camp

The theatrical group entertained quarterly. The cast of the play *Köpenicker Strasse 120*. Werner Blanck is fifth from the left standing between the two "ladies." Hans-Joachim Böttcher is to the right of the bearded man holding a pencil. (Courtesy of Werner Blanck)

The POW orchestra and chorus gave frequent performances. (Courtesy of Werner Blanck)

a two-week period in September 1945, the camp orchestra and a collection of variety acts staged six shows. POW companies topped off the events with lotteries that awarded candy bars, ping-pong balls, and other prizes to the best performers.[13]

At least three times a week, the POWs crowded into company barracks to watch the latest American movies. They included *Road to Morocco, Seven Sinners, Abe Lincoln in Illinois, Thirty Seconds Over Tokyo, Gulliver's Travels,* and, of course, the comedies of Abbott and Costello.[14]

One form of recreation strictly *verboten* by American camp officials was drunkenness among the POWs. Beer was available at the canteen on a limited basis: one bottle a day, per man. However, when prisoners abused the privilege, the sale of beer was sometimes suspended. In either case, a few adept POWs turned to the clandestine making of moonshine. This prompted shakedowns of the barracks by American guards looking for illegal drink and other forms of contraband. Relations between the guards and the POWs, which were normally cordial, became acutely tense during these searches.[15]

Although the War Department and relief agencies provided much of the recreational equipment enjoyed by the prisoners, another available source used to purchase or rent additional items such as indoor games, handicraft tools, motion picture films and projectors, and theatrical accouterments was the camp prisoner of war trust fund. The fund was supported by profits from POW canteens and was managed by a trust fund council headed by the POW camp commander.[16] Between January and June 1945, more than $18,000 was withdrawn from Camp Cooke's trust fund for entertainment and educational purposes. Of this amount, $4,631.11 funded activities at the main camp. The nine branch camps at that time each received varying amounts—Lamont, $4,507.61; Shafter, $2,690.68; Tulare Fairgrounds, $1,944.78; Boswell, $1,186.89; Tagus Ranch, $1,133.41; Goleta, $972.86; Lakeland, $474.00; Tipton, $334.41; and Saticoy, $313.98.[17]

The secret reeducation program at Camp Cooke effectively began with the arrival of First Lieutenant (later Captain) John T. Harris in December 1944. Officially, he was assigned to the staff of the POW camp as the assistant executive officer. But Harris's veiled assignment was to organize a reeducation program among the prisoners at Cooke and its branch camps. Assisting Lieutenant Harris was Sergeant Manfred Lewinnek. A Jewish émigré from Nazi Germany, Lewinnek came to the United States in 1938 and enlisted in the Army four years later. His native

Sgt. Manfred Lewinnek, 1945. (Courtesy of Anne Hurwitz)

language skills made him an ideal recruit for duty at the German POW camp at Fort Devens, Massachusetts, in 1944, and then a few months later, at the age of thirty-two, as the interpreter-supervisor at Camp Cooke. His duties included selecting suitable German publications for the POWs, screening prisoners to determine their political ideologies (to include identifying Gestapo agents) for possible separation to other camps, and selecting POW instructors and study directors in the base and branch camps. He was also the supervising editor and political advisor for the POW camp newspaper, *Der Lagerspiegel*, directing its editorial writers toward helping the mission of the Army's Special Projects Division. Finally, Karl Wagner, himself a POW in the camp and a certified engineer in civilian life, was appointed director of studies by popular vote with the concurrence of Lieutenant Harris and Sergeant Lewinnek. He helped organize and promote educational and recreational activities within the camp. At least nineteen other prisoners who qualified were selected as teachers. Among this passel were lawyers, architects, university students, and merchants. Each instructor was paid an hourly wage, which did not exceed the standard pay of 80 cents a day.[18]

Under the leadership of Lieutenant Harris, an extensive education system developed at Camp Cooke. Besides the required reeducation curricula of English, American history and civics, and American geography, prisoners could study other subjects including accounting, art, biology, bookkeeping, calculus, chemistry, economics, French, German, geometry, Latin, mathematics, physics, sociology, Spanish, and statistics. Technical instruction in agriculture, building and construction, machinery, radio repair, and tailoring were also available.[19]

Another educational option accessible to all prisoners at Cooke, and approved by the Provost Marshal General's Office, was group correspondence courses. Offered by the University of California at Berkeley, at least fifteen courses were available including art appreciation, zoology and general biology, differential and integrated calculus, and mechanical engineering. The camp prisoner of war trust fund paid for these courses.[20]

The POW library at Cooke offered a wide selection of German and English books donated by the War Prisoners' Aid Committee of the YMCA, the International Red Cross, and the German Red Cross. Using POW trust funds, Lieutenant Harris purchased many additional titles for the library, including German literature banned by the Third Reich. In August 1945, he bought twenty-four German books from Nobel laureate Thomas Mann. An outspoken critic of National Socialism, Mann had fled his native Germany and during the war lived in Pacific Palisades, California. The library at this time had about 1,500 books on its shelves, most in German, with an additional 2,500 volumes distributed among the branch camps. Other reading material, particularly text and reference books used in education courses, was obtained free of charge through interlibrary loans with the University of Southern California in Los Angeles.[21]

German language newspapers and magazines were enthusiastically received in the camp, and at least twenty-eight of these publications were subscribed to at Cooke and were available at the canteen. Prisoners who could read English also gravitated

UNITED STATES ARMY

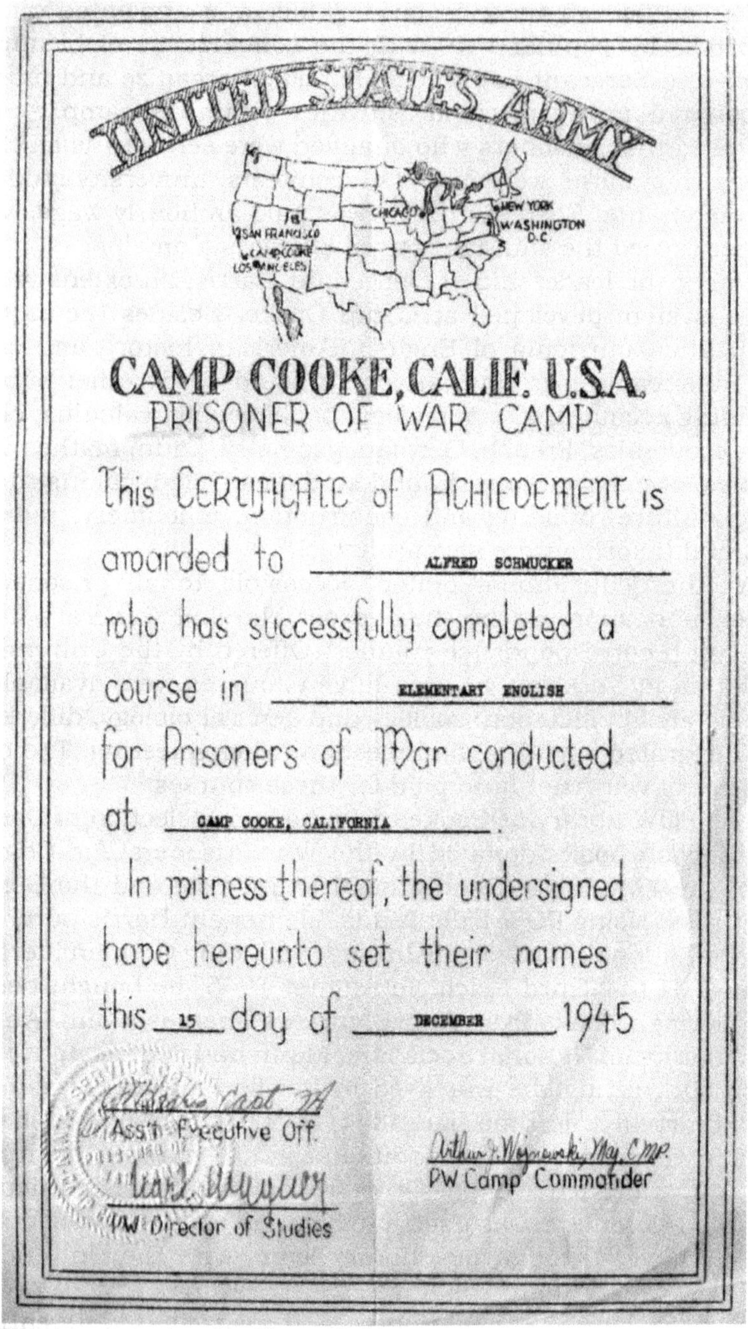

CAMP COOKE, CALIF. U.S.A.
PRISONER OF WAR CAMP

This Certificate of Achievement is awarded to ALFRED SCHMUCKER who has successfully completed a course in ELEMENTARY ENGLISH for Prisoners of War conducted at CAMP COOKE, CALIFORNIA.

In witness thereof, the undersigned have hereunto set their names this 15 day of DECEMBER 1945

Ass't Executive Off.

PW Director of Studies

Arthur F. Wojnowski, Maj. CMP
PW Camp Commander

The prisoners were issued certificates of achievement for education classes they completed at Camp Cooke or at any of its branch camps. (Courtesy of Alfred Schmucker) toward the *New York Times, Newsweek, Time,* and *Life,* as well as other leading publications. They were amazed at the uncensored reporting of war news and the diverse political opinions freely expressed. By providing the opportunity for POWs to discover for themselves examples of freedom of speech and freedom of the press in American democracy, the PMGO hoped that along with other aspects of the reeducation effort, a new, enlightened attitude would emerge among this core group of men and gain traction in postwar Germany.[22]

Another source of intellectual diversion and information in the camp was a public-address system. Under the supervision of camp officials, the POWs at Camp Cooke began operating the system in July 1945. News, talk shows, radio plays, live and recorded music, and poetry readings were broadcast from the camp every day between six-thirty and eight p.m. The news was announced in English and German, with German commentary. Similar arrangements were established at some of the branch camps, including the ones at Edwards Ranch and Shafter. News reporting and music were the most popular programs, and the favorite song of all the POWs was Bing Crosby's recording of "Don't Fence Me In."[23]

Between June and December 1945, the POWs at Camp Cooke published their own biweekly newspaper, *Der Lagerspiegel* (*The Camp Mirror*). The paper, which was also distributed to the branch camps, encouraged the prisoners to openly express their democratic thoughts. It featured short stories, geography descriptions of the United States, poetry, songs, crossword puzzles, a calendar of events, sports news, clever jokes, practical English lessons, announcements of plays, concerts, and films, and lengthy editorials usually about politics and philosophy that were consistent with the national anti-Nazi POW newspaper, *Der Ruf*.[24]

In nearly every edition, the paper exhorted its readers to recognize the disastrous consequences of National Socialism and to adopt democratic ideologies. In one instance, it reminded its readers to accept responsibility for the horrible crimes perpetrated against civilization by Nazism and to work for the readmission of Germany into the circle of civilized and democratic nations of the world. Another article referred to the Third Reich as "an aberration of reason and justice." "Such insanity," it went on to say, "must never repeat itself. We owe it to our children."[25]

How successful was the reeducation program at Camp Cooke in eradicating Nazi racial and anti-Semitic sentiments? Lieutenant Harris and Sergeant Lewinnek attempted to answer these questions shortly after the war by conducting a survey of one thousand prisoners (four companies) at the main camp. While the responses they received provide interesting quantitative data on the attitudes of the prisoners, the survey's conclusions must be tempered. Given the prisoners' circumstances, they were sometimes evasive or inclined to offer answers to questions in a way they believed likely to benefit their situation. The survey and its results, which appear in the appendix of this history (page 229), indicate a small but distinct Nazi presence in the camp.[26]

ALFRED SCHMUCKER

Within the POW compound, we had the opportunity to attend various education courses. This is where I learned to speak English. Attending movie shows also helped to improve my English language skills. Twice a week we could see a movie at a cost of 15 cents (in canteen coupons). Our favorite female stars were Ingrid Bergman, Deanna Durbin, and little Margaret O'Brien.

We also had access to American newspapers and magazines and could subscribe to *Life* and *Time* magazines. *Der Ruf* was another type of newspaper sold in our canteen. If I remember correctly, it cost 5 cents a copy. The paper was published by a select group of POWs who were at a camp in one of the New England states. It was a highly sophisticated paper that reported on plans to instill democracy in Germany. It also informed us about the intent of the United Nations. Ninety-five percent of its content was of a political nature. We, behind the fence, were more interested in other things: What's left in Germany, to what occupation zone does our town belong, and when can we expect to be repatriated? For this reason, the paper was not a bestseller. On the other hand, we had a German language paper, published in New York, which told us a lot more about conditions in postwar Germany.

After duty hours and on Sundays, we had various recreational activities. We could play chess, cards, soccer, go to the library, receive music lessons, or listen to records for hours in one of the recreation rooms. We also had a theatrical group and an orchestra. Within our barrack we all contributed some money and bought a small radio through our canteen. We used it to listen to the news and the popular songs of the time. I remember a few of these songs such as "I'm Always Chasing Rainbows," "Five Minutes More," "Bell Bottom Trousers," "You Are My Sunshine," "Shine On Harvest Moon," and, by the way, our favorite song, "Give me land, lots of land under starry skies above, don't fence me in."

We had quite a large number of pets in Camp Cooke. Our company had a dog called "Lady." She gave birth to several puppies, and it seemed she was constantly pregnant. After the animal population had become too large, we received orders to get rid of them. In our barracks we had a cat. The trash disposal unit took her several times for a thirty-mile ride to set her out. The poor thing returned after several days three times.

One day, Doris Bailey, Corporal Bailey's wife, brought me a little dog. We called him "Tiny." I kept him in the labor office overnight, and that way he was not subject to the disposal ban. When we transferred to Montana, I had to leave him behind, and my heart was bleeding. Doris promised to look after him.

HEINRICH KERSTING
We had our own theatrical group that gave nice performances, and several times a week we saw motion picture films. Our favorite American celebrities were Betty Grable, June Allison, Judy Garland, Ava Gardner, Bing Crosby, Bob Hope, and many others. Many different types of sports were played in the camp, including soccer, handball, volleyball, boxing, baseball, softball, tennis, and ping-pong. Education classes were also offered in mathematics, German, engineering, and more. There were plenty of opportunities for beginners and for those continuing in these fields.

WERNER BLANCK
I was a member of the stage performance group at Camp Cooke. We used to rehearse two or three times a week, and we gave five or six stage performances during each calendar quarter. Many of us would also get together and have fun playing poker and listening to the fabulous songs played on the radio. During other times we played handball. We also had a camp orchestra of twenty musicians. In addition to performing German classics and operettas, they played popular American tunes, including songs by Cole Porter, Irving Berlin, Glenn Miller, and others. Both the orchestra and the theatrical group received many of their outfits and instruments from the International Red Cross and the YMCA. These agencies did many good things for us.

In addition to music concerts and stage performances, we watched Hollywood movies at least once a week. Many of us also took advantage of the education classes offered to us in English, French, Spanish, mathematics, physics, and much more. I enrolled in a Spanish course, but dropped out. Those who completed a class received an education certificate from the American camp administration. As far as I know, however, these certificates had no value in postwar German schools or universities. For most of us, our time at Camp Cooke was by far the best part of our military experience.

HANS-JOACHIM BÖTTCHER
Our theater at Camp Cooke was originally designed to be a chapel, but the Afrika Korps troops in the camp modified the building for nonreligious entertainment in August 1944. They constructed a large stage at one end of the building and revamped the floor so that it slanted toward the stage. Just in front of the stage, they dug an orchestra pit that seated about twenty musicians. The main portion of the barrack was then lined with benches.

The most memorable thing about our theatrical group was not so much the plays, but rather the harmony that existed within the group itself. As a member of the theater cast, we celebrated all sorts of events together, and after rehearsals or performances we would meet backstage for coffee and drinks. The Americans frequently attended our performances and occasionally would stop in for an "inspection." During these visits they never rejected an invitation for a drink, although alcohol was officially forbidden. Sometimes we were caught playing a game of poker, but there were never any repercussions. The GIs enjoyed seeing our "girls" in underwear, and you can imagine the sort of jokes that followed. On one occasion the camp commander came in with his staff while the girls were getting ready. Incidentally, our theater costumes were supplied to us by a company in the Los Angeles area.[27]

The camp recreation area included a soccer field (also used for handball), a tennis court, and a boxing stage. There was never much tennis or boxing in the camp, but the boxing stage, an elevated platform, was repeatedly used for speech making.

In the fall of 1944, a circus came to Camp Cooke and staged performances in the sports arena on the main post.[28] We attended a special performance and many of the international artists introduced themselves in German, telling us where they had starred in prewar days, places like the Wintergarten in Berlin and the Hansa-Theater in Hamburg. They almost made us feel at home. Many of us came from Hamburg and knew the Hansa-Theater. My family were almost regulars at this place. Nearly the whole camp attended the circus performance. We were taken to the arena by the same buses that took us to work in the mornings.

On Christmas Eve, December 24, 1945, we had a comical game of soccer in which those occupying the left row of beds in barrack 15205, played against those in the right row. Everybody was dressed in amusing costumes (bakers, butchers, market women, school children, etc.); one team wore hats; the other didn't. The feature star on one of the teams was "Peppi" Buchner—an Austrian, I believe—a humorous character who was always good for a joke. He was dressed in a Louis XIV costume. Heinz Schröder was referee. He wore a hula dress and did plenty of kicks that drew riotous cheers. Throughout the day and evening, the camp broadcast system filled the air with festive music.

That evening our entire company celebrated in the mess hall and later in the theater. The stage was wonderfully prepared with plenty of chairs and tables for our foods. Hans Loewen and Jürgen Bleckert prepared the decorations. We had an open bar with free beer, whiskey, rum, and homemade wine for everybody. Our bartender was Günter "Picco" Hebestreit. We exchanged presents and had a fantastic celebration. On Christmas Day we enjoyed another soccer match, and the winner received a special holiday trophy.

While at Camp Cooke, I completed classes in American geography and chemistry (no experiments). Since we had a good library at our disposal, I became an avid reader. One of the newspapers available to us at the canteen was *Der Ruf.* Most POWs were reluctant to buy this paper, some because they didn't (yet) like its anti-Nazi tendency and others because they didn't want to be seen with this paper although they may have agreed with what was written. In the long run, and especially after 1945, the paper was generally accepted. Finally, partners were always available for a game of cards (skat), checkers, etc.

I wasn't directly involved in the activity of making wine in the camp, but I think it was produced by some POWs using raisins and grapefruits. Whiskey was occasionally "imported" into the camp by various means. One method involved the POW trash unit, which smuggled whiskey into the camp in empty garbage cans. They knew the guards and vice versa, so I guess the POWs were waived through the gate without being searched.

Outside the camp on the main post was a tortoise pond. One day a group of POWs from the paint shop caught a few of these animals and stenciled swastikas on their shells.

Regardless of politics, one sentiment shared by all POWs was homesickness. It was most evident among POWs who had their own families. Nevertheless, considering the wartime circumstances, most of us were glad to be in the United States and not in Russia or France.

HERBERT SCHAFFRATH

We always had plenty of activities to occupy our free time in the evenings after work. We could continue our education by attending any of the several free courses available in the camp, or we could watch one of the many original movies that was playing in our theater. Since I did not have the good fortune of working in the laundry during the day, I spent many of my evenings washing my clothes. Sundays, however, I played handball in the morning and soccer in the afternoon.

In the autumn of 1944, we had a very decent camp commander who one Sunday morning allowed us to attend a performance on the main post given by an itinerant circus. We marched in formation from the camp to the sports arena for a ten o'clock show. We had a wonderful time, and for a while it was almost like being back home.

In the camp we had both an orchestra and an amateur theatrical group. I attended and greatly enjoyed all their productions. Especially memorable to me were the individuals who played the female acting roles. They were so convincing in their speech and mannerisms that one got the impression they had to be women. For us young people, these artistic performances introduced our hearts and minds to a world free of politics and martial music. Even today, I have the greatest respect for those people who with profound devotion to their craft made our time at Camp Cooke considerably more pleasant.

The song "Don't Fence Me In" was a popular melody among the POWs in 1945. For one talented POW working in the drafting room of the post engineering headquarters building it sparked a creative idea. He shaped a dog out of clay, painted it very colorfully, fastened a large chain on its neck, and wrote on the dog the lyrics "Don't Fence Me In." To the Americans this was a humorous and artistic expression. For us POWs it was wishful thinking.

We celebrated Christmas Eve 1944 with a lively concert by our camp orchestra and choir. Communal singing of "Stille Nacht, heilige Nacht" topped off the evening. On Christmas Day all the POWs in the camp shared in a huge holiday meal. This was in contrast to the 1945 Christmas celebration when each company celebrated separately. In my company we had singing and poetry readings, punctuated by friendly conversations over cups of coffee. Our artists had decorated the mess hall with all sorts of beautiful Christmas ornaments. The festival meal consisted of a bouillon soup, chopped turkey, mashed potatoes, fresh vegetables (cauliflower, peas, carrots, green salad), rice with raisins, steamed fruit, coffee, oranges, and pastry. Cigarettes were handed out after the dinner.

Birthdays were another special event celebrated in the camp. The birthday boy would invite his friends to join him in the mess hall for coffee and a delicious cake prepared by our kitchen personnel. After the main event, the party would move to our barracks where we would sit around talking and drink Coca-Cola. This is how I celebrated my twenty-first birthday at Camp Cooke.

Perhaps I was too young at that time, but in my barrack we never made any wine or schnaps. The only thing we ever fermented was milk, which we used to make curd cheese for spreading on our bread.

Having a pet dog or cat in our barrack gave each of us a wonderful feeling of homeliness. When we returned from work in the evenings, our little dog was always waiting at the door to greet us eagerly. In return, we looked after him with the same affection. We fed him with food from our mess hall and built for him a doghouse that was large enough for a full-size Shepherd. When the animal population in the camp became too large for sanitary reasons, the Americans rounded up our pets and removed them.

Despite all the pleasant activities available to us at Camp Cooke, we all had days when our only thoughts were to be reunited with our loved ones back home. Generally though, we had a wonderful time at Cooke and enjoyed the moderate California climate.

ADOLF KELMER

After work, our evenings were open to all sorts of recreation and entertainment in the camp. One could play soccer, ping-pong, practice boxing, or participate in arts and crafts. We had some remarkably talented artisans in the camp whose skilled hands transformed scraps of wood into beautiful decorative items. Much of my free time was spent reading or walking around the camp watching people.

We also had an amateur theatrical ensemble supported by a competent camp orchestra that performed several popular comedies on stage. At other times, the theater was used for showing movies. For a nominal amount of camp money, we could watch the latest Hollywood releases or a variety of older films. In our recreation barrack, where we often played ping-pong, silent comedy films from the early days of cinematography were occasionally shown. These films were sent to us from the International Red

Cross and came in intervals of several weeks apart. Sometimes we received up to ten reels at a time. They played one reel after another on the same evening. It took a lot of endurance to sit through this film marathon in a barrack that was often filled with cigarette smoke. Few people aside from myself appreciated this art form.

On a few occasions, I watched some exceptional movies in the large cinema outside the POW camp at Camp Cooke. To get to the cinema from our compound, our company has to assemble and march in close Prussian-style formation. Our group was divided into four sections according to the uniforms we were wearing. The first few rows were men from the Afrika Korps. Following them were the Luftwaffe, the navy, and finally those like myself without a German uniform, but wearing our best POW clothing and looking smart because it was still a uniform. I was told that our American company commander, Captain Everett, came up with the idea for these outings that were always a lot of fun. People stopped to watch as we passed by, and a crowd would form near the front of the cinema to hear the shouts of "halt," and the commands that followed. Now as I think back to those marches, I hope they were viewed for what they were, harmless entertaining spectacles. Of all the people marching and watching, I think Captain Everett got the most enjoyment out of this Prussian-style marching game. He was a good man and had our respect.

Father FRANZ GÖDDE
Sports occupied much of our free time at Camp Cooke. Chess and card games were also popular. Since we had plenty of books, magazines, and newspapers available to us, I devoted my time to reading and was never bored. I also completed a course in advanced French and received a certificate from the camp administration. I don't think the various courses offered in the POW camps were officially recognized by the German education system after the war. Courses in English or French, however, might have been helpful in finding work in certain professions that required knowledge of foreign languages.

WERNER GILBERT
We had all sorts of recreation available to us at Camp Cooke. I usually played soccer, chess, and halma. Alcoholic beverages in the camp, however, were another matter. I remember that one day a crew of POWs were unloading cans of pineapple juice from a railroad car and smuggled many of the cans into the stockade.

The juice was easily transformed into good tasting schnaps. A kettle, a spiral, cold water to cool the drink, and soon we had that liquid refreshment dripping into empty Coca-Cola bottles. Of course, after that you could smell the alcohol odor throughout much of the camp.

GEORG KROEMER
In Camp Cooke, I played soccer and attended classes in basic English and Spanish.

LEONHARD REUL
The American administration at Camp Cooke had a splendid idea when it offered reeducation courses for German POWs. The majority of the younger POWs, including myself, grasped with both hands these opportunities to improve our education. I also considered them as reliable weed killers against dictatorships in the future. All the teachers, including the then-POW director of studies at Camp Cooke, Karl Wagner, visited our branch camp at Tagus Ranch about once or twice every two weeks. They usually stayed the night outside the POW camp in rooms the Americans had set aside for them. The teachers aroused a strong sense of enthusiasm even among the slowest learners. I completed courses in American civics, American history, American geography, and advanced English.

HEINRICH SCHÜNEMANN
We had few recreational activities available to us POWs at Camp Old River. For instance, we didn't have a music band or a theatrical group. We passed the time by reading or playing soccer, cards, or other games. The prisoners who picked cotton during the day were usually too tired to play soccer after work. Almost every week we could see an American movie in our little tent "theater." We enjoyed the shows and the opportunity it gave us to learn more about America and the character of its people. On Sundays, we had religious services that were conducted by a civilian minister and attended by a small group of men.

On January 5, 1946, I was transferred from Camp Old River to another branch camp at Lamont. Since the repatriation process began a few weeks later, none of us received work assignments outside the camp. We occupied our time playing sports, reading, or just walking around socializing with friends. To help pass the time, the camp commander told us to form teams and learn to play baseball. Our instructors were the American guards.

It was my job to translate the difficult rules of this game from the instructors to the players.

HELMUT WOLTER
Adjacent to the barracks at Camp Chino was a recreation field that we used for soccer. When we first got to the camp, we noticed that the usual white markings were missing from the field. We asked the guards if they had chalk to make the lines. They didn't have chalk, but offered instead laundry detergent or baking flour. We were totally amazed that after years of war these valuable items would be so plentiful in America and available to us for use in preparing a soccer field.

KLAUS HEBEL
During my free time at Camp Cooke and Edwards Ranch, I played ping-pong. In the evenings, especially at the main camp, we had all kinds of education classes. I completed courses in English language skills and stenography. For me the combination of work and meaningful leisure activities was the best medicine against homesickness.

I think it was at the Delano branch camp that late one night we were awakened by a popping noise in our barrack that sounded like gunfire. It turned out that hidden behind the false ceilings of our barracks were bottles of homemade wine. When the cider began to ferment, it blew the stoppers off the bottles, and sent the contents dripping to the floor. Boy, did we laugh like crazy when we realized what was actually happening.

RUDOLF HINKELMANN
Our favorite pastime at Tagus Ranch was playing soccer. We also saw American entertainment films, played cards, and read. Although I didn't get too involved with the illegal schnaps brewing in the camp, I heard from others that the utensils for making the drink were hidden underneath the doghouses.

Four or five POWs in my company at Cooke each had a dog. During the daily roll call, these dogs would always sit beside their respective masters. The camp administration tolerated the animals. The only objections occasionally came from other POWs. At night, coyotes, who smelled the dogs in the camp, would come right up to the fence and howl all night. This was especially common during a full moon. Our dogs were deathly afraid of the coyotes and often cowered in bed with their masters or hid under the barracks yelping. The same situation also occurred at Tagus Ranch and at Camp Warner. The guards in the towers were not allowed to shoot at the coyotes for fear of starting a gun battle that might mask an escape or other disturbance in the camp. In short, we had many nightly concerts.

• Reaction to Nazi Atrocity Films •

On June 4, 1945, the prisoners at Camp Cooke were rounded up and marched a short distance to Theater 3 on the main post to view one or more Nazi atrocity films. To be sure there was no misunderstanding, the film commentary was translated into German. The intent of this mandatory viewing was to instill a sense of collective guilt or at least a sense of responsibility for starting the war and for the Holocaust. Lieutenant Harris, who supervised the showing, later told a visiting inspection team from the International Red Cross and the U.S. State Department that reactions to the film varied considerably. "The soldiers obeyed orders," some said. Others indicated, "We could not divulge what happened." He remarked that some prisoners of war expressed displeasure, while others labeled the pictures as "propaganda." He also stated that privates generally reacted differently from noncommissioned officers to what they saw on the screen, but he did not elaborate on the differences.[29]

After viewing the films, many prisoners who felt shame and guilt for the war crimes of Hitler's regime, looked into the mirror of moral responsibility and collectively donated the considerable sum of $8,298.68 to the International Red Cross, the American Red Cross, and the War Prisoners' Aid Committee of the YMCA. Most of the money was designated for the survivors of concentration camps.[30]

Father FRANZ GÖDDE

Not long after the war, the Americans at Camp Cooke showed us concentration camp films.[31] Attendance at the post theater to view these films was mandatory and covered a few hours. The films were extremely disconcerting to the POWs. Afterward, we had hot discussions about this topic. Only the incorrigible Nazis did not want to believe that something like this was possible.

Almost none, of course, had ever heard of concentration camps—so they said. Actually, it was well-enough known, only the scale of the crimes we did not know. The films were shown only once as far as I remember.

WERNER BLANCK
I remember very well the day we were taken to see films about German concentration camps. At first we couldn't believe it. We thought it impossible that human beings could commit such terrible and criminal things. We were very depressed.

HERBERT SCHAFFRATH
We were not told in advance about these documentary films, which everybody in the camp had to watch. For many days thereafter, these films were the main topic of heated discussions. Many of the men were not ready to believe that the German people could perpetrate such crimes. Like most of my fellow captives, I knew nothing about the concentration camps, but the images of those horrible deeds were inescapable. Privately, I cursed those Germans who had participated in those crimes.

GEORG KROEMER
During the reeducation program at Camp Cooke, we were shown films of the horrible deeds that occurred in the German concentration camps. We were totally shocked by these films. In the beginning, almost all of us said it was impossible, and yet it was true. The evidence was just too obvious and irrefutable. Only a small number of men continued to believe that it was all propaganda and falsehoods.

    I knew that the Jews were housed in concentration camps, but had absolutely no idea of their suffering. Soldiers like myself who were usually knee-deep in mud and were then captured knew nothing of what went on inside the camps. After seeing these films, many of us were ashamed of our leadership.

ADOLF KELMER
I had seen many films while at Camp Cooke, but none affected me as much as the concentration camp newsreels. At first, many of us didn't understand why we had to see these films. (Nobody was excused for any reason.) Many of my comrades immediately dismissed the films as propaganda. It took me a long time to accept the authenticity of the films.

HANS-JOACHIM BÖTTCHER
We were brought to the post theater and I happened to get a seat in the front row. I became the target of a photo-journalist who

watched for our reactions. Naturally, I tried to control my face, but a picture of me and some comrades appeared in one of the local newspapers with the inscription "A super Nazi." Anyway, we were shocked by what we had seen on the screen. We knew, of course, that individuals were punished in concentration camps, but nobody had suspected this had happened to such an extent.

ALFRED SCHMUCKER
One day we were told not to go to work, but to be ready to go to one of the large movie theaters outside the POW stockade. Our names were called out to make sure that everybody was present because attendance was obligatory. In the theater we were shown concentration camp films. When we left the building, pictures were taken of the POWs by Army photographers.

WERNER GILBERT
I vaguely recall that we had to view films at Camp Cooke about concentration camps. When one had not been in the homeland for four to five years, as was the case for most of the German Afrika Korps troops, one could not form an opinion about these films.

RUDOLF HINKELMANN
What did we *Afrikaners*, who were transported [to North Africa] as early as the summer of 1941, know of what was happening at home, of how the Jewish citizens were being mistreated?

HELMUT WOLTER
After the war we were shown a newsreel about the concentration camps. Everybody at Camp Chino had to attend, and all were deeply moved by what they saw on the screen.

KLAUS HEBEL
I was at the branch camp near Goleta [Edwards Ranch] when we were shown these films. The POWs who had been in captivity for several years, such as the Afrika Korps troops, could not imagine those horrors and did not want to believe what they were shown. On the other hand, those of us who entered the war later had already heard about or at least suspected the reality of Nazi atrocities and the existence of death camps. We knew that all Jews from Germany had been deported to some unknown destination. It was a crying shame.

HEINRICH SCHÜNEMANN
There were always rumors about concentration camps in Germany after 1939. My parents never talked to me about these things. As a young soldier stationed in Germany, Belgium, and France, I did not witness anything about the camps. Soldiers on the Russian Front and in Poland knew more about these things. I don't recall having seen any of the German concentration camp films while in America. In Norwich, England, however, we were shown these films and were given additional information by an English officer. Later, back home, I watched concentration camp films on television. Both my wife and I were hit hard by what we saw, and even today we carry with us the guilt of what happened under Hitler's rule.

• *Nazi Influences in the Camps* •
During the first few months of its operation, Camp Cooke housed a sizable number of ardent Nazis. For the most part, but not exclusively, they were Waffen SS men and Wehrmacht soldiers with prior membership in Nazi partisan organizations such as the *Sturmabteilung* (SA), commonly known as the Brownshirts. They made their presence in the camp well known to other POWs and to American authorities. Raymond Feinberg, a lieutenant and company commander at the POW camp, distinctly recalls the SS prisoners. "They were a rough bunch of POWs. They stated that ten Americans were not as good as one of them. According to their bluster, the only reason they had been captured or surrendered was because they had run out of food, water, and ammunition."[32]

The Army realized that for the prisoner of war reeducation program to succeed, it had to establish a learning environment in the camps that was relatively free of intimidation by Nazi groups. This meant segregating leading Nazis into separate camps, a measure not always successful or appreciated by some American officers. At Camp Cooke, officers from the main post sometimes hampered the segregation effort because in some instances it meant breaking up trained work details assigned to the installation. Despite their opposition, many of the Nazi troublemakers were eventually removed from the camp, undoubtedly to the relief of other German POWs.[33]

Horst Schneider was one of the rabid Nazis at Camp Cooke. On at least one occasion, he attempted to slip past Army censors a hidden message to the intended receiver of his letter by using the familiar Nazi metaphor "parasites" to characterize Jewish servicemen at Cooke, and to gleefully cheer the annihilation of German Jewry. His letter was confiscated by Sergeant Lewinnek, whose job in the reeducation program at Cooke included screening all POW correspondence. Lewinnek fled from Nazi Germany in 1938, but was unable to secure similar passage for his parents. Shortly after Germany's surrender in May 1945, he learned they had died in a Nazi camp near Riga, Latvia, three years earlier in March 1942. One can imagine the anguish and animus that Lewinnek felt as he read Schneider's foul missive.[34]

TRANSLATION

January 15, 1945. Dear Hedi!
How time flies, one week after another. I'm already here six months and I'm still with the old comrades. One has already adjusted to this life, however, it is not a feeling that free human beings have. One experiences harassment and chicanery from many sides. This has to be tacitly accepted and cannot be changed. Everything would be quite good if only there was not a Parasite who keeps hating us. Thank God he was eradicated in our Germany. We feel his influence here, but this does not bother us. Let us hope that after this [the war?] he loses all authority. Now I hope that you understand me correctly because then you can imagine how it is here. I would love to hear from you sometime soon. Sometimes I doubt that you receive my letters. Everything is fine with me; I have what I need. Happy greetings to all acquaintances.
Greetings from Horst.

Father FRANZ GÖDDE

We found out about the failed plot to assassinate Hitler (July 20, 1944) the following day. The situation in the camp was very tense. I remember that many of us whispered, with hands covering our mouths, "Too bad it didn't work." Others in the camp felt differently. For that reason, after the assassination attempt, we had to use the Hitler straight-arm salute for all military greetings. We were instructed by the U.S. military camp commander to use only the Hitler salute. I assume that the American authorities had been instructed by the German government via the International Red Cross to get this new policy to the POWs. Previously, the Hitler salute was given only when entering a room with cap or helmet

German Prisoners of War at Camp Cooke, California

Some German POWs steeped in Nazi racial ideologies tried to slip these views past Army censors in letters addressed to family and friends back home. An example of this subterfuge is this letter from Horst Schneider, confiscated by Sgt. Manfred Lewinnek at Camp Cooke in January 1945. (Courtesy of Anne Hurwitz) removed. All other times we used the standard military salute. Of course, once the war ended the salute problem solved itself.

Although the Afrika Korps comprised many Nazi sympathizers, they were not excessive in their thinking, and one could converse and live peacefully with these people. This changed for a few months beginning in November 1944 when the first POWs captured in France began arriving at Camp Cooke. Among this group were members of the Waffen SS. These people would not accept that the war was lost for Germany and continued to believe in Hitler's ultimate victory.

On one occasion a few of these staunch Nazis, or *Schlägertruppen*, as we called them, planned to enter our barrack late one night and beat up one of our friends. We found out about this in advance and were ready for them. Sure enough, they arrived around midnight. As they approached their intended victim the lights went on and the sluggers got slugged. They were from Company 3 or 4. The incident was never reported to the American authorities because they remained neutral in such matters. This encounter happened around November or December 1944 and was the last of its type in our company.

HEINRICH KERSTING

The news of the attempted assassination of Hitler in July 1944 caused a great deal of consternation and uncertainty among the POWs in the camp. Although it wasn't spoken aloud, some of us felt that his death would have been better for everyone concerned. The war would have ended much sooner, the senseless dying would have ended, and we POWs could have gone home sooner. After the assassination attempt, we were told by the Americans to use the Hitler salute and not the standard military salute. This order probably originated from higher-ups in Germany.

HERBERT SCHAFFRATH

We had at Camp Cooke some incorrigible Nazis who as late as the fall of 1944 still believed in a German military victory. Having experienced the superiority of the Western Allies in North Africa a year and a half earlier, I was convinced that our promised victory was an illusion.

HANS-JOACHIM BÖTTCHER

There was a definite difference in attitude between the *Afrikaners* and those captured after the Normandy Invasion about the eventual outcome of the war. Except for some staunch characters, the *Afrikaners* had already seen and experienced enough to know that the U.S. could not be defeated. On the other hand, we were still under the influence of German propaganda.

RUDOLPH HINKELMANN

During the time that I was at Tagus Ranch we had at least two Communist sympathizers in the camp. When Romania and Bulgaria dropped out of the [Axis] Alliance, these two individuals became drunk and loudly proclaimed their political affiliation. This later touched off quite a few political arguments with other prisoners, and one night around midnight in mid-September 1944, gunshots rang out.[35]

Since I was the camp spokesman, I was called to the main gate where I saw two wounded POWs hanging on the barbed-wire fence. The two prisoners were the Communist sympathizers. They had been shot by the guards, who thought an escape attempt was in progress. Actually, the two were trying to get away from the camp *Schlägertruppen*. While I was standing at the fence in my pajamas, one of them bleeding from the mouth suddenly looked at me and yelled at the top of his lungs, "Geh zurük du Nazischwein!" ("Get back you Nazi pig!")

He said this in the presence of the American camp physician, Dr. Goldman. I was insulted so I immediately walked back to my barrack. Nevertheless, this remark was enough for Dr. Goldman to brand me as a Nazi. A short time later two American guards roused me out of my bed. They told me to pack my possessions and to go with them. Together with a few other prisoners, I was placed in the guardhouse under tight security. A day or two later I was transported in a railroad car to Camp Clark, Missouri. I had been stamped as a full-blooded Nazi by the Americans.

HEINRICH SCHÜNEMANN

It may have been about November 1945 when a young and rather slightly built POW at Camp Old River told the camp spokesman that he had found little slips of paper with swastikas scattered around his bed and personal belongings. He identified the few Waffen SS men in the camp as the ones responsible for the threatening notes, but the SS men denied the accusation. The Americans were notified and responded immediately by sending in guards to surround the young POW's tent. They also posted a few Army vehicles around the camp perimeter and ordered everyone in the camp to line up for roll call and to remove their shirts. We then had to raise our left arm so that the guards could check our armpits for the SS tattoo, the group's blood sign. In the end, this young POW was escorted from the camp by the Catholic chaplain and never returned. The rest of us resumed our daily activities.

Friends of this fellow later told us that he was a poor cotton picker who often complained and had fabricated the whole story so he could be transferred to a different camp. Sure enough, in March 1946, we ran into this POW at Camp Lamont. He admitted to falsifying the entire incident to get the transfer.

• *Religion* •

Religion was another device used to reach the social consciousness of the prisoners. But religion was not on the minds of most prisoners, as Maurice Perret of the Swiss Legation discovered after visiting Camp Cooke in September 1944. In fact, the prisoners had turned down an offer from American Army chaplains to conduct religious services in the camp. Since religion (Christianity) under National Socialism was subjugated to state control, dedicated Nazis resented its practice outside party-sanctioned gatherings. Some stayed away because they feared participation would invite reprisals from Nazi stalwarts in the camp. Others were simply indifferent.[36]

Until the defeat of Nazi Germany in May 1945, only a tiny minority of POWs regularly attended religious services at Camp Cooke. At first, Catholic services were conducted in the theater barracks and Protestant services in a schoolroom. After the war, when the number of worshipers increased significantly, both congregations held regular gatherings in a chapel outside the POW camp. Lieutenant Harris obtained the services of German-speaking civilian clergymen for both Catholic and Protestant worship. According to the POW newspaper, *Der Lagerspiegel*, the Protestant pastor was from San Luis Obispo and every Sunday brought a floral arrangement with him. Catholic services were sometimes accompanied by a violin soloist, fellow prisoner Kurt Meyer. In areas where it was sometimes difficult to obtain local clergy, German POW lay leaders led the congregants. By the end of May 1945, all the branch camps had some form of organized religious practice.[37]

The prisoners occasionally received more attempts at soul-saving than they cared for. Helene De Groodt, the widow of Lieutenant (later Captain) Franklin T. De Groodt who was assigned to Camp Cooke and to several of its branch camps, recalls one such incident at the Delano camp:

Once when Frank was commanding the Delano camp, a churchful of storefront fundamentalists decided they were going to go down to the POW compound (which wasn't far from the center of that little valley town) to "save them Nazi sinners." In those times many of the migrant workers who had come to harvest crops and stayed in the valley towns were dust bowl Okies, etc. They had little education, a lot of gullibility, and a strong founding in one sort of fundamentalist religion or another. Most of them, when they got to California, formed little storefront churches and had frequent revival meetings.

After whipping themselves up into a frenzy of revival fervor one night, they poured out of the church and marched down the streets singing their own version of gospel songs and speaking in tongues, headed straight for the compound. Curious, the prisoners filtered out into the yard to see what was happening. When they saw all these frenzied and strange-looking hordes advancing, pressing up against the wire fence with faces all contorted by zeal, shaking their fists and threatening the wrath of the Lord in a strange language, the prisoners thought a mob had come to kill them. They got the Lagersprecher to go to the camp commander and beg him to send those murderers away! Of course the camp personnel had been keeping an eye on things but thought it was pretty funny when some of the loudest-talking Germans in camp came begging for protection from a bunch of religious fanatics.[38]

HERBERT SCHAFFRATH
For us young people in Germany, the education system under National Socialism was so exacting and all-pervasive that Christian values were increasingly relegated to the background. In time, the personal need for church worship had been replaced by dedication to the state.

HANS-JOACHIM BÖTTCHER
Religion was not encouraged by the [Nazi] government, but also not suppressed. The church was partly a secret center or refuge of the opposition.[39] Most POWs at Camp Cooke were indifferent about religion.

GEORG KROEMER
Religion was not much in demand at Camp Cooke. After all, the origins of Christianity are rooted in Judaism.

HEINRICH KERSTING
Religion was clearly not a top priority among the POWs at Camp Cooke. Most of our energy was directed at sports and thinking about the homeland. We did, however, have religious services in the camp, and for a time I acted as a translator for a Catholic priest.

Father FRANZ GÖDDE
Every Sunday at Camp Cooke religious services were held for Catholic POWs. At first, these services were conducted in the theater barracks, and later they were conducted in a chapel outside the camp. We would gather by the entrance gate and patiently wait for our guard to escort us to and from the chapel. The civilian priest who conducted the services was from Dortmund, Germany. He had to leave the homeland to escape being thrown into a concentration camp.

Before the end of the war, maybe six or seven POWs at Camp Cooke attended regular services. After the war we had more than one hundred worshipers. Now that the crazy reign of the Nazis was finished, people were finally coming back to the old religious beliefs.

HELMUT WOLTER
Religious observance in Germany before the war was not forbidden, but we youths had little interest in the subject. After the war, religious observance, which was encouraged by the Americans at Camp Chino, was fairly well received.

HEINRICH SCHÜNEMANN
At Camp Old River we had Sunday services conducted by a civilian minister and attended by a small group of worshipers.

• *Escapes* •
One of the most pressing concerns of the War Department in transporting thousands of enemy prisoners to America was the possibility that gangs of Nazi prisoners could escape from the camps and cause widespread terror and sabotage in the civilian

community. Through countless publications, the War Department directed POW camp commanders to enforce strict security measures to prevent prisoner escapes. Machine gun towers equipped with searchlights, frequent shakedown inspections of prisoner barracks, censorship of prisoner mail, and in some camps, the use of guard dogs became standard practice.[40]

In actuality, the threat of escape was more imagined than evidenced. Apart from the Army's security measures, most prisoners were prepared to sit the war out in relative comfort while enjoying a full range of recreational and educational activities made available to them by the War Department and relief agencies. The train ride to the camps had also convinced many POWs of the substantial distances involved in any escape attempt.[41]

Still, for some POWs imprisonment under any circumstances was unacceptable. Indeed, prisoners escaped from Cooke and its branch camps for a variety of reasons. Sometimes it was a matter of principle. Others were motivated by a curiosity to see America and mingle with its people. Some were simply homesick.[42]

Those who escaped with the intention of returning home usually headed south, hoping to slip into South America, where they could find a sympathetic captain who would hide them on a ship bound for Germany. Their chances of success were woefully small for a number of reasons. First of all, they grossly underestimated distances in the United States and lacked suitable maps. Often they had no means of travel other than by foot, and if stopped, they were likely to arouse attention by their thick accents and POW garb.[43]

Nevertheless, between August 1944 and April 1946, Camp Cooke reported nine escapes involving seventeen prisoners. Most fled in pairs at night by cutting through, going over, or rolling under the barbed wire fences. Others slipped away from work details. They remained at large until they were captured, usually after a couple of days, or surrendered to the police when their food ran out. American camp officials humorously, but privately, referred to these types of escapes as "Appreciation of America" tours.[44]

One such escapade occurred at the Old River branch camp on November 4, 1945. According to the *Cooke Clarion* and the investigation report prepared by Captain John T. Pellew and Lieutenant Harold W. Wolff, four men identified as Franz Frankenberger, Juergen Stender, Kurt Plath, and Erich Schaefer escaped from the camp by crawling under the compound fence at about ten-thirty p.m. They made their getaway by stealing a private automobile.

When the car ran out of gas, they stole another. With the second car also low on gas, the hapless fugitives drove into a gas station, and one of the English-speaking prisoners asked that the tank be filled. When they drove off without paying for the gas, the attendant notified the state police, who apprehended the four the next evening near McFarland, some twenty-five miles north of the camp. Questioned by FBI agents and Army authorities, they cited poor and insufficient food and housing as the reasons for their escape.[45]

An article published in the *Los Angeles Times* on March 9, 1945, provides an interesting if not humorous anecdote about three German POWs who coordinated their escapes on the same day, one from Camp Cooke and the other two from a work detail at the Johns-Manville plant in Lompoc. Kurt Meier and Josef Kuhner were captured on March 8, two days after their escape. They were discovered hiding in the Southern Pacific Railroad yard in Santa Barbara, about fifty miles southeast of Cooke. At police headquarters, they reportedly gave the Nazi salute and said that 'Hitler will rule the world.' The third prisoner, Gustav Apel, they said, was heading for Argentina. When informed that Argentina was only a few miles south of the city, both men reportedly "beamed" over Apel's good fortune. Apel surrendered the next day to law enforcement at gunpoint after jumping from a freight train.[46]

Georg Kroemer, a three-time escapee, managed to elude sentries each time when he slipped out of Camp Cooke and two of its branch camps on two prior occasions. Kroemer's first escape occurred on January 12, 1945, when he and Richard Martin vanished from the Boswell Ranch camp near Corcoran. Their goal was to reach Fresno and then turn themselves in, thinking they would be returned to Camp Cooke where living conditions were more favorable. The men traveled on foot at night and slept during the daytime. Two days later they turned up on the doorstep of E. M. Stevens in the Clovis district of Fresno. They identified themselves as escaped POWs and asked that the sheriff be called. Kroemer's next escape was in April from the Edwards Ranch camp near Goleta when he and Oskar Köhnlein hopped a train they thought would take them to Mexico. Captured in the stockyards north of the camp between Santa Maria and San Luis Obispo, Kroemer was taken to Camp Cooke and placed in solitary confinement. He escaped on May 5, made his way to Los Angeles, and spent ten days at liberty until surrendering on May 15 to police officer William A. Smith. Questioned by FBI agent Richard B. Hood, Kroemer told Hood that the only purpose for his escapes "was to do a little sight-seeing [sic] while he was in America."

Returned to Camp Cooke, Kroemer was put on a train to Camp Rupert, Idaho. The details of his exploits are best told later by Kroemer himself.[47]

The longest period of escape from Camp Cooke was accomplished by Adolf Kelmer and Horst Stellbrand, who were also the only prisoners from this camp to reach Mexico. Their flight began on November 17, 1945, when by subterfuge they walked out the main gate of the POW compound and were not seen again until their recapture by border patrol officers on December 9–10 during a routine identification check south of San Diego at the Tijuana river bottom near the Mexican border. The escapees had crossed into Mexico and became lost. A few hours later they unknowingly reentered the United States and were apprehended by law enforcement officers.[48]

Another group of prisoners dug a tunnel at Camp Cooke that started from under one of the barracks and extended to almost the compound fence. American authorities learned of the tunnel from one of the prisoners before its completion. Lieutenant Raymond Feinberg vividly recalls the tunnel: "It was a beautiful engineering job complete with shored walls, tracks, and electric lights." This was all the more incredible because Camp Cooke was built on sandy soil.[49]

Following their recapture, the POWs were questioned by Army G-2 intelligence officers and FBI agents. Punishment usually consisted of confinement to the guardhouse, loss of privileges, and a restricted diet of bread and water for up to two weeks. Repeat offenders or those considered incorrigible Nazis were transferred from Camp Cooke to other camps. For instance, in October 1944, the Army had shipped to Camp Clark in Missouri sixty-seven POWs, most of whom were involved in constructing the tunnel at Camp Cooke.[50]

FBI Director J. Edgar Hoover repeatedly warned the American public that escaped POWs would cause sabotage and endanger American citizens. In reality, there was not a single recorded case of these offenses committed by an escaped POW. The most serious crime was stealing an automobile, or some small item needed for the getaway.[51]

GEORG KROEMER

After a few comfortable weeks in the main camp at Camp Cooke, I was transferred to the branch camp at Boswell Ranch, Corcoran, to pick cotton. I had no interest in doing this type of work. Besides, I wanted to experience America from outside the POW camp. One day while working in the cotton fields, I ran away from the camp with my comrade, Richard Martin. We expected to blend in with the working population because our khaki-colored clothes were the same as those worn by American GIs, farmers, laborers, and other types of workers. Ours, however, had on the arms, legs, and back in big letters "PW." We put these letters on ourselves with toothpaste so that later it was easily removed after we had escaped. While on our own, we lived off candy, bread, water, and whatever we found in the fields. We stayed overnight in cattle sheds and in open fields. After three days we turned ourselves in to the police. The FBI questioned us, gave us food, and offered us cigarettes.

We were returned to Corcoran and placed in a tent directly under the guard tower for fourteen days. On the fifteenth day, before being moved back into the main camp, the American guards played a macabre joke on us. With six other men who were with me in this tent, we had to climb into the back of a GMC truck. Off it went followed by a jeep with guards. Out in the field somewhere, we had to kneel down, and the guards then aimed their rifles directly on us from a distance of about sixty feet. Fortunately, they didn't pull the trigger. My comrades were frightened, and I was not in good humor myself. This was truly a very macabre joke that should never have been allowed to happen.

After my official punishment, I was back picking cotton. Shortly thereafter, my comrades nominated me as the camp spokesman. Amazingly, the American camp administration agreed to this proposal. I held that job until the end of the cotton harvest, around the spring of 1945.

I was then sent to Camp Cooke for a brief time before ending up at the Edwards Ranch camp along the Pacific Ocean. We spent some beautiful days at this camp before my comrade, Oskar Köhnlein, and I decided to go to Mexico. We escaped on April 4, 1945, shortly before my birthday. While most of the camp was out swimming under the supervision of American guards, Oskar and I slipped away from the group. That evening, after we had escaped, we chased an animal into the brush. We didn't know it was a skunk until I got a direct hit in my face and also on my clothing. All that night, good old Ossi, my co-conspirator, wouldn't share his blanket with me. Even after I washed in the ocean and washed my clothes the next day, the penetrating stink would not diminish.

The next morning we climbed aboard an open railroad car heading south. In a small rail station the trains were switched, and a locomotive was coupled directly in front of our car. One of the rail workers spotted us but didn't say anything. We assumed everything was fine. As our train rolled into the next station, however, we were delivered into the waiting arms of the military, who had surrounded the train. Our dreams of Mexico, sorry to say, were finished.

We were taken to a camp that was probably a prison for wayward GIs, and assigned to a work detail with the soldiers removing weeds from the camp grounds. After reveille in the morning, everything was done in double time. We received the same plentiful meals as the GIs.

After three days at this penal camp we were taken by jeep to Camp Cooke. We were housed in a well-guarded barrack that was isolated from the main stockade by fences and situated under a guard tower. We received bread and water, and every three days a warm meal.

Using the knife that came with my warm meal, and which I did not return, I worked for several days cutting a hole in the bottom back wall of the barrack directly behind my bed. I covered the hole with the headpiece of the bed and the rolled-up cover. When the opening was large enough, I squeezed out of the barrack at night and climbed over the fence into the POW camp without being noticed by the guard in the tower. I went into one of the barracks where I had some good friends and went to sleep. In the morning, after my friends had given me money and candy, I stood as the eleventh man in a row during roll call. These men worked outside the stockade on the grounds of the main GI camp. Sometime later that day I wandered away from the work detail and hid under one of the barracks until nightfall. I then set out by foot, heading for Los Angeles. I slept and hid during the day and traveled by night. Every time I saw the headlights of an approaching motor vehicle, I would dive for cover.

At a steep upgrade in the road [probably Conejo Grade south of Camarillo] I jumped onto the back of a small, slow-moving truck loaded with fruits and vegetables, and hid between the wooden crates. When it arrived in Los Angeles, I jumped off at a traffic light. There, I moved around the city freely, but only to buy the necessities for eating. At night I slept in wrecked automobiles in an auto dismantling yard.

After about a week, when the dollars and candy that were given to me were exhausted, I walked up to a police officer and said to him, "I am an escaped German prisoner. Please take me back." Even today, I can still see the terrified and flabbergasted expression on his face as he froze for a long moment and then left the traffic intersection to its own devices while he frantically waved to a fellow officer who took me into custody. This was going to be my last escapade because after my return to Camp Cooke I was sent to the penal camp, Camp Rupert, in Idaho.[52]

WERNER BLANCK

In January 1945, I was transferred with several other prisoners to Boswell Ranch at Corcoran, to pick cotton. I didn't want to go because I had a much better job working at the PX warehouse. Besides, all my best friends were at Camp Cooke so I decided to escape from Corcoran. I saved part of my meals, and after work on the second day I didn't go back to the camp. Instead, I hid in the cotton fields until nightfall. I walked at night and slept during the day. After three days I became too hungry and decided to surrender. At a nearby town, I met an old man standing in front of his house and asked for directions to the sheriff's office. I then surrendered to the sheriff and told him that I was an escaped POW. He welcomed me and allowed me to bathe. He then invited me to have breakfast with his family. Several hours later two FBI agents came and took me to a prison in Fresno.[53]

The sheriff at Fresno was a nice elderly gentleman. Whenever he had spare time, he allowed me into his office and we talked. I remember that he ordered food for me from the cafeteria across the street. Two or three days later, Army guards from Camp Cooke escorted me back to the camp. I was questioned and sentenced to twenty-one days in the guardhouse. In spite of my punishment, I was glad to be back at Cooke.

ADOLF KELMER

In November 1945, Horst Stellbrand and I escaped from Camp Cooke. I first met Horst a few months earlier while working in the laundry on the main Army post. Horst was a peaceful, quiet, even taciturn individual who before the war worked as a deck hand aboard various small ships plying the coast. After several weeks of getting to know each other, Horst told me about his idea of going to Mexico and asked if I wanted to accompany him. I immediately said yes. From that moment on, all our thoughts and actions were directed at preparing for the trip.

All summer and throughout the fall of 1945, we diligently collected the items needed for a successful escape. Starting with K rations, we also acquired a compass, two canteens, civilian overalls, sleeping bags, cigarettes, a sewing kit, a small cache of first-aid medicines, a map of California, and snack foods. Most of these articles we concealed near one of the buildings outside the prison compound or tossed over the camp fence a few days before our escape. During the weeks of preparation, we became so obsessed with our escape plans that we completely withdrew from other POWs, even friends.

Our initial escape plan involved digging a tunnel that would extend in an easterly direction from under one of the barracks and exit at an empty building on the outskirts of the prison compound. Equipped with only small hand tools, we began our digging late one night in October 1945. Night after night the work continued until finally we had the beginnings of an actual tunnel.

After a few weeks of strenuous toil, Horst said that we could stop digging because he had found an easier way to vanquish the fence. He kept the details of the plan to himself, but said that we would be leaving soon and that I should be ready to go on a moment's notice. Our tunnel was maybe fifteen feet long, but only wide enough for one to crawl through on his stomach. The dirt that we removed we scattered under other buildings in the camp.

The next weekend we closely observed the procedures and work schedules of the guards at the front gate. On the following Saturday [November 17, 1945], Horst said to me, "We go after roll call this evening." It was like a sudden jump into cold water. I was thrilled, but numb with anticipation. Horst had chosen this time because it was the last roll call of the week until Monday morning. This would give us an extra 24 hours away from the camp before our absence would be noticed by the guards.[54]

That afternoon, Horst obtained a typewriter from somewhere in the camp and brought it into his barrack. The machine was essential to Horst's escape plan. Toward evening we each went back to our respective barracks and quietly prepared for our departure. After donning regular Army overalls under my POW uniform, I stuffed a few matches into my pocket and headed out the door to meet Horst. Having worked in the laundry on the main post, I found it relatively easy to get military clothing and jackets without "PW" markings.

Shortly before the changing of the evening guard, Horst and I walked to the main gate. Horst was carrying the typewriter. On duty at the gate were two guards, the senior of whom we both knew well as "Charlie." He was an affable fellow who had made the Army his career. Horst concocted some plausible, but spurious story that he had borrowed the typewriter earlier that afternoon from an office outside the compound and wanted to return it before it got too late. Unaware of our real intentions, the two guards agreed to let us go if we signed their log book and promised to hurry back. We signed our names and filled in the departure time. We also entered our return time as ten minutes later. Since these guards were near the end of their shift, we hoped they would not look too closely at the log book and would forget to tell their relief team that we were still outside the compound. Personally, I felt a little ashamed of myself for having deceived Charlie, but we had no way of knowing he was going to be on duty that evening.

Once outside the fence, we walked briskly away from the compound, disposed of the typewriter, and disappeared into the darkness. Groping our way from barrack to barrack, we finally came to the location where a few days earlier we had hidden our travel provisions. After searching the grounds for what seemed like hours we came up empty-handed. At this point we abandoned the search and left the camp, taking with us the few items already in our possession. Between us we had a pound of bacon, a few cigarettes and matches, a compass, a small frying pan and a few knives from the mess hall, two canteens, and $50. We had accumulated the money by exchanging with other POWs our camp script for hard currency. We also found money while working in the laundry and going through the pockets of GI clothing. With our limited provisions, we headed south through the thick, brush-covered hills and back roads of northern Santa Barbara County.

The first couple of days we traveled at night and slept during the day. Although we later occasionally reversed this pattern, in most instances we continued on foot by night and searched for a suitable hideout between early morning and noon. Most of our sleeping was done in intervals of a few hours at a time and sometimes in shifts, with each of us taking turns at guard duty.

As an additional precaution, we always chose a route that seemed to be the safest and most practical, whether it was following the coastline, secondary roads, or rail lines. When we couldn't find a suitable rest area in the vicinity of one of these routes, we sometimes detoured as much as fifteen miles along a country lane leading into the mountains. On such occasions, we then slept undisturbed for several hours at a time and without the need for standing guard.

On the second day of our escape, we followed a road that ended at a small rural farm. Standing at the top of a hill, we looked down and saw a group of men and their dogs near a cattle corral.

The dogs sensed our presence and immediately began to bark. We turned and ran in the opposite direction. We found a large storm drain and followed it through to a dried riverbed, where we stumbled upon the parched bones of several dead cattle. Was it water scarcity or animal predators that had caused this, we wondered? We couldn't stop to think; we just had to go on.

After about six days, we exhausted our pound of bacon and our fresh water supply. We managed to get through another day by licking the morning dew from dusty branches. By this time we were already about forty miles southeast of Camp Cooke and felt reasonably safe changing our route to travel along the coast. We also figured that our prospects of finding fresh water, food, and other provisions would be greater along the beach, where residences were likely to be located. I vividly recall our stepping out from the hilly countryside after seven days and seeing the beautiful Pacific Ocean glistening beneath a bright blue sky.

One morning while walking along a solitary stretch of beach, we noticed a collection of small wood-frame cabins ahead of us. The buildings appeared vacant and may have served as cabanas for vacationers during the summer months. Farther off in the distance we observed a small hamlet, but its presence did not alarm us. After carefully watching the area for some time, we entered one of the cabins. Once inside, we lay down and propped our feet squarely against the door to keep out intruders. We had barely closed our eyes when suddenly a watchman began banging on the door, trying to force his way in. From the other side of the door, we heard in angry, unmistakable Spanish a command for us to open the door. We kept silent. The more he pushed on the door the more determined we became to defend our new-found freedom with all our might.

After a few minutes, the watchman stormed off in the direction of the hamlet, undoubtedly with the intention of seeking reinforcements. He was almost out of sight when we dashed from the cabaña, heading west along the beach, and disappeared behind the slopes of cliffs that extended out into the ocean. After a short rest, we climbed the cliffs and were delighted to find the railroad tracks at our feet. We followed the tracks southeast, and somewhere along the trail we crossed a narrow railroad bridge. Before stepping onto the bridge, which incidentally did not have handrails, we listened for trains and then we quickly crossed to the other side.

The following morning just before sunrise, we settled down to rest next to a large bush in a field. About noontime we heard a group of German POWs, probably from the branch camp near Goleta, who were harvesting tomatoes in a field nearby. Since we wanted to remain undetected, we kept a watchful eye on our hardworking neighbors until late afternoon when they returned to camp. That evening we ate so many of the tomatoes still hanging on the vines that we became terribly sick.

A few nights later we were again on the beach, this time under a bright, moonlit sky. Ahead of us we noticed a small animal waddling along the sand, and it quickly disappeared behind some rocks. Thinking it was a rabbit and eager to catch it, Horst began taking large, fast steps to overtake the animal. Just as he was about to pounce on it, this cute, furry little creature, raised its bushy tail, took aim, and hit Horst point blank in the face with a full load of its malodorous brew. Horst, badly shaken and alternating between shades of green and alabaster, fell over a three-foot-high rock from this suffocating attack. He spat and choked and for several minutes struggled to recover his breath. Even I, standing a few feet behind Horst, was hit by the spray from this skunk.

The fetor from the attack was so overwhelming that we stripped down to our undergarments. We then tied the contaminated clothes together and dragged them through the ocean water in a desperate attempt to remove the odor. Despite repeated washings and the open air, that heady aroma remained with us for several more days.

Meanwhile, a day or so later we reached the suburbs of Santa Barbara by following the railroad tracks. Late that evening we arrived at the freight railway station, where we planned to stow away on a train headed for Mexico. After spending considerable time observing the station, we approached three passenger coaches parked on the tracks. We slipped inside one of the cars and quickly fell asleep on its plush upholstered seats.

We got up a few hours later and left the comfort of our coach to scrounge for food. Our noses led us to a bakery, where parked behind the plant in neat rows was a fleet of small delivery trucks. Written on the side panel of each vehicle was the name "Weber's Bread." Horst immediately struck up a conversation with the man who was loading the trucks, and soon he too was pushing a handcart carrying bread from the building to the trucks. This went on for at least a half hour while I watched from a safe distance. Finally, Horst brought out two large loaves of fresh bread, and together we returned to our railroad coach. We slowly savored each slice of bread until our hunger disappeared and we were again overcome by fatigue.

With the arrival of dawn a few hours later, we awoke to the sound of railway people operating a switching car near our coach. A large locomotive had been coupled to a row of freight cars and was preparing to leave the yard. Without hesitation, we ran from our car and jumped aboard an empty cattle car whose doors were wide open. Except for the floor and the roof, which were made of solid pieces of metal or wood, the body of the car consisted of widely spaced parallel strips of metal that allowed one to see out of and into the car. The train began to move, but very slowly. Meanwhile, the sky was getting lighter, and we were becoming increasingly concerned that our presence would be noticed. As the train approached its first stop a few minutes later, we jumped off and ran quickly in the direction of the city.

For the time being, we decided to follow small secondary roads. That night we hitched a ride with a gentleman driving an early model automobile. Horst sat in the front seat, and I sat in the back. The man didn't bother to ask us where we were going, but instead immediately started babbling. Unfortunately, I didn't understand a word he said. Horst, on the other hand, did much better. In fact, the two of them carried on a conversation. One could easily see and smell that the driver was in good spirits that evening. After a certain distance, we parted ways with the driver and happily said our farewells as if we were long-time friends.

A short time later we again reached the shoreline. At a pier that extended out several feet into the ocean, we discovered a school of clams in the shallow sandy waters. We collected a few dozen of these creatures and tried eating them raw. For me this was an unpalatable experience. Fortunately for us, we didn't go hungry that night because a short distance from the pier we found a walnut grove. We devoured these nutritional and good-tasting nuts until our stomachs rebelled.

As the number of small towns and hamlets along the coastline increased, so too increased our opportunities to raid various gardens in search of fruits and vegetables. On one occasion I found a tree whose fruit was really delicious and was of a type I had never eaten before. Years later when I described this fruit to friends, they told me that I had probably eaten figs.

During our continual search for food and safe resting places away from populated areas, we came across a large building. From a safe distance, we observed the building for a long time before deciding to enter. It turned out to be a horse stable, and the lone resident standing inside its stall didn't seem to mind our presence. Above the stable and extending over half its length was a hayloft. We climbed up to the loft, made ourselves a cozy bed, and rested until late that afternoon, when we resumed our journey.

By this time I had developed a large and painful blister on my right foot, which caused me to limp and walk behind Horst. I could see from Horst's stoic expression that my slower pace did not fit his plans. I didn't understand his frustration because we usually got along very well.

During the next day or so, we passed through additional small communities. In one of these towns, whose crooked side streets and back alleys we roamed, we landed in a narrow driveway behind several hotels and businesses. We searched their garbage cans for food and for anything else that could be useful for our journey. Across the street and perpendicular to the driveway was a jeep with four or five soldiers inside. When the vehicle began to move, one of the GIs stood up and pointed us out to his buddies. Despite his fascination to find out who we were and what we were doing there, we could see from the facial expressions of the other soldiers that they didn't care. They glanced at us and drove away. Nevertheless, we became very uneasy and quickly left town.

Hours later we were in the countryside far away from most civilization. At one point we ventured off the road and walked toward a clearing in a forest. We discovered a vacant campsite with empty cans scattered about and a wooden box containing meatballs and a loaf of bread. With sunset rapidly approaching, we were eager to find a place for the night. We stepped over a small wire fence and headed up a hill. At the top of the hill was a pile of stones that we pulled together and made a small hut. We then collected branches and covered our little villa with a roof.

Early the next morning we were jolted out of our sleep by all sorts of gunfire and explosions. Since we always slept fully clothed, taking off only our shoes, we grabbed our meager belongings and doubled-timed back toward the fence. Clearly posted in large letters was a sign warning trespassers that this was an exercise area for Army artillery and infantry. Relieved to have survived that experience, we walked back toward the town and found the road heading south.

One or two evenings later we again hitched a ride. This time the invitation came from a woman who stopped her car, opened the door, and smiled at us. She and Horst carried on a nice conversation. After a short drive, our paths parted.

The next couple of nights Horst and I slept in parked cars. None of these cars were locked. We never damaged anything, and the only thing we ever took from these cars was an apple or some other small inexpensive item.

As we got closer to Los Angeles, we again looked for railroad tracks, hoping to get aboard a southbound train. One evening we found the tracks, but the first train we saw steamed by too fast. We caught the second train near an incline when it began slowing down. We hid in the bushes until the train was in front of us and then sprang to our feet. Running as fast as I could, I grabbed onto the handrail and pulled myself up. Although the train was moving slowly, it felt as if my arm was being ripped out of its socket. After a few terrifying moments, I had both feet firmly planted on the step. Horst, meanwhile, was already on the railroad car behind mine, but walked across the moving car to where I was standing.

We were on a flatbed car loaded with slabs of sheet metal. With every movement of the car, the metal shifted back and forth and from side to side, making for a very hazardous situation. Since this was an open car, the cold wind blew the thick black smoke of that coal-fired steam engine directly into our faces. We walked toward the rear of the train and took shelter in a car that was partially enclosed. Around morning, we arrived in Los Angeles. We climbed down and got away from the large railroad yard as quickly as possible.

After a few minutes, we got ourselves oriented again and headed out on foot toward Long Beach. The first hours of this new day nothing much happened. We walked toward the coast, me limping a short distance behind Horst. After a period of time, Horst stopped, and one could plainly see that he had had enough of my slow pace. "Take the damn shoe off," he said. He looked at my foot, looked at the shoe, shook his head, and then pulled out his knife. He cut out the piece of the shoe that had caused a blister the size of a half dollar to form on my foot. When he was done, he handed me my shoe without saying a word and began walking away. At least now I was able to walk again, only the shoe was a little worse for wear.

That night we came to an area with many small food warehouses. Parked at one of the loading docks was a large truck partially filled with cardboard boxes. While I acted as lookout, Horst quietly approached the truck, and with one big slash of his knife, he opened a carton and pulled out three or four glass jars. As we fled the scene, we imagined all sorts of delicious foods contained in those jars. We ran across a lawn, where I tripped and somehow activated the water sprinkler system. Soaking wet, we continued on to a secluded area, where we feverishly unwrapped the packages only to find empty drinking glasses. The whole episode was so ludicrous that we laughed our heads off.

Several hours later we came across a large machine with the word "ICE" written across the front. We immediately envisioned chocolate or vanilla ice cream. The large machine didn't arouse our suspicion because we thought of America as a country with large possibilities. I deposited the requested 5 cents into the machine and out came a tray about two feet long. Then from within the machine came a rumbling sound. A few seconds later a large solid block of ice, nicely wrapped in a carton, dropped onto the tray. What, we asked each other, are we going to do with a block of ice? We each chipped off a small piece for drinking water and put the rest of the ice into a container next to the machine.

The next afternoon we got to the shore at Long Beach. We bummed around at an amusement park but did not participate in any of the festivities. Throwing our money away for something like this didn't make any sense to us. We held on to our money and planned to spend it only in the event of an emergency.

That night we came to a small rural residence. Horst, who always had a good sense for finding food, now targeted two chickens. He whispered a command to me, but I refused. I didn't want to steal a poor family's chickens. A twisted frown came over Horst's face that quickly turned into an expression of malevolence. Without uttering a sound, he sneaked up to the chicken coop and quickly snatched two hens. For the next day and a half, he carted around those live winged delicacies.

About seven miles south of Long Beach, the terrain became very flat. At one point we came to a large, dense belt of reeds. This seemed to be an ideal place to rest for several days and a likely area to find drinking water. We carefully pushed our way through the reeds so we wouldn't create a trail. At some point we found a good spot and built a reed hut. As far as we could stretch our arms, we bound the tops of the six-foot high reeds together and left a man-high opening. We then flattened the reeds inside the hut creating a thick mattress. By the time we finished, it was a very well-constructed edifice with plenty of room for both of us.

We soon found the main watering hole, but it turned out to be brackish. That night I walked back toward the village to get fresh water. I left the hut about an hour after sunset (we did not have watches), leaving Horst behind with his two clucking hens. The passageway through the reeds to the road was easy to find. I had to place inconspicuous markers at the roadside, however, so that I could find my way back to the hut.

I remained at the edge of the reed belt until darkness before walking toward the village. Since it was too dark to see anything and most of the residents were still awake, I waited until about midnight when the illumination from the moon was at its brightest. While I was waiting, I climbed to the top of a tall watchtower along the beach and slept a few hours. Finding water wasn't too difficult, but collecting it without arousing the neighborhood dogs was tricky. During my foray I also gathered carrots and a few other vegetables.

I was back at the hut before daybreak, and that is when I discovered that Horst had eaten both chickens. Over a very low flame were the sad remains of chicken wings floating in a frying pan filled with water. When I questioned Horst about the chickens, he claimed that they belonged to him because I had refused to help catch them. I overcame his momentary act of selfishness for the sake of getting to Mexico, but our friendship was never quite the same. The campsite was no longer comfortable, and we left the next day. We were still many miles from San Diego and even farther from Mexico. Along the way we passed many small communities, sometimes close together, other times far apart. Near San Diego, we collected potatoes, onions, one sweet potato, and a few other items. Around lunchtime, we camped behind a large thorny bush, somewhere in the field, and prepared our meal. We filled our frying pan with a potato-vegetable mixture and cooked it over a small campfire we built using dry twigs. Peering through the bush, we could see off in the distance a farmer plowing his field with a mule pulling a simple plow. The farmer went about his work singing and whistling, the image of a contented man.

Later that day we arrived at the harbor in San Diego and marveled at a beautiful sailing ship. The following night we crossed what we thought was the border into Mexico. There were no signs or buildings to indicate an international crossing, however. For reasons I no longer recall, we had to leave the beach at San Diego, our main reference point, and migrate inland. By this time our compass had stopped working, and overhead, for the first time during our entire journey, the sky was completely obscured by a thick blanket of fog. We were completely lost. Around midnight we came to a well built-up street with sidewalks and lights. The street curved, and just as we reached the apex of the curve, we noticed a brightly lit building. We later learned it was the U.S. border checkpoint.

Without saying a word, Horst and I made an abrupt about-face and started walking back down the street. Suddenly the parked car that we had passed a few minutes earlier came to life. All four doors flew open and out jumped five or six civilian-clothed agents. They shouted, "Hands up!" and wanted to know where we were going and our identities. At first we said nothing. I then whispered to Horst if we should dive into the ditch alongside the road. Horst shook his head and looked at me as if I had lost my sanity. At least half of these big guys had one hand in their pockets and were obviously not holding their small change.

A few seconds later Horst and I were handcuffed to separate agents and carted off to that brightly lit station house at the end of the road. We were led into a room, given cups of coffee and cigarettes, and told to empty our pockets. As we did, the agents' eyes grew wider. Hidden inside our double pairs of overalls and underneath that thick jacket that Horst was wearing was an assortment of paraphernalia. We each had daggers and small knives that we had taken from the mess hall at Camp Cooke, as well as machetes that we had picked up along the trail. The arsenal elicited expletives of amazement from the agents. We also had a small frying pan, drinking cups, spoons, forks, salt and pepper shakers, and various other items in our pockets.

Surrendering these items wasn't too difficult, but parting with the $50 that we had carefully cherished for emergency money was very painful. For the next two hours, they asked us all sorts of questions such as where we were from, where were we headed, and what were our intentions. At first we were evasive, and didn't want to tell the truth. We talked in *Plattdeutsch*, trying to convey the impression that we were from the Netherlands. Without papers to prove this, however, it was useless. During the interrogation, the agents told us we had approached the checkpoint at the American border from the Mexican side. At that moment we gave up the charade and told them we were escaped POWs from Camp Cooke. They became even more incredulous about our story, but a short time later everything was finally cleared up. We were again handcuffed and taken to a jail in San Diego.

At the calaboose we went through the usual processing procedures, including fingerprinting and photographs. Sometime after three o'clock in the morning, we were led to a large hall and placed in a holding tank where all kinds of people who had been arrested during the night were being held. Except for the small crack of light seeping in from the doorway, it was pitch black in this corridor. Inside the tank we quietly tiptoed past several other people and found a large open space to lie down. I woke up later that morning to the laughter of people in the cell. I was lying next to the toilet in the corner of the room with my arm wrapped around it as if it were something wonderful to hold.

During the early part of the day, people were constantly entering and leaving the holding tank. Sitting near me were several men with dark complexions who were conversing in a language unfamiliar to me. Even though we communicated only through gesture, these very kind people, who by their threadbare clothes were clearly impoverished, shared with me the cake they were eating. I later found out they were Indians from the mountains of Mexico.

After a few hours in this tank, Horst and I were moved to a different unit in the jail. The cellblocks were aligned along the walls and were segregated by race, with the whites below and the blacks upstairs. During the day we mixed freely in the day room that was on the outside perimeter of the complex and had a window facing out to the street.

I think it was the second day of our incarceration that a pair of newspaper reporters came to interview Horst and me. They took several pictures and asked many questions. At first, we were apprehensive about the interview, but the two reporters did their best to put us at ease.[55]

After perhaps a week, Captain Everett and Charlie from Camp Cooke came to collect us. Their greeting was rather frosty. On the promise that we would not attempt to escape, they allowed us to make the trip back to Camp Cooke without handcuffs. Along the way, Captain Everett became more sociable toward us. Charlie, however, remained aloof and continued to give us occasional stern glances.

Back at Camp Cooke, we were tersely sentenced to four weeks of bread and water in solitary confinement, and our hair was clipped off. Housing conditions in the cellblock were not comfortable, but there were enough distractions throughout the day to help pass the time. For one thing, we were allowed outside in the exercise room one hour a day. It also took a lot of time to read the numerous notes and messages written on the walls of the cell. Finally, when we searched the washrooms we found all sorts of hidden items such as tobacco, cigarette paper, and matches that were left behind by our predecessors as small gifts.

After four weeks of confinement, the guards released us into the main camp population. My bed, empty for so long, was returned to me along with all my personal belongings. Everything had been placed in storage, and nothing was missing. Our company spokesman handed these things to me and at the same time lectured to me about the difficulties our escape had caused him and the other prisoners in the camp. I listened attentively and didn't say a word.

Friends in my barrack later told me about the situation in the camp after our escape. The Americans knew that two prisoners were missing, but not until further checks were they able to identify the pair by name. They began applying all sorts of little punitive measures on the innocent prisoners in the camp. Knowing this, it was not surprising that my fellow prisoners greeted my return with ambivalent feelings. After a few days in the general camp population, however, the hard feelings and the cold shoulders that I felt in the beginning began to disappear. Incidentally, when Horst and I got back to the camp we went our separate ways.

ALFRED SCHMUCKER

You could hardly call this an escape, but I did leave Camp Cooke on an unauthorized trip. At the risk of being court-martialed, Corporal Bailey took me out of the camp one Saturday. He hid me on the floor behind the front seat of his Buick and covered me with a blanket until we passed the gate. Then I moved up front, and he showed me Santa Maria and part of the surrounding area. We were only gone for about two hours, but for me it was a great experience. It was the only time that I was outside Camp Cooke.

HEINRICH KERSTING

I never attempted to escape from Camp Cooke because I considered it senseless to try such a thing. A return to the homeland by this method was, in my opinion, impossible. I seem to remember that even our camp translator, Helmut Hahn, who spoke a fantastic English, was back "home" again after spending only a short time outside the camp during an escape attempt.[56]

HERBERT SCHAFFRATH

I tried to escape when I was in French captivity in Algeria. After my recapture, I was placed in solitary confinement for three weeks. Based on that experience, I had no interest in attempting to escape from Camp Cooke.

• POW Canteens •

In accordance with Article 12 of the Geneva Convention, every prisoner of war camp in the United States had a canteen where, during certain hours, POWs could buy foodstuffs, sweets, soft

Canteen coupons. (Courtesy of Alfred Schmucker and Heinrich Schünermann)

drinks, beer, cigarettes, personal care items, inexpensive leather items, jewelry, and locally grown produce. The merchandise was sold at fair market value, and all profits made by the canteen were deposited into the POW trust fund. The money was used to purchase items and services that benefited the general POW camp population. At Camp Cooke, this included commercial movie rentals, at least two camp radios, a phonograph and records, and carpenters' tools. A portion of the canteen profits were also used to pay the kitchen helpers. In general, the canteen was a self-supporting enterprise, operated as far as possible by prisoner of war personnel. The POWs were supervised by an American canteen officer, who procured the merchandise and audited the business records.[57]

All purchases from the canteen were made using canteen coupons (script). Coupon books were issued to prisoners through payroll deductions and withdrawals from personal trust fund accounts. Each book was in dollar denominations and contained 1-, 5-, and 10-cent coupons. On the cover of the book was the name of the issuing camp, the date of issue (last day of the payroll month), the date when the book became invalid, the name of the prisoner to whom it was issued, and authentication by the camp commander.[58]

The coupons were intended to be nontransferable, and were accepted by canteen personnel only when presented undetached from the book. Since POWs staffed the canteen at Cooke, this regulation was usually ignored. To discourage the hoarding and counterfeiting of coupons, they were valid only for a period of two calendar months after the end of the month they were issued. Each new series of coupons was printed using a different style and paper color from the previous edition.[59]

Coupons were needed to make purchases at the canteen and for admission to plays, concerts, movies, and other forms of entertainment in the camp. Prisoners could also donate a portion of their monthly coupons to other prisoners employed as kitchen police, latrine orderlies, or as members of permanent fatigue details. These positions were often filled by elderly or medically infirm prisoners who were unfit for full-time labor. The process was handled by an American officer who would collect the coupons and issue to each member of these details a canteen coupon book in dollar amounts according to his apportioned share. The remuneration was not to exceed the going rate of 80 cents per working day. At the same time, the POW could be paid his monthly gratuitous allowance of $3. Prisoners transferred to other camps could have the value of their coupons transferred to the receiving camp. Upon repatriation, coupons could also be deposited into the prisoner's individual trust fund.[60]

• Food •

For the most part, the prisoners of war who arrived in the United States were impressed by the quality and selection of foods that were available to them in the camps. Grievances did arise, however, when they received foods that were completely unknown to them or which simply did not reflect their national tastes. For example, when kitchen crews at Camp Cooke received cranberries to be served with the dinner meal, no one thought to tell the POWs how to prepare the fruit, so they attempted to eat the cranberries raw.[61]

At the urging of the War Department, the Army sought to correct these problems by allowing each POW camp to develop its own specialized menu. The only restriction was that the quantity and food selection could not exceed what was available to American soldiers. At Camp Cooke, the Army issued menu change request cards to the prisoners and prepared a menu based on their responses. Canned corn, for instance, was overwhelmingly rejected in favor of more potatoes. The Army also distributed to every camp a list of foods generally disliked by the POWs and recommended omitting these foods from the new menus. One such listing appeared in the War Department's Technical Manual 19-500, "Enemy Prisoners of War" and consisted of oysters, corn meal, dry cereal (except corn flakes), celery, corn and hominy, eggplant, green peppers, sweet potatoes, pumpkin, squash, peanut butter, tomato juice, and all canned fruit juices. The manual had also recommended that the following foods be served more frequently: frankfurters, salami, bologna, cheese, fresh fish, cabbage, lentils, lettuce, white potatoes, sauerkraut, spinach or leafy greens, and bread.[62]

When the American press got wind of the food menus, journalists Drew Pearson and Walter Winchell charged the Army with "coddling" the POWs. The War Department denied the charges, saying that it was complying with the rules of the Geneva Convention and hoped that its concessions to the prisoners would be reciprocated toward American captives. It also reasoned that if the POWs received the type of food they were accustomed to eating back home, less would be thrown away. This was particularly important at a time when the federal government was promoting food conservation and rationing everything in the civilian community from sugar to gasoline.[63]

Criticisms escalated when Allied forces entered Germany, and discovered in some instances neglected and starving American soldiers in enemy POW camps. Worse yet, American troops liberating concentration camps discovered the grisly deeds of the Nazi regime. Although many high-level U.S. government officials had known earlier about Nazi atrocities, nothing was done to prepare the Army for what it encountered. Army leadership and rank and file were so revolted by what they had witnessed they often saw little difference between a Nazi SS concentration camp murderer and any other German soldier.[64]

To counter charges of coddling, and because of a worldwide food shortage by the spring of 1945, the Army had substantially reduced the POW menu and cut back on the number of items available for sale in the canteens. Cheaper grades of meat were served, often in smaller quantities and less frequently. Butter was replaced by margarine. Other foods were also reduced. The Army substituted loose tobacco and cigarette rolling paper for packaged cigarettes. In adopting a stricter policy toward the prisoners, the War Department concluded that it was still abiding by the Geneva Convention. Most of these restrictions at Camp Cooke were later repealed.[65]

Everyday Life in the Camp

The POW company mess halls at Camp Cooke were always clean and perfectly organized. Note the artwork on the walls. (Courtesy of Hans Rosenthal)

The kitchen crew for Company 2. (Courtesy of Werner Blanck)

Many German POWs misinterpreted the reduction of rations at the end of the war to mean that the American Army was no longer concerned about reprisals against its soldiers in German hands. Further, it was using the situation as a measure of revenge against German prisoners. Still, few POWs could point with any validity to food shortages in the camps, which were, after all, routinely inspected by visiting members of the Swiss Legation, the International Red Cross, and the YMCA. Moreover, prisoners found ways to circumvent the restrictions and in most instances left America several pounds heavier than when they were in the Wehrmacht.[66]

RUDOLF HINKELMANN

I remember an incident that was indicative of the extent to which the American administration at Camp Cooke was willing to go to satisfy us. On Friday or Saturday afternoons, we received from the food commissary on the main post freshly sliced meat or cutlets. On one occasion, the cooks in our company feigned great anger and refused to accept the meat that was delivered. They said they were planning a meal that required a different type of beef. About an hour later, the Americans replaced the meat with the requested type.

During the time that I was at Camp Cooke and Tagus Ranch, food was always very plentiful. For example, at Tagus Ranch one evening, I noticed in the corner of our mess hall an eating contest involving sausages and potato salad. Suddenly there was a pushing crowd and a call for medics. It turned out that the contestant had eaten thirty-six sausages, thereby winning a bet that he could not eat more than thirty-five. The winner had to have his stomach pumped.

Every POW received on his birthday a delicious pastry prepared by our German chefs. In the afternoon or in the evening, the birthday boy would invite his friends to join him in celebrating his birthday with coffee and pastry.

HANS-JOACHIM BÖTTCHER

At Camp Cooke we were all well fed—much better in fact than the Europeans on the Continent. After the capitulation of Germany and for about three or four weeks thereafter, maybe a little longer, there were some reductions in the amount of food that we received. Meat was reduced and was limited to liver and pork ribs. Fortunately, our cooks invented a variety of ways to prepare these meals so that the restrictions didn't become a problem. We also received dried fruit instead of fresh fruit. In the canteen, Coke, ice cream, chocolate, and beer were some of the items that vanished from the shelves for some time. Nevertheless, I cannot think of any real hardships. Besides, many of the POWs who worked in U.S. Army kitchens, bakeries, food stores, and elsewhere on the main post smuggled foods into our camp.

A few of the food items were unknown to us before coming to America. These included corn flakes, peanut butter, white bread, certain types of sausages (there was one called "baloney," that wasn't bad), and some of the fruits.

HERBERT SCHAFFRATH

Generally, we did not have a favorable opinion of American food. The sausages were tasteless, and the white bread was too soft and lacked sufficient grain. On the other hand, we had corn flakes for breakfast, which I liked very much. Also on our menu were plenty of fresh fruits and vegetables, notably grapefruits and sweet potatoes.

We were shocked when our meals were suddenly cut to a [legal] minimum. We were all miffed and were of the opinion that now the American Army was showing its true face. Since the war was over and the Americans had their soldiers back from German captivity, we felt that perhaps we were now being punished for the concentration camps. To a large extent, however, the food shortage was offset by the actions of Captain [Robert L.] Everett and the professional culinary skills of our own cooks. According to rumor, Captain Everett had connections with Army kitchen personnel and was able bring more food into the stockade than was authorized. The provisions were then shared equitably with all the POW kitchens.

ALFRED SCHMUCKER

Toward the end of the war, our mess halls/kitchens stopped receiving prime cuts of meat and butter. It did not mean that we were put on a starvation ration because we still had plenty to eat. They just cut out the finer things. For example, in lieu of steaks, we received lung. Margarine replaced butter. Peanut butter had been available before the reduction, but increased after May 1945. It was pretty sticky in the palate, and not all of us liked it. Since President Roosevelt had died about this time, we called it "Roosevelt Memorial Butter."

But as things go, once in a while a piece of meat is desirable. I began asking myself how I could use my jeep from the labor office to improve the food situation. I got the idea of removing the back seat from the jeep and installing the largest garbage can I could find. Together with our kitchen personnel, some of whom also worked on post in the U.S. kitchens, we devised a plan. If a white apron was hanging in the kitchen window, it was a signal that the American supervisor was gone. I would then come by with my jeep and replace the empty garbage can with a filled one. On top of the can, the KPs had placed a layer of garbage. Beneath the trash in well-sealed packages were steaks, chicken, turkey, or whatever their daily menu offered. When I returned to the camp, the guard lifted the lid off the can, spotted the garbage, and waved me on. The guards never stopped to think about what was going on. Garbage was normally taken from the camp, but never brought into it, except for my special trips. Three or four excursions were sufficient to feed a whole company of POWs for one day. These special missions were done whenever the coast was clear and lasted until I lost my driver's license in April 1946.

HEINRICH KERSTING
We always had generous amounts of appetizing food in our camp until after the capitulation of Germany. At that time our meals were noticeably reduced, but were still sufficient.

WERNER GILBERT
When the war in Europe ended, our meals at Camp Cooke were reduced practically overnight. Some POWs had a difficult time adjusting to the change. Until that time we had everything: In the morning it was bread, butter, jam, eggs, sausage, milk, and coffee. The noon meals consisted of meat, potatoes, vegetables, and dessert. In the evening the same or cold cuts. To compensate for the smaller meals, some POWs filched food from American cupboards, sometimes with the cooperation of the GIs. After a couple of months, the food situation improved.

ADOLF KELMER
In the days following the capitulation of Germany, there was a noticeable change in the attitude of the Americans toward the POWs. Whereas before the surrender an almost friendly atmosphere existed, now the feeling was more reserved. Also, the abundance and diversity of our meals, which we had taken for

granted, was suddenly stinted. Even our canteen was affected. For a time it stopped carrying some of our favorite items.

Father FRANZ GÖDDE
At war's end, our meals were reduced and some items such as packaged cigarettes were unavailable to us at the canteen. We turned to the business of bartering. In exchange for soap, candy bars, toothpaste, and other items that we could buy in our canteen, we received cigarettes from the GIs who worked alongside us in the labor office. This went on from May to August 1945, when cigarettes were again sold in our canteen.

LEONHARD REUL
At Tagus Ranch we received sliced sausages that we nicknamed "Truman cutlets" [for President Harry Truman]. They were breaded and deliciously prepared by our two professional cooks. Toward the end of the war, our meals were curtailed, but this did not result in any serious deprivations.

KLAUS HEBEL
Around June 1945, our kitchen at Edwards Ranch began receiving smaller amounts of food. Certain items, such as sugar, had to be rationed by our kitchen. To offset the reductions, the POWs who worked in the American kitchen smuggled into our camp butter, sugar, and other victuals. With these ingredients our chef prepared a wonderful cake for us every Sunday morning.

• *Medical and Dental Care* •

The Army went to great lengths to safeguard the health of its prisoners as mandated in the Geneva Convention. Of immediate concern was preventing the spread of infectious diseases. Shortly after arriving at his first POW camp in America, each prisoner received a complete physical exam. It included vaccinations against smallpox, typhoid, paratyphoid, and tetanus. At least once a month thereafter, Army medical corps officers inspected the prisoners for communicable diseases and vermin infestation.[67]

At Camp Cooke, POWs with minor medical problems were treated at the camp infirmary. A German-speaking American doctor and German medical corps soldiers staffed the infirmary. In the San Joaquin Valley, where most of Cooke's branch camps were located, two Army medical officers made routine rounds attending to POW patients. Outside the valley, the branch camps at Edwards Ranch and Saticoy each had small infirmaries that received routine visits by a medical officer from the main camp. Serious medical problems at the branch camps that required hospitalization were referred to nearby military installations, or to the post hospital at Cooke where two wards were set aside for prisoners.[68]

The most significant medical problem in the San Joaquin Valley branch camps in 1945 was the high incidence of coccidioidomycosis. More commonly known as Valley Fever, it is endemic to the dry soil of the San Joaquin Valley and to other parts of the American southwest. Infections are acquired by inhalation of spore-laden dust that affects the pulmonary system. It is usually not fatal if treated properly. Migrant workers and German POWs who worked in the fields in Kern, Tulare, and Kings counties digging, hoeing, and picking potatoes, cotton, and cultivating other crops were susceptible to infection. The peak season for the disease was between July and August when the fields were their dustiest before the start of fall or winter rains.[69]

The outbreak of coccidioidomycosis among the prisoners began in the latter part of May 1945. By mid-August, 162 prisoners had been admitted to the station hospitals at Camp Cooke, Minter Air Field, and Lemoore Air Field. The latter two Army installations were located near the branch POW camps in the San Joaquin Valley. The incidence of coccidioidomycosis started at the Lamont branch camp, and quickly expanded to the Shafter camp. Together they comprised the majority of the cases. The other valley camps at this time at Tipton, Boswell, Tagus Ranch, Tulare, and Lakeland all experienced fewer cases of coccidioidomycosis. This was because the prisoners at these camps were mostly working in the orchards and in places with adequate ground cover.[70]

Moved by the meteoric rise in coccidioidal infections at Camp Cooke's branch camps, Lieutenant Colonel Arthur P. Long, director of the Epidemiology Division, Army Surgeon General's Office in Washington, D.C., wrote to the base camp commander on August 7, expressing his concern and called out for urgent solutions to end the problem as soon as possible. In calling for a detailed situation report, he informed the commander that the incidence of coccidioidomycosis at Cooke was "greater than the total for all United States Army troops in this country." In the weeks that followed, the infection rate steadily dropped off as new precautions were taken and seasonal adjustments reduced the level of harmful airborne spores.[71]

Dental care was another vital health service provided to the prisoners. At the base camp, an American dental officer assisted by a German prisoner devoted his full time to the treatment of prisoners. In March 1945, he had 280 sittings in which he performed four hundred fillings, two hundred extractions, and inserted or repaired between thirty and forty dentures. By April 1945, additional dental clinics were established at Lamont and Tulare. Prisoners from nearby camps were also treated at these clinics.[72]

Herbert Schaffrath, who was confined to Camp Cooke, amusedly recalls: "Some of the men who received full or partial dentures would run around the camp proudly showing off their new teeth to anybody who cared to see."[73]

• *Sanitary Inspections* •

At least once a month, an Army medical officer conducted sanitary inspections of the main POW camp at Cooke and its branch camps. Infractions at the base camp were few and nearly always minor. Branch camps, on the other hand, because of their rural settings were more susceptible to sanitary problems. Between February 13 and 17, 1945, the assistant medical inspector at Camp Cooke visited the six branch camps that were under the jurisdiction of Cooke at that time. Among the inspected items were the food supply and its preparation, the water supply, the sewage system, garbage disposal, and insect and rodent control. Only branch camp #5 at Boswell Ranch in Corcoran received an unsatisfactory rating and a recommendation that it be closed. Colonel Wilson C. von Kessler, chief surgeon at Camp Cooke, concurred with the findings and notified the post commander that a new camp was being constructed at another location.[74]

Sanitation at branch camp #2 at Tagus Ranch in Tulare, branch camp #4 at Edwards Ranch near Goleta, and branch camp #7 at the fairgrounds in Tulare were all found to be satisfactory. Branch camp #6 at Shafter and branch camp #8 at Lamont, however, both had nonpotable water supplies. The report recommended the water storage tanks be cleaned and sterilized and hypochlorinators be installed in the water systems. Until these changes were implemented, camp officials were to boil all water intended for human consumption.[75]

A follow-up inspection in May 1945 involved five of the original camps inspected in February, as well as the new Boswell Ranch branch camp and three new camps activated during this month: branch camp #9, the Lakeland camp located on the Elmer C. von Glahn Ranch in Corcoran; branch camp #10 at Tipton; and branch camp #11 at Saticoy. The report singled out water systems, sewage systems, and insect infestation as topics of concern. While the water at the Tipton camp tested consistently potable, questionable water samples were taken from the Boswell and Lakeland camps. Both camps were instructed to boil all drinking water until the complete potability of the water supplies could be assured. To make the well water that supplied the Saticoy camp potable, a chlorinator was installed and the entire system was sterilized prior to the activation of the camp in the latter part of May 1945.[76]

The May 1945 sanitary report also noted that all the branch camps initially had pit latrines, but in most instances these were converted to waterborne latrine systems.[77]

Flies were ubiquitous at all the camps. To combat the problem, traps were set, DDT was sprayed, and screening went up in the camps. The report mentioned that earlier in the month medical officers from Cooke conducted a survey to determine (1) the prevalence of mosquitoes around the seven branch camps in the San Joaquin Valley, (2) the incidence of malaria in the local population, and (3) the extent of local mosquito control. While mosquitoes were present at all the camps, only Shafter and Lamont reported having large numbers. The medical staff issued mosquito repellent to all personnel at these two camps.[78]

Malaria had not been reported in any of the counties where the POW camps were located. This was due largely to municipal abatement programs. In addition, the Hooper Foundation of the University of California was conducting a control program in Kern County (site of the Shafter and Lamont camps) with the objective of eliminating the Culex tarsalis, the vector of equine encephalomyelitis. Despite these promising measures to eradicate the problem, the Army took no chances and routinely tested all guards and prisoners assigned to or leaving this area for signs of the disease.[79]

• *Death and Burial* •

In September 1944, a prisoner of war cemetery was established at Camp Cooke near the POW compound. During the two years that Cooke administered its POW camps, ten German prisoners were buried in the cemetery. Death certificates located for eight of the men indicate that half of them died at Camp Cooke from illnesses. One of these deaths was from pneumonia, precipitated by a self-imposed hunger strike. The four other POWs were from camps at Fort Ord and Los Angeles, outside the administration of Camp Cooke.[80]

Everyday Life in the Camp

The German POW cemetery at Camp Cooke, November 1945. (Courtesy of Hans-Joachim Böttcher)

One of the two for whom a death certificate is unavailable is Ernst Hupe. On February 9, 1945, the *Bakersfield Californian* reported a German prisoner of war was found hanged that morning at the branch camp in Lamont. Although the name of the prisoner and the cause of death were not released, the individual was undoubtedly Ernst Hupe and was buried at Camp Cooke. Cemetery records lists his date of death as February 14, 1945, but this was probably the date of initial internment.[81]

In an interview published in the *Arvin Tiller* on August 10, 1977, Carl Sands recalled the hanging incident but not the prisoner's name. As a civilian employee with the U.S. Forest Service, Sands supervised German POWs cultivating the government's guayule crop. He recalled that among his group of prisoners was an incorrigible Nazi whom the Americans had nicknamed "Little Hitler." "Whenever this prisoner was told to do something he would give the straight-arm salute and shout, Heil Hitler," Sands added.[82]

One morning while preparing to take a truckload of prisoners out to work, Sands noticed that Little Hitler was missing from the group. He notified the guards, who immediately ordered the prisoners back into the camp and organized a search of the compound for the missing prisoner. They found the prisoner hanging from one of the buildings. Next to him was a ladder. Sands said the guards then rounded up about thirteen prisoners suspected of being involved in the lynching. According to Sands, many of the men had scratches on their faces, and one had his thumb wrapped in bloodied bandages. Sands never saw any of those men again, nor did he learn the results of the Army's investigation.[83]

The POWs that were buried at Camp Cooke all received full military honors. On the death of Willie Berkemer from acute respiratory infections, the German camp newspaper, *Der Lagerspiegel,* reported the German camp spokesman and an American Protestant pastor presided over the funeral with more than one hundred POWs in attendance.[84]

On November 26, 1947, the Army exhumed the remains of all ten POWs and reburied them at the Golden Gate National Cemetery in San Bruno, California. Placed above each grave is a simple granite headstone inscribed with the individual's name, nationality, date of death, and in some instances a military rank. The ten names and the circumstances of their deaths are presented in Table 2.[85]

Table 2. German POWs Initially Buried at Camp Cooke[86]

Name	Age	Date of Death	Place of Death	Cause of Death	Date of Reburial
Hupe, Ernst	--	Feb. 9, 1945	Lamont	Hanged?	Nov. 26, 1947
Berkemer, Willie	25	May 25, 1945	Camp Cooke	Acute bronchitis with secondary pneumonia	Nov. 26, 1947
Krafthofer, Ernst	--	Aug 21, 1945	Los Angeles	Motor vehicle accident	Nov. 26, 1947
Heinze, Georg	35	Aug. 22, 1945	Los Angeles	Peritonitis, resulting from a motor vehicle accident	Nov. 26, 1947
Maierhofer, Georg	31	Aug. 24, 1945	Fort Ord	Acute leptomeningitis	Nov. 26, 1947
Haussler, Longin	30	Nov. 9, 1945	Los Angeles	Meningitis?	Nov. 26, 1947
Mangold, Richard	23	Dec. 3, 1945	Fort Ord	Gunshot wounds	Nov. 26, 1947
Rosenberger, Hubert	26	Jan. 14, 1946	Camp Cooke	Meningitis	Nov. 26, 1947
Mattick, Walter	26	Feb. 27, 1946	Camp Cooke	Lymphosarcoma	Nov 26, 1947
Deul, Georg	37	Mar. 14, 1946	Camp Cooke	Aortic insufficiency with cardiac decompensation	Nov. 26, 1947

A sample death certificate relating to one of the German prisoners initially buried at Camp Cooke. (Courtesy of California Department of Health Services)

CHAPTER 7

The Branch Camps

APPROXIMATELY 155 base camps and 511 branch camps were constructed across the United States to accommodate the influx of POWs. Base camps were large compounds established for the duration of the war, and they served as the administrative headquarters for branch camps in a particular area. Wherever possible, existing housing on military installations was used as base POW camps. These camps were located in areas that assured maximum employment for prisoners. Branch camps, usually much smaller in size, existed on a semi-permanent or temporary basis to satisfy a specific work need at sites remote from the base camp.[1]

Although the use of military installations for POW camps was strongly encouraged, service commanders in coordination with local camp commanders were authorized to select housing owned by other federal agencies, state and local governments, and private individuals. These facilities varied in type from barracks and mobile units to tentage. In all cases, the facilities had to be in accordance with the Geneva Convention and comparable to the housing that was furnished to American troops living under similar conditions.[2]

While the War Department would fund the conversion of federal properties to POW camps, it would not do so for alternative sites. This, however, did not deter companies or farm associations who were willing to establish a camp at their own expense in return for POW labor. Whether this involved new construction or the modification of existing facilities, camp preparations were supervised by Army engineers and often included the use of POW labor teams. Items needed for the camps that were difficult for civilian firms to obtain because of wartime exigencies were supplied by the Army. These might include electrical fixtures, wire, and generators. The Army also provided cots, dishes, and other paraphernalia for use in all the camps. These articles would be removed or disposed of as military surplus after each camp was shut down.[3]

Because of their temporary use and remoteness from populated areas, branch camps were generally less comfortable and had fewer recreational and educational amenities than their base camp. Nevertheless, they developed a surprisingly diverse collection of activities. With very few exceptions, Camp Cooke's sixteen branch camps all had an education program, weekly film shows, a recreation field for sporting events (mostly soccer), a library that included German and English language newspapers, and a public-address system for broadcasting music, news, and other forms of entertainment and information. The duration and size of each camp determined the scope of these activities. Depending upon the available talent in the camp and the enthusiasm of the prisoners themselves, most camps also boasted a theatrical group, a band, and a chorus.[4]

Table 3. Camp Cooke's POW Detachments
(Branch Camps)

Camp Name	Activation Date	Deactivation Date
Tagus Ranch, Tulare	July 29, 1944	Feb. 13, 1946
Chino	Oct. 6, 1944	Apr. 1, 1945*
Edwards Ranch, Goleta	Oct. 20, 1944	Dec. 4, 1945
Boswell Ranch, Corcoran	Dec. 1, 1944	Oct. 5, 1945
Shafter	Dec. 11, 1944	Mar. 28, 1946
Tulare Fairgrounds, Tulare	Dec. 11, 1944	Jan. 24, 1946
Lamont	Dec. 18, 1944	Oct. 5, 1945
(Reactivated)	Jan. 7, 1946	Mar. 23, 1946
Lakeland, Corcoran	May 8, 1945	Oct. 5, 1945
(Reactivated)	Jan. 3, 1946	Feb. 15, 1946
Tipton	May 24, 1945	Feb. 4, 1946
Saticoy	May 27, 1945	Unknown
Old River	Oct. 18, 1945	Mar. 26, 1946
Buttonwillow	Oct. 24, 1945	Jan. 14, 1946
Delano	Oct. 25, 1945	Mar. 26, 1946
Tachi Farms, Corcoran	Nov. 21, 1945	Jan. 2, 1946
Rankin, Tulare	Dec. 1, 1945	Jan. 31, 1946
Lemoore	Dec. 8, 1945	Apr. 11, 1946

*The camp remained open, but its administrative jurisdiction was transferred on this day to the base POW camp at the Army's Pomona Ordnance Depot located on the grounds of the Los Angeles County Fairgrounds.

Camps that were in operation for only a few weeks, such as Tachi Farms near Corcoran and Rankin Field in Tulare, offered POWs little beyond the basics in the way of organized social activities. Regardless of their size, all the camps provided medical services and a canteen that sold many of the same items available at the base camp.[5]

The prisoner population at Camp Cooke's branch camps varied from about 212 men (Edwards Ranch) to more than 900 (Lamont). Rarely and then only briefly did the assigned number of men ever exceed a camp's capacity. The American contingent at each camp was usually headed by a captain and included one or two lieutenants and a guard detachment of thirty to fifty enlisted men.[6]

Contracts signed between Army officials and farmer associations requesting prisoner of war labor were written for the duration of the harvesting season for one or more crops. They could and often were renewed if follow-up work was available and local free labor remained in short supply. Otherwise, the camp would be deactivated and the prisoners and staff sent to other locations.[7]

Growers seeking POW labor from Camp Cooke sent their eligibility requests to the farm labor offices of the U.S. Department of Agriculture's Extension Service. Applications approved by the Service would be forwarded to the Army for final approval or disapproval by the Ninth Service Command. In Tulare County, the Tulare Procurement Association was the contracting agency for growers seeking prisoner of war labor for the camps at Tulare Fairgrounds and Tipton. In Santa Barbara County, the Coast Farm Labor Association arranged to bring prisoner labor to Edwards Ranch near Goleta. Similar agreements were worked out with additional associations in Kern, Kings, Ventura, and San Bernardino counties where Camp Cooke's other POW branch camps were established.[8]

In general, the prisoners proved to be willing workers and produced satisfactory results, saving crops that might otherwise have been plowed under because of the free labor shortage. Only in the cotton harvest did the Army often have to resort to "administrative pressure" for nonperformers.[9]

Cotton picking was backbreaking work. It also required a skill and physical dexterity of the hand that some prisoners lacked, were unwilling to learn, or were incapable of performing because of war injuries. Some of the more politically inclined prisoners attempted to exploit this situation by claiming that the cotton was being used in the manufacturing of munitions. They invoked Article 31 of the Geneva Convention, which prohibited war-related work by prisoners. These same individuals associated cotton picking with black slavery in the United States and were indignant that Aryans, Germans no less, should be assigned to so demeaning a task.[10]

Officials from the International Red Cross and other welfare and social service organizations periodically inspected Camp Cooke's branch POW camps. Overall, they reported favorably on camp conditions and noted high morale among the prisoners. Rarely did their inspections find a problem. When they did, the Army moved promptly to correct it. One such example occurred at the Shafter branch camp, where the German camp spokesman claimed one of the guards was "beating on prisoners who were working in the field." When asked by the visiting inspector about the allegation, camp commander Captain Dan W. Brown denied the "beating" of any prisoners. He indicated that the guard had only "pushed one [prisoner] around" because he had become "provocative." Brown added that the guard had since been reassigned to other duties in the camp.[11]

The relationship between prisoners and guards was, for the most part, cordial and would sometimes extend to trading inexpensive items or services as recalled by Spencer Stallings, a guard at the Shafter branch camp. "I would buy glue and other materials the prisoners needed but couldn't get in their PX [canteen], and trade these things for haircuts or for wood carvings they made."[12]

As American servicemen returned home after the war to civilian jobs, the need for contract prisoner labor declined. For the War Department this meant evacuating prisoners as quickly as possible from areas where free labor had now become available. In almost every instance, the process began with the closing of branch camps and relocating prisoners to areas where their labor was still needed. At Camp Cooke, prisoners who were not immediately shipped to camps in other service commands found themselves at the main camp or at one of its remaining branch camps, especially Lamont and Lemoore. Both of these branch camps became important staging areas for the repatriation of German prisoners. By April 1946, the last of Camp Cooke's branch camps, Lemoore, had closed its gates forever.[13]

• *Detachment #2, Tagus Ranch, Tulare* •

The first branch camp under the jurisdiction of Camp Cooke was activated at Tagus Ranch on July 29, 1944. The camp was about ten miles north of Tulare on the west side of the Southern Pacific

German Prisoners of War at Camp Cooke, California

Aerial view of Tagus Ranch POW camp, October 3, 1944. (Courtesy of John Pellew)

Front gate at Tagus Ranch POW camp, October 3, 1944. (Courtesy of John Pellew)

Railroad tracks off Highway 99 in the San Joaquin Valley.[14] Construction began in early June when the Tagus Ranch Company, which contracted with the Army for prisoner labor, began erecting Quonset huts to house POWs and the American staff. The California Department of Agriculture supplied the Quonsets. A work crew of twenty able-bodied German prisoners from Camp Cooke assisted in the construction of the stockade fence, the guard towers, and the installation of floodlights in each of the towers and around the camp perimeter. They would later perform similar work at many of Cooke's other branch camps. At the end of July, state employees installed the last major item in the camp—a water system.[15]

The prisoners' quarters consisted of sixteen Quonset huts, each designed to house about sixteen men. The other facilities included one administrative barrack, one kitchen/mess hall, a canteen, and buildings for latrines and showers.[16]

On August 1, 1944, a truck convoy carrying the first contingent of about 238 German POWs threaded its way through the narrow and mostly desolate roads between Camp Cooke and the Tagus Ranch branch camp. With them was a cadre of sixteen armed U.S. Army guards under the command of First Lieutenant (later Captain) John T. Pellew. The five-hour journey ended that evening with their arrival at the camp. After a few days of settling into their new quarters, the prisoners were put to work pruning deciduous trees on Tagus Ranch. Covering seven thousand acres, Tagus Ranch was reportedly the world's largest peach, apricot, and nectarine orchard. Later that year, the prisoners harvested cotton.[17]

Medical care at the Tagus Ranch camp was dispensed by an American Army physician and two German medical corps soldiers. Prisoners requiring immediate hospitalization were transported to the Army air station at Lemoore, about twenty-five miles west of the camp.[18]

In addition to the usual dogs and cats found in all the camps, the prisoners at Tagus Ranch also had several pet doves in a cage. The birds were probably captured in the orchards.[19]

On November 7, 1944, Captain Claude L. Curtis relieved Lieutenant Pellew as commander of the Tagus Ranch camp. First Lieutenant Glenn E. Michael remained second in command. Shortly after the opening of the camp, the guard detachment had nearly doubled to about thirty men. Except for the shooting incident recounted earlier by Rudolph Hinkelmann, no other major problems or disturbances were reported at this camp. The camp closed on February 13, 1946.[20]

• *Detachment #3, Camp Chino (Ayers), Chino* •

Located in the city of Chino, Camp Ayers began life prior to American entry into World War II as a state relief administration project to shelter transients and the unemployed. After the Japanese attack on Pearl Harbor in December 1941, the State Guard took control of the camp for use as a training base. It became the headquarters of the State Guard Quartermaster Department until the original guard organization was mustered out and reorganized. In 1943, the camp was turned over to the Farm Production Council and housed Mexican nationals employed in agricultural work throughout the area. Known as guest workers, they were required to return to Mexico at the conclusion of their contracts.[21]

At the request of the Farm Production Council, and with its assistance, the Army established a German prisoner of war camp at the old housing site on October 6, 1944, and renamed it Camp Chino. The camp, which was enclosed by a newly erected security fence and guard towers around the perimeter, encompassed the barracks, mess hall, and power plant, but not the warehouses and other buildings on Central Avenue that were occupied by the Council. A staff of about forty enlisted men and officers ran the camp under the command of Captain Charles S. Fletcher Jr.[22]

Accompanied by a detail of military police, the first contingent of three hundred German POWs detrained at the Southern Pacific Depot on Central Avenue on October 7. Garbed in blue denims with "PW" markings and carrying barrack bags slung over their shoulders, the prisoners reportedly sang and whistled German songs as they marched down the avenue to the camp under armed guard. They had come from the POW camp at Florence, Arizona.[23] Within a week of their arrival, most of the prisoners were working in the vineyards of the Southern Grape Growers Association. Many others were contracted out to the Farm Production Council to harvest tomatoes, oranges, lemons, sweet potatoes, and more.[24]

In January 1945, facilities at Camp Chino were expanded for an additional 240 prisoners, raising the POW population to about five hundred men. To accommodate the additional guards that were brought in, extra Quonset huts and a mess hall were constructed outside the stockade.[25]

Almost no documentation exists about the education and recreation programs at this camp. But since these programs were mandated and standardized by the Provost Marshal General's Office, the activities at this camp would have been on par with those offered at Camp Cooke's other branch camps. One indication of this occurred in November 1944 when Captain Fletcher appealed to local residents for the loan of musical instruments of all kinds. The instruments were to be used by prisoners hoping to form an orchestra. How or if the community responded is unknown.[26]

On April 1, 1945, Camp Cooke transferred responsibility for Camp Chino to the POW base camp at the Army's Pomona Ordnance Depot, located on the grounds of the Los Angeles County Fairgrounds. Captain Fletcher was reassigned to the base POW camp at Cooke as adjutant.[27]

About three weeks after the transfer, Captain Lyle T. Dawson of Service Command Unit 1909 in Los Angeles conducted an inspection of the camp, the record of which gives some insight into the difficulties of managing the POW labor program. He reported that the many pro-Nazis among the prisoners were exerting considerable pressure on fellow POWs to keep production down. In an attempt to bring production back up to targeted levels, the newly appointed camp commander, Captain Royce L. Dixon, took the Army's policy of "no work, no eat" literally to include no bread. He also ordered the prisoners to perform two hours of outdoor close order drill. It is unclear from the report whether these disciplines preceded or followed a general labor strike that occurred on April

5. Regardless of which occurred first, the situation resulted in his replacement by Captain Almon F. Rockwell on April 18. Under his command, Rockwell shipped out seventeen physically unfit POWs. When another group of POWs attempted to test his resolve by refusing to accomplish their assigned task, Rockwell put them on a diet of bread and water for seven days. Production levels in the other work details increased immediately.[28]

• *Detachment #4, Edwards Ranch, Goleta* •

The prisoner of war camp at Edwards Ranch overlooked the Pacific coast near Goleta, approximately eighteen miles northwest of Santa Barbara and forty-nine miles southeast of Camp Cooke. The camp was originally built to house 180 Mexican nationals as seasonal guest workers. When workers could not be obtained for the fall harvest, growers turned to the Army, which approved their request for POW labor. The growers enlarged the camp for about 250 prisoners and a staff of U.S. Army personnel. On October 12, 1944, a labor team of twenty prisoners from Camp Cooke assisted in the construction of a security fence, guard towers, and other modifications to the camp.[29]

Eight days later, on October 20, the Army activated the camp. Camp facilities consisted of fourteen Nissen huts (each capable of housing about eighteen men), a shower room, a combination kitchen/mess hall, a canteen, an administration barrack, an infirmary, a tent with a ping-pong table, another tent for storing theatrical equipment, a third tent for recreational use or living space, and a small soccer field.[30]

Inside the mess hall, the prisoners built a large stage for various shows and performances, including regular concerts by the camp's eight-piece orchestra. Their other artistic creations included wood sculptures, paintings, and horticultural projects

The POW camp at Edwards Ranch. (Courtesy of John Pellew)

POW Nissen huts at Edwards Ranch. (Courtesy of John Pellew)

that featured flower, fruit, and vegetable gardens. Inspecting the camp on June 16, 1945, Paul Schnyder of the International Red Cross remarked: "The entire camp looks like a garden, adorned by massive red geraniums and water fountains. We have never seen a small camp decorated with as much taste and love of nature."[31]

Nearly all the POWs enjoyed the camp phonograph, radio (receiver), and library, which had the usual mixture of German and American books, newspapers, and magazines. After work and on weekends POWs would stroll down to the beach for a swim under armed guard.[32]

A POW education director, assisted by five prisoner instructors, carried out the American-directed education program in the camp. The prisoners attended courses in English, history of the United States, geography of the United States, constitutional law, stenography, accounting, economics, science, and other subjects. Religious services for the two principal Christian confessions were conducted in the camp every Sunday by a priest from Goleta and a lay leader from among the prisoners.[33]

The camp infirmary was staffed by an American medical officer and German POW medics, and was visited weekly by a physician from Camp Cooke. Urgent cases would be handled by a civilian physician on call in Goleta. An Army ambulance was available to transport patients to Camp Cooke for advanced care. Prisoners requiring dental treatment were also taken to the main camp.[34]

The POWs at Edwards Ranch worked in the orchards harvesting lemons, tomatoes, and other produce, as well as gathering walnuts. In late 1945, a cadre of about 250 POWs were dispatched to the Army's Hoff General Hospital in Santa Barbara to help dismantle and pack hospital equipment. The hospital began closing down in early November, shipping its belongings to supply centers and to other military hospitals.[35]

During its nearly fourteen months of operation, the POW camp was under the command of several different officers, including Captain Curtis E. Fahnert, Lieutenant John T. Pellew, Captain Franklin T. De Groodt, and Captain William H. Phillips. POW Detachment 4 at Edwards Ranch was officially deactivated on December 4, 1945.[36]

• *Detachment #5, Boswell Ranch, Corcoran* •

The first of three POW branch camps at Corcoran was established on the J. G. Boswell Ranch in the El Rico District of Kings County on December 1, 1944. Two days later, more than four hundred German prisoners arrived at the camp and were ordered to set up tentage. Within the next few days, they were picking cotton on the Ralph Gilkey and J. G. Boswell ranches. The American detachment consisted of about fifty-six enlisted men and officers under the command of Captain David Scofield, and later Captain A. S. Nicewanger.[37]

In April 1945, the prisoners and staff were relocated to a new camp on the Los Poso Ranch, also a J. G. Boswell interest, one and a half miles west of Corcoran. Originally built and used to house workers in the Civilian Conservation Corps, its transformation into a prison involved refurbishing the buildings, and erecting a security fence and guard towers around the entire camp. At the time of its activation on May 1, the stockade measured 400 feet by 700 feet and could house 500 men. The commanding officers were Captain Robert J. Brown and, beginning on June 27, 1945, First Lieutenant J. D. Mitchell. Camp recreation included a POW theatrical group and music band.[38]

For reasons not entirely clear, the branch camp at Boswell Ranch had more reported escapes than the main camp at Camp Cooke or any of its other branch camps. Between December 1944 and the first week of May 1945, eleven escapes occurred involving twenty prisoners. One prisoner escaped from the camp three times, another at least twice. Hermann Kuehne attempted the first escape from the camp on the El Rico Ranch on December 28, 1944. He walked away from a cotton-picking crew on the pretense of being ill, and made his way through the cotton fields where he thumbed a ride into Corcoran. Local police picked him up later that evening, asleep in the railroad station. On January 1, 1945, an escaped POW attempted to seize the car of rancher Gordon Hammond. Hammond had noticed the man walking along the road toward Corcoran and offered him a ride. Suspecting he was an escaped POW, Hammond decided to take him back to the prison. The POW realized what Hammond had in mind and grabbed the wheel, attempting to wrestle control of the vehicle from Hammond. The car had come to a stop when fellow rancher H. G. McKeever, driving by with four laborers in his vehicle, pulled over and quickly joined the struggle. They subdued the prisoner, tied him up, and delivered him back to the prison camp. The most spectacular break from the Boswell camp occurred around midnight on January 3, 1945, when Wilhelm Ruh, Richard Dedow, and Karl Aemmler scaled the prison fence amid a fusillade of bullets fired by the guards and vanished into the night. A fourth prisoner, Robert Barbian, escaped a few hours later during the early morning of January 4. Hungry and cold, all four men surrendered on January 6 to W. J. Bensburg, foreman of the La Hacienda Ranch twenty miles south of Corcoran. Bensburg telephoned the sheriff's office to collect the prisoners.[39]

Boswell Ranch and two other branch camps, Lamont and Lakeland, closed on October 5, 1945. The POWs and the American staffs at these camps were transferred to Camp Cooke and to other Army facilities at Ft. Ord and Stockton, California.[40]

Temporarily, the three vacated camps were filled by Japanese prisoners of war headed back to Japan from Camp McCoy, Wisconsin, and Camp Clarinda, Iowa. The Army activated Service Command Unit 1946 at Lamont to take over administration of the three Japanese POW camps in the San Joaquin Valley. When the POWs departed in early January 1946, the Army closed the Boswell camp permanently. The Lamont and Lakeland camps reopened with German POWs under the administration of Camp Cooke.[41]

• *Detachment #6, Shafter* •

In November 1944, local cotton gin companies in Shafter and Wasco, and the Farm Labor Office of the Agricultural Extension Service in Kern County contracted with the Army's Ninth Service Command to bring German POW laborers to the small farming town of Shafter. The companies participating in the program and raising $4,000 for the establishment of a POW camp included Producers Gin, Camp-West-Lowe Farms, D. C. Moore Gin, and Coberly West Ginning Company (all based in Shafter), and Co-Operative Gin and Producers Gin of Wasco.[42]

The POW camp at Shafter, 1945. (Courtesy of Spencer B. Stallings)

The process for employing prisoner labor at Shafter was fairly complicated, and was similar to the process employed at some of Camp Cooke's other branch camps. The growers who cooperated with the sponsoring gins to have their cotton picked under this program formed the Shafter Procurement Association. Each grower would pay ten cents per prisoner per day into a special fund to defray overhead expenses of the five gins. Part of the money would also be used to pay a coordinator to act as a middleman between the gins and the growers. His duties included developing and implementing a plan for allocating groups of prisoners to handle the work. The growers would then hire the coordinator to represent their interests with Army officials at the POW camp for the training and placement of work crews. Finally, the growers would pay the federal government the prevailing scale for cotton picking, $2.25 per hundred pounds.[43]

On December 2, 1944, a crew of about thirty POWs from Camp Cooke, under the supervision of Second Lieutenant Raymond Feinberg and six military police, began modifying the federal government's former guayule camp at Shafter into a POW camp. The camp was a half-mile south of the town, and about twenty-two miles northwest of Bakersfield. The prisoners modified the barracks, installed a 13-strand, 8-foot high barbed wire fence around the camp, and erected guard towers outside the fence at each of the four corners of the camp and at the main entrance. The men completed the project in about a week and returned to Camp Cooke.[44]

The completed POW compound measured 765 feet by 316 feet and could house up to 600 prisoners. Each lodgment was

Lunch break for a group of POWs at Mr. Reimer's farm in Shafter. From right to left, Mr. Reimer, an American guard, and fourth, prisoner Gustav Thielemann. Note the farmer's two children in the front holding their pets. (Courtesy of Gustav Thielemann)

partitioned into six rooms and accommodated approximately thirty-six men. Included within the stockade were a carpenter's shop, an electrical shop, a paint shop, and an infirmary for minor medical problems. Serious cases were cared for by the Army medical corps at Minter Field, four miles northeast of the town.[45]

The Shafter branch camp opened on December 11, 1944. Three days later, some six hundred German prisoners of war under armed guard descended on Shafter from Camp Rupert, Idaho. According to the *Shafter Press*, the prisoners disembarked from a Santa Fe special train at nine a.m. and "paraded down Central Avenue, four abreast, singing a German song" on their way to the stockade.[46]

On December 18, most of the prisoners were sent out on labor details to about thirty different growers and got their first experience picking cotton. Each prisoner was required to pick 150 pounds of cotton per day. By March 1945, the cotton harvest was complete. A new contract negotiated between the Army and several growers in the district had the prisoners in short order harvesting sugar beets, peas, and potatoes. About three-fourths of the POWs toiled in the fields at any one time while the others worked inside the camp.[47]

Spencer B. Stallings, a guard at the camp, recalls: "The farmers furnished transportation for the prisoners between the camp and the work site, and we provided one field guard to each group.

Sometimes we didn't have enough guards available, but the groups went out anyway."[48]

In August 1945, a small band of POWs under the supervision of American Private First Class Leon Alex, camp clerk and interpreter, began operating a combination radio/public-address system at the Shafter branch camp. Given the abbreviation ABSIS (American Broadcasting Station in Shafter), the "station" would broadcast two hours every day a combination of live and recorded music, news, commentary, and other programs of interest. As a primary source of information and a welcome entertainment medium in the camp, broadcast radio had the power to influence political and cultural views. Since radio was already swayed by wartime propaganda, it fit auspiciously into the Army's reeducation program of prisoners.[49]

In September 1945, Camp Cooke's *Der Lagerspiegel* reported that with the cooperation and support of the American camp administration, the POWs were making major improvements to the physical and social environment of the camp. In addition to using surplus material to spruce up the appearance of each barrack, the prisoners had placed decorative flowerbeds and sundials between the barracks. A fully equipped barbershop was set up, and an entertainment room with a phonograph and games also graced the camp. The camp boasted two handball courts and a soccer field. Especially notable was a large vegetable patch and a pen for raising pet rabbits.[50]

Pastoral services were held in the camp every Sunday, led by a Lutheran minister from Bakersfield, and a Catholic priest from Wasco.[51]

In June 1945, the Army detachment at the Shafter POW camp consisted of three officers and forty-six enlisted men commanded by Captain Dan W. Brown.[52] Spencer Stallings vividly recalls how the camp was organized:

> Lieutenant J. D. Mitchell was in charge of inspecting the field guards and took care of the work details. Lieutenant Frank De Groodt was the camp officer who kept an eye on the prisoners during the day. The prisoners were divided into two companies with an American sergeant in charge of each and a German NCO as leader of each POW company. The POW kitchen was in a separate building from their quarters and was manned entirely by the prisoners. Our mess hall was outside the stockade, but was managed by a staff of POWs who did all of our cooking and

The Branch Camps

Left to right, Lieutenants Mitchell and De Groodt with four guards at Camp Shafter, 1945. (Courtesy of Spencer B. Stallings)

Spencer B. Stallings, third from left, with fellow guards armed with carbine rifles and preparing to go on duty, 1945. (Courtesy of Spencer B. Stallings)

KP duty. The prisoners ate very well, and so did we. They had a garden and grew many of their own vegetables including corn, which they cultivated for us because they wouldn't eat it.[53] [The prisoners considered corn as swine food because in Germany it was typically fed to pigs.]

And of the guards, Spencer Stallings recalls:

The camp guards were not the sharpest of people. Every Saturday and Sunday night, Captain Brown had to put two men on MP duty in town to make sure that the guards were back in camp to pull tower duty. If a guard missed his shift he had to pay his replacement $1.00 per hour and pay back the hours he didn't put in. This arrangement was worked out between the men and the sergeant of the guard. For discipline, you could expect to work guard duty from the water tower during Sunday soccer games. The prisoners played soccer on a field outside the compound and a guard was required to watch them from the tower.[54]

We were given the option of having field guard during the day or tower guard. Since some of the men complained about their feet hurting while out in the field, they often got tower guard.[55]

During the night it was not unusual to hear guards firing their weapons from the towers at jack rabbits around the compound. One evening about midnight, I was going on duty when a guard opened up with his .30-caliber machine gun. When I got up in the tower he laughed and said that despite all the shots he had fired, he missed at least eight rabbits. These incidents would wake up the people who lived across the road from the camp. The next day they would ask us what happened and we would just laugh and say, "Nothing, no one escaped and no one was shot."[56]

In fact, I don't remember any shootings ever involving POWs. They never gave us any serious trouble and were glad to be out of the war and to be treated decently. They did, however, occasionally test us by sneaking up to the tower and from a blind spot toss pebbles at the window to see if we were on the job.[57]

Army life as a POW guard at Shafter did not follow strict military regulations. For example, one rule that was never carried out was to turn in our weapons at the end of a shift. Instead, we usually hung our fully loaded rifles from nails in the wall near our beds. This would explain why most of our barracks had bullet holes in the ceiling, but why no one was accidentally shot still amazes me.[58]

Helene De Groodt, the widow of Captain Franklin T. De Groodt, held a mostly favorable opinion of the prisoners. As she recalls:

> We got to know and respect them [the POWs] as human beings. Often they showed us pictures from home and told us about their families. This of course, was only at the branch camps where the atmosphere was less formal. Frank's orderly at the Shafter camp was a kind old fellow in his fifties. He was actually sort of a surrogate nanny to our baby, and showed me how to cure diaper rash with cornstarch. He could see I was pretty young and inexperienced, and pediatricians were scarce during the war. Before the birth of our son, he advised Frank to put a lump of sugar on the windowsill to attract the stork and hurry things up. Of course, there were other POWs that had been less than friendly.[59]

When Camp Shafter closed on March 28, 1946, the staff and prisoners were relocated to Camp Cooke.[60]

• *Detachment #7, Tulare Fairgrounds* •

In 1942, the Tulare County Fairgrounds in Tulare served as a temporary detention center for Japanese-Americans and Japanese immigrants forced from their homes in the area by the federal government and sent to internment camps for the duration of the war. Two years later, when a shortage of Mexican guest workers increased the risk of crop losses in Tulare, German POWs were brought in to supplement the harvesting of cotton and produce. They were housed in eleven barracks at the fairgrounds. As a POW camp, the fairgrounds could confine up to 350 prisoners, but typically held less than 250 men. Surprisingly, this relatively small camp included an Army dental clinic that also served other branch camps nearby. Captain Rudolph J. Daley was the commanding officer of the POW camp when it opened on December 11, 1944. His staff consisted of First Lieutenant (later Captain) Robert L. Everett, Second Lieutenant John Ryan, two other officers, and thirty-three enlisted men.[61]

The fairgrounds camp closed on January 24, 1946. Its staff and prisoners transferred to the Tagus Ranch and Tipton camps. Three months later Tulare County auctioned off the buildings, leaving behind no trace of the POW camp.[62]

• *Detachment #8, Lamont* •

On December 18, 1944, the Army opened the Lamont prisoner of war camp about seventeen miles southeast of Bakersfield. The camp was set up behind Ribier Market on DiGiorgio Road at a facility formerly used by the U.S. Forest Service to house workers cultivating guayule. The complex consisted of three groups of buildings of the same type used at the Shafter camp, where guayule was also grown.[63]

Apart from harvesting guayule for the federal government, the prisoners picked cotton, vegetables and fruits, and performed other types of agricultural labor under an Army contract with a farmer's cooperative called the Lamont Prisoner of War Labor Association.[64] Carl Sands, a farmhand employed by the U.S. Forest Service at Lamont, recalls supervising groups of German POW workers:

> They were good, hard-working boys. Only during the cotton season did we have problems. They didn't want to pick cotton. They did a very good job picking potatoes and then loading them onto trucks. The truckers would sometimes slip them 50 cents or a dollar to hurry up. Since the drivers were paid by the packing company per load, the more shipments they made to the warehouse the more money they earned.[65]

With a capacity of one thousand POWs, the Lamont camp was the largest branch camp under the jurisdiction of Camp Cooke. In June 1945 it held 945 prisoners. Much like other camps, its population fluctuated with the movement of prisoners between facilities. The American watch force at this time consisted of seventy-two enlisted men and five officers. Among the camp commanders at Lamont were Captains William H. Montford and C. W. Chappell.[66]

Leisure activities for POWs at Camp Lamont were almost as diverse and plentiful as at Camp Cooke. Two of the most popular education courses attended by POWs were agricultural sciences and automotive repair. The camp library reported a brisk book circulation of between seventy and a hundred titles per day. Many of these titles were reference manuals for farming (cattle raising), general agriculture, professional baking, and various artisan books. Popular, but scarce in the collection, were German language novels. Using money authorized from the POW trust fund to purchase musical instruments, a talented group of POWs established a small orchestra. Their repertoire of contemporary tunes and classical music attracted large audiences. At other times, they provided musical accompaniment to the camp's stage shows.[67]

To gauge the level of POW interest in religious activities at the branch camps, Camp Cooke's post chaplain, Lieutenant Colonel Herschel R. Griffin, rode the circuit of camps to interview staff and prisoners. Stopping at Lamont in September 1945, he discovered that about 140 men, or roughly 24 percent of the current camp population of around 600, regularly attended camp services conducted by visiting Catholic and Lutheran clergy. Had the Army conducted the same survey before as well as after the capitulation of Germany it would have undoubtedly discovered a lower percentage of congregants in the first survey. Of this we can be certain because overt displays of spirituality outside of Nazi-sanctioned gatherings risked interpretation by Nazi stalwarts in the camp as a sign of wavering loyalty to the regime. Fear of reprisals from this group would be enough to keep some POWs away from the pulpit until the war ended.[68]

On October 5, 1945, the camp was turned over to the base POW camp at the Pomona Ordnance Depot, an element of Service Command Unit 1946, for temporary use as a Japanese prisoner of war camp. The German POWs and the American staff were temporarily relocated to Camp Cooke and its other branch camps. They reclaimed the camp on January 7, 1946, after the departure of the Japanese. In the final weeks leading up to its closure on March 23, Lamont served as a staging area in the San Joaquin Valley for the repatriation of POWs.[69]

• *Detachment #9, Lakeland, Corcoran* •

The Lakeland branch POW camp was originally intended to house one thousand Mexican guest workers. They were expected in October 1944, in time to begin harvesting cotton on the fourteen thousand-acre von Glahn-Boswell tract in the center of the dry Tulare Lake bed. In preparing for their arrival, agribusinessman Elmer C. von Glahn, president of the von Glahn Lakeland Company Inc., purchased a former sugar beet refinery and completely refinished it into a four-story dwelling called the Casa Grande Labor Hotel.[70]

When it became evident that large numbers of Mexican guest workers would be unavailable to assist in the harvest, von Glahn contracted with the Army for prisoner of war labor. After installing security fencing and guard towers, the "hotel" camp with a revised capacity of seven hundred men opened for German prisoners on

May 14, 1945. The POWs picked cotton and later worked in the fruit orchards for many other growers. Captain John E. James was the camp commander at Lakeland. His cadre consisted of three officers and forty-four enlisted men.[71]

On October 5, 1945, the Lakeland branch camp was vacated and turned over to the Pomona base camp, Service Command Unit 1946, for temporary use as a Japanese prisoner of war camp. After the Japanese departed, Camp Cooke reclaimed the camp for German prisoners on January 3, 1946. Less than six weeks later, on February 15, the Army closed the camp permanently.[72]

• *Detachment #10, Tipton* •

The POW branch camp at Tipton, south of Tulare along Highway 99, originally housed Mexican migrant workers who were hired to harvest crops, but were now in short supply. To overcome the labor shortage, the Tulare Procurement Association arranged with the Army's Ninth Service Command for prisoners of war to pick cotton, vegetables, and fruits for growers around Tipton. As part of the agreement, the association paid the cost of modifying the existing housing camp for German POWs. When the POW camp opened on May 24, 1945, it could hold up to five hundred men, but the actual number of prisoners at the camp averaged between three hundred and four hundred.[73]

Manuel Faria Jr. was sixteen years old when his father brought German prisoners of war to work on the family farm at Tipton in 1945. He recalled:

> We had up to ten POWs who worked in our cornfields preparing silage. Every morning my dad or I would drive to the camp and pick them up at about 7:00 and return them to camp in the evening. We never had any guards with us and never had problems with any of the POWs. During lunchtime they would sit with us around the table and eat whatever meal my mom had prepared. One or two of the men spoke a fair English, which made it possible for us to communicate. They were a fine bunch of guys who were also extremely talented.[74]

The U.S. Army detachment at Tipton consisted of Captain Edmund J. Trottier, Lieutenant Harold J. Klouser, and thirty enlisted men. When the camp closed on February 4, 1946, the prisoners and some of the enlisted cadre moved to the POW camp at Lemoore. The remaining staff received new assignments at Camp Cooke.[75]

• *Detachment #11, Saticoy* •

The successful use of POW labor at Chino, Goleta, Tulare, and elsewhere prompted the Saticoy Lemon Association, a co-op of twenty-two major citrus ranchers in Ventura County, to request prisoner of war labor from the Army. The local farm labor office routed their request to the Agricultural Extension Service, which confirmed the need for labor. A board of Army engineers provided the association with the design requirements for constructing POW housing. Next, state and county officials with representatives from the association selected a coastal strip of land for the camp at Seaside Park in Ventura.[76]

The proposed location did not sit well with the Ventura Chamber of Commerce. Urged on by a different segment of the business community, the chamber harangued supporters of the plan and claimed the camp would encroach on events at Seaside Park. One month later, in February 1945, camp proponents found an alternative site outside the Ventura city limits that received construction approval. The camp would be established on eighteen acres of land between El Rio and Saticoy, about ten miles east of Ventura.[77]

Using a detachment of German prisoners and contractor labor, construction of the camp started in February, and it opened for use on May 27. Each "caterpillar-shaped" green barrack in the compound housed up to fifty prisoners and collectively gave the camp a capacity of about five hundred men. Captain Mark H. Phillips was the first commanding officer of the camp. He was succeeded by Major Arthur J. Wojnowski on August 31, 1945.[78]

The language barrier between POWs and agricultural labor bosses was one of the most difficult impediments to work efficiencies and was never entirely resolved. To help maximize the results from POW labor by improving communications, the farm labor office of Ventura County introduced a training program for all prisoners assigned to the citrus fields and for personnel directing their work. The program was reportedly the first complete course of its kind in California. Prisoners viewed films with German soundtracks instructing them on the proper method to harvest fruits. Four German-speaking citrus men from the state extension service served as instructors. Supervisory training was conducted for foremen and picking bosses, and included the teaching of simple German phrases.[79]

During their free time, the POWs at the Saticoy camp enjoyed a modest program of educational and recreational activities. For those religiously inclined, two worship services were conducted every Sunday in the recreation hall. The Reverend A. J. Bueltmann of Ventura conducted Protestant services in the morning. He was succeeded by the Reverend E. Athrops of Oxnard. Monsignor Anthony Jacobs of the Santa Clara church in Oxnard held Catholic services on Sunday afternoons and furnished the hall with an orchestral organ.[80]

The exact date when the camp closed is unavailable, but likely occurred at the end of the spring harvest between March and April 1946. On May 1, the Army's Stockton Ordnance Depot took over the facility.[81]

• ***Detachment #12, Old River*** •
The POW branch camp at Old River was located in an unincorporated area of Kern County, about twelve miles southwest of downtown Bakersfield. Construction of this tent camp started in early October 1945, when the 1021st Engineers Treadway Bridge Company from Camp Cooke graded a patch of vacant land and installed a barbed wire enclosure with guard towers, a water system, and other basic structures. On October 18, the camp received about five hundred German prisoners of war. Accompanied by a hundred guards and officers, the prisoners detrained at Bakersfield and boarded trucks that took them the rest of the way to the branch camp. Many of these men had come from Camp Lodi in Wisconsin.[82]

Housing for the prisoners and the American staff consisted of tents, which the prisoners set up on their first day in the camp. After a few days of settling into their new quarters, the POWs were organized into details and sent out to work, mostly on the cotton fields.[83]

Camp Old River closed on March 26, 1946, at which time the prisoners were probably sent to the camps at Lamont or Lemoore in preparation for their return to Germany.[84]

• ***Detachment #13, Delano*** •
In late October 1945, an advance group of German POWs under the supervision of military police arrived at Delano to help set up a prisoner of war camp adjacent to the vacated Army airfield. The work consisted of stringing wire fences around the existing barracks, constructing guard towers at the corners of the stockade, and installing sixteen 1,500-watt floodlights to illuminate the campgrounds at night.[85]

On October 25, 1945, five hundred German prisoners of war arrived at the Delano camp. They had reportedly come from a camp in Ohio. Within a week of their arrival, most of the men were at work harvesting eight thousand acres of cotton in the McFarland district about six miles south of Delano. They were brought to Delano at the request of the Prisoner of War Labor Association chaired by Lawrence H. Bendoski, manager of the Producers Cotton Oil Company at McFarland. The association was composed of cotton growers in need of additional labor in the district.[86]

Early in November 1945, the Delano branch camp also became a supply base for Camp Cooke's other German prisoner of war camps in the San Joaquin Valley. In this capacity it was known as the Delano Sub-Depot and included a camp inspector and branch sections for engineers, education, supply, and a medical dispensary.[87]

The prisoner population at Camp Delano peaked at about 750 men in early January 1946. By this time, the seasonal cotton harvest was complete and the need for prisoner labor sharply diminished. Later that month the movement of prisoners to other camps got underway, and on March 26, one day after the last twenty-five prisoners departed, the camp closed. Captain Franklin T. De Groodt was the commanding officer at Delano during these final weeks.[87]

• *Detachment #14, Buttonwillow* •

Almost no documentation is available about the POW tent camp at Buttonwillow. Located in a small farming community about twenty-six miles west of Bakersfield, the camp was activated on October 24, 1945, and closed less than three months later on January 14. Its commanding officer was Captain Leland F. Stanfel. The POWs assigned to this camp undoubtedly worked in the cotton fields.[89]

• *Detachment #15, Tachi Farms, Corcoran* •

Of all the camps managed by Camp Cooke, the POW camp at Tachi Farms had the shortest operating span. It only existed for forty-two days between November 21, 1945 and January 2, 1946. The tent camp was located in the Tulare Dry Lake bed near Corcoran, and housed approximately 250 prisoners sent from a POW camp at Glasgow, Montana. The men worked in the valley picking cotton. The American staff consisted of about thirty enlisted men and two officers.[90]

• *Detachment #16, Rankin Field, Tulare* •

Rankin Aeronautical Academy was about seven miles southeast of Tulare near Highway 99. Established in May 1941 by John G.

"Tex" Rankin, the academy was one of more than sixty private flying schools that were under contract to the federal government to train pilots during World War II. Some 10,400 cadet pilots received their primary training at Rankin, including such aces as Major Richard I. Bong and Lieutenant Colonel Robert B. Westbrook. By the summer of 1945, the war was winding down and with it the need for additional combat pilots. For the War Department it meant terminating its contract with Rankin, which contemporaneously resulted in the closing of the school in July 1945.[91]

Four months later, on November 16, the San Joaquin Agricultural Labor Bureau signed a contract with the Reconstruction Finance Corporation, the new owners of Rankin Field, for use of the facility to house 750 German POWs. The bureau, meanwhile, had already signed a contract with the Army, assuming all expenses in bringing the prisoners to the area for use in harvesting cotton.[92]

A hastily prepared security fence went up around the existing housing barracks in time for the arrival of the first group of four hundred German prisoners on November 30, 1945. Two days later, when the camp was officially activated, a second group of 350 POWs entered the camp. Within short order, the prisoners were at work harvesting cotton for local growers. Less than two months later, on January 31, 1946, the camp was deactivated.[93]

• *Detachment #17, Lemoore Field, Lemoore* •

Lemoore Army Air Field opened on December 7, 1941, and served the Army Air Forces first as an installation of the Western Flying Training Command and, beginning in June 1944, as a processing station for the Fourth Air Force. On September 30, 1945, Lemoore Field was deactivated and became a sub-base of Camp Pinedale. Two months later the base was transferred to the Ninth Service Command, and on December 8 the Army activated part of the installation as a branch prisoner of war camp assigned to Camp Cooke.[94]

In addition to housing more than eight hundred German prisoners, Lemoore became a sub-base of Camp Cooke on January 9, 1946. For this purpose, a forty-truck convoy was established at Lemoore to move prisoners and supplies from outlying branch camps that were closing in the Bakersfield-Tulare areas. Some of these prisoners rotated through the Lemoore camp or Camp Cooke before being placed aboard trains headed for ports of embarkation. The Lemoore POW camp closed on April 11, 1946, shortly after the last prisoner had left the San Joaquin Valley.[95]

CHAPTER 8

Auf Wiedersehen

IN AUGUST 1945, Undersecretary of War Robert P. Patterson dispatched letters to the secretary of agriculture and to the chairman of the War Manpower Commission asking them to urge "all employers of prisoner of war labor the necessity of immediate action on their part looking toward replacing prisoners of war with free labor." In September, the War Department announced that it expected to return the last of all prisoners of war to their homelands by the spring of 1946.[1] News of this decision brought mixed reactions from the same public segments who had earlier favored or opposed the POW labor program. Patriotic groups and union labor organizations demanded the immediate deportation of prisoners, while farmers in certain areas of the country who were still experiencing critical labor shortages argued for delaying the withdrawal. For example, in the San Joaquin Valley of California, farmers suggested the establishment of a "parole plan" for German prisoners. The scheme would operate in much the same way that Mexican nationals were managed as contract workers under the Bracero Program. The prisoners would be retained in the valley to help produce food to be sent to their homeland.[2]

Despite enormous pressure from both sides of the labor issue, prisoners of war were withdrawn as work contracts terminated and sufficient free labor became available. The rate of repatriation was guided by available transportation and concern for military and industry requirements.[3]

Prisoners leaving from Camp Cooke or from one of its branch camps were usually sent directly to Camp Shanks in New York and then to the port of embarkation. Others were detoured to labor camps in California, Montana, and elsewhere for a few weeks while awaiting transportation to Camp Shanks. Some prisoners were sent to Oakland, California, and then directly to Europe via the Panama Canal. The more "cooperative" prisoners, especially those who were receptive to the U.S. Army's reeducation program, usually went to Fort Eustis, Virginia, where each was then reevaluated. Clandestine Nazi sympathizers and those listed as undecided were sent to the regular POW camp at Fort Eustis.

POW medical evacuees file across the deck of a harbor boat in New York before boarding the U.S. Army hospital ship *Frances Y. Slanger*,[4] bound for Germany. (Courtesy of National Archives)

The remainder were enrolled in an intense six-day course that promoted democracy. At the end of the course they went to the port of embarkation in New York.[5]

Each man was permitted to take with him fifty-five pounds of personal baggage plus ten pounds of books and papers. Most prisoners simply understood this to mean a total of sixty-five pounds was authorized. The prisoners who left from Camp Cooke were allowed to take with them the following quantity of canteen articles:

> *Ten* cartons of cigarettes (no popular brands)
> *Fifteen* packages of tobacco
> *Twenty-five* packages of razor blades (off brands)
> *Ten* bars of soap[6]

On January 1, 1946, the POW population at Camp Cooke and its branch camps stood at 8,700. The first group of about five hundred prisoners left Camp Cooke around January 26. The majority of these men had come from branch camps in the Bakersfield-Tulare areas where by this time most of the seasonal contracts for agricultural work had ended. The steady movement of prisoners leaving Camp Cooke for ports of embarkation continued through early 1946. By March 21, the main post still held 860 prisoners with an additional 2,600 distributed among the branch camps. The last account of POWs at Camp Cooke was on May 2, 1946, when the Army reported that three prisoners, Bertram Ronner, Manfred Thome, and Christian Zwilling had escaped from the stockade at Cooke on April 29. They were probably apprehended a few days later, but local newspapers did not cover the story. On May 18, 1946, Headquarters Camp Cooke closed the POW camp at Cooke.[7]

Nationally, the last shipload of German prisoners left the United States on July 23, 1946. Remaining behind were 141 men who were serving prison sentences, 134 who were in hospitals, and 25 escapees. All of these men were eventually returned to Germany.[8] Arriving in Europe and longing to return home, many prisoners were dismayed to find themselves handed over to British or French authorities. The prisoners were whisked away to prison camps and organized into labor groups. The least fortunate of these men remained prisoners until 1948. The luckiest of the POWs with hometowns in the American occupation zone were sent to discharge centers in Germany and released within a few days.[9]

After completing separation forms, the prisoners received their discharge certificates and 40 *Reichsmark* ($4) in cash. This pay was separate from the check they received from their trust fund account upon leaving Camp Cooke. A shuttle train operating in the American zone stopped at each discharge center several times a week and offered the newly released prisoners free passage to the station nearest their residences. Those who lived near the centers often received rides to their hometowns in American Army trucks. Similar transportation arrangements existed in the British occupation zone. Eager to return home, some prisoners simply set out on their own. Almost all the men dreaded the thought of being sent back to their hometown if it happened to be in the Russian zone. They did whatever they could to convince American authorities at discharge centers that their residence was in the American zone.

ALFRED SCHMUCKER

In January or February 1946, the first group of POWs were sorted out and began their trip back to Germany. The majority of these men were past forty years of age. I have no idea why these people were picked for early repatriation. The selection, to my knowledge, was made without hearings or recommendations from the German camp administration. It turned out that many Nazi sympathizers as well as individuals whom the American camp administration wanted to get rid of (troublemakers and people unwilling to work) appeared on that repatriation list. The rest of us remained in Camp Cooke and continued our assigned work until it was our turn to leave.

In April 1946, we boarded a train and went via Oakland and Sacramento across state lines to a small village in northeast Montana. Here we stayed for six to eight weeks and worked on farms hoeing sugar beets. When we were told that our daily quota was to hoe two rows of sugar beets a day, we figured this could be accomplished without much effort. We were used to the size of fields in Germany, where you could almost spit from one end to the other. Our eyes grew bigger when we faced the facts. These rows measured 1.8 miles in length; one row to hoe in the morning and the second on the way back in the afternoon. To make matters worse, we received a hoe that had a handle about twelve inches long. All day long we had to bend down just to use this tool. Oh, my aching back. In addition, we could hardly see what to hoe and what to leave growing. It was not a pleasant job.

At the end of May 1946, we went by train to Camp Shanks in New York. From there we boarded a Liberty ship that was going to take us home. One of us had to repeat his way up the gangway several times to satisfy the press photographers who were looking to get a decent shot. We arrived at Le Havre, France, and went by U.S. trucks to an American POW camp called Bolbec. We stayed at this tent camp for about three weeks while our discharge papers were executed. Each of us also received the fabulous 40 *Reichsmark*, our military discharge money. We were then separated and sorted out by occupation zones. Each zone, American, British, French, Russian, and the Bremen Enclave, had its own compound.

Whenever there were a sufficient number of POWs to fill a train headed for a respective zone, people would leave Bolbec. I got on a train that took several of us to Marburg, a town approximately fifty miles north of Frankfurt, in the American zone. We had to wait here until there were enough people to fill a train of boxcars headed for Garmisch-Partenkirkchen, the southernmost point in Germany. The train ride was free, and we were supposed to stay on the train until we reached the station nearest to our hometown. The first stop was Giessen, approximately

Auf Wiedersehen

German clerical workers processing forms for POWs about to be released from Discharge Center 26 at Bad Aibling, Germany, June 1946. (Courtesy of National Archives)

Former POWs board one of the special round-robin boxcar trains available in the American zone to take them to the station nearest their homes, February 1946. (Courtesy of National Archives)

nineteen miles south of Marburg. Here I decided to say farewell to three years of captivity as I hopped another train that took me to Frankfurt. Early the next day, I found a train that got me to my parents' house in Heidelberg on August 18, 1946. My discharge paper served as my train ticket. I received meal ration tickets after I returned home.

Normally, our monthly paychecks at Camp Cooke were issued in coupons. Our pay for the last month in the United States was given to us as a check, which read "MPO" (military payment order). It was supposed to be redeemable in U.S. dollars upon return to Germany. As it turned out, we all got cheated by the German government because we had to turn in our MPO one year prior to the Money Stabilization Act of June 1948. My MPO of $24.15 was paid in *Reichsmark* (RM). To make a long story short, the RM 80.50 that I received had a purchasing power worth one package of cigarettes on the black market.

HANS-JOACHIM BÖTTCHER

My work at the ordnance shop at Camp Cooke ended on March 9, 1946. We were told to pack our belongings and to be ready to leave because we were going home. During this time we were allowed to mail parcels home. I had bought some valuable books on physics and chemistry, and I posted them to my parents' house in the Russian zone together with all sorts of other things, including soap. All the packages arrived safely.

From March 16–21, 1946, we traveled by rail to Camp Shanks in New York. The morning after we arrived, we embarked on the SS *Chapel Hill Victory* that docked at Antwerp, Belgium, on April 1. The next morning we went by rail in boxcars, and like cattle, were herded into Camp 2218 near Brussels. Three days later we moved to Camp 2221, not far away from where we were already living. At this camp we reunited with friends from Camp Cooke who had been shipped out to the branch camp at Lemoore. At Camp 2221, German *Lagerpolizei* and British guards confiscated from us whatever they considered valuable, including toiletries, tobacco, underwear, and sports equipment—despite our receipts from Camp Cooke. We didn't expect such a welcome.

On May 1, 1946, we returned to Antwerp and then went by ferry to the docks at Tilbury, England. During the next nineteen months, I stayed at various camps in the Hampshire/Wiltshire areas, working on farms sometimes by myself and later with other POWs. I also spent six weeks at PW University in Wilton Park. As part of the so-called reeducation program, we attended very interesting lectures concerning British, German, and European historical and economic topics. Our evening discussions featured politicians as special guest speakers.

When our branch camp closed, we were moved to the main camp at Romsey/Hampshire. During the day we were allowed out of the camp, and many of us used this generosity to visit Southampton to shop for coffee, tea, soap, spices, and other things to take home. In preparation for our return to Germany, we were grouped according to our length of captivity. For instance, having been captured in August 1944, I was placed in Group 20 and was scheduled for repatriation in December 1947.

On December 31, we were sent to Moreton-in-the-Marsh. We then proceeded to Harwich and caught a ferry to Hoek van Holland. We then crossed the border by train to the old German army training camp at Munsterlager for separation. Since my hometown was now in the Russian zone, I used the address of my relatives in Hamburg on the forms that I filled out at Munsterlager. This way I was released to the British zone. Had I gone to the east, the Russians would have sent me to a quarantine camp for brainwashing. From the home of my relatives in Hamburg, I would later go "black," as we used to say, and secretly visit my old village. All the time I would be dodging Russian guards and police.

On January 6, 1948, I received my discharge certificate and 40 *Reichsmark*. I remember that a few of us got impatient waiting for the arranged transportation. To get home sooner, we bribed a truck driver with cigarettes to take us to Hamburg. Money in those days would not have helped. I returned home to Hamburg on January 7. Here I received my food ration tickets for two days from the special office for passengers in transit.

WERNER BLANCK

Like most other POWs at Camp Cooke, we were glad the war was finally over and that our families in Germany were no longer in danger. Naturally, all of us were eager to return home as soon as possible, but our joy was tempered by thoughts of an uncertain future.

I left Camp Cooke in March 1946 and was sent to Camp Shanks in New York. The POWs whose hometowns were now in the British occupation zone of Germany, of which I was one, went to England where we had to stay for another year. At the camp in England, I worked as an interpreter and camp spokesman. The POWs whose hometowns were in the American, French, and Russian zones were released directly to Germany. When we departed

Camp Cooke we were allowed to take all our personal belongings, including goods we had purchased in the canteen. British soldiers in the camp later confiscated many of these items.

Shortly before our departure from Camp Cooke, we each received a check for the full amount in our savings account. My check was for $68.90. Back in Germany, the *Reichsmark* had such little value that the money was almost worthless. It didn't make sense to exchange it, and so at some time or another I lost my check.

When I arrived in Hamburg in April 1947, I was relieved that my parents' home and business had only received minor damage. I immediately started work in their hairdressing shop. In the beginning it was difficult to earn a living, but we managed.

Father FRANZ GÖDDE
Early in March 1946, we left Camp Cooke by train and passed through the southern states to Fort Eustis, Virginia. We stayed at this camp for about a week while attending a course designed to deepen our understanding of democracy. We then moved to Camp Shanks, New York, for a few days before boarding a ship that sailed to Le Havre, France. Arriving at the port city on April 7, we went by truck to Camp Bolbec [in Le Havre] for three weeks. At the end of the month, we reached the discharge center at Bad Aibling [Germany] in the American zone. A week later, we traveled in a truck convoy to the discharge center at Munsterlager in the British zone. Here the British told us loud and clear that we were now under their control and would be sent to England to work. Fortunately for me, a few of the POWs arranged with an American officer to gain our release. Those of us with a certificate from Fort Eustis had only to remain in this camp five more weeks. Those such as myself, from Westfalia, then went by truck to Münster/Westfalia and were released the next day on June 6, 1946.

I left Münster on a train to a city approximately five miles from my hometown. Since public transportation was unavailable, I walked the last stretch. Back home on the farm, I assisted my dad, who was seventy-four. This work helped me make the transition back to civilian life.

HERBERT SCHAFFRATH
My last workday at Camp Cooke was March 8, 1946. About this time, we were grouped according to our hometowns with respect to the occupation zones in which Germany had been divided.

I was reassigned to another company in the camp with fellow POWs whose hometowns, like my own, were now in the Russian occupation zone. In preparation for leaving the camp, we were directed to wear our black uniforms with the familiar white letters "PW" painted on them.

We were allowed to take all our belongings. Cigarettes were hoarded even by nonsmokers because these would later become valuable bargaining chips in Germany. All of us were elated to be going home, but at the same time apprehensive of what we would find when we got there.

On March 16, we left Camp Cooke by rail and five days later arrived at Camp Shanks, New York. During the ride the guards constantly reassured us that we were going to be shipped directly to Germany. I don't think that most of us believed the journey would be direct to the homeland. In any event, our travel cross-country was made more memorable by one of our guards who pointed out cities and areas of scenic beauty. For me, this was another sad reminder that we were parting from a great and beautiful country.

Camp Shanks was a spacious, bustling transit station for American soldiers and German POWs. After five days in this camp, we were put aboard the SS *Williams Victory* that delivered us to Antwerp, Belgium, on April 5. Straight off the ship we fell into the waiting hands of the English, who immediately put us aboard a train to Brussels. Carrying our packs, we then walked about five miles to Tent Camp 2218. Three days after arriving at this camp, we were transferred to Camp 2228 near Waterloo.

Six weeks later, on May 19, we returned to Antwerp to Camp 2225. Only a few days had passed when we were whisked away in the middle of the night. This time we went by ship to Tilbury, England and then traveled by train to Camp Cranwich. We remained at this facility for over a year, working at various agricultural jobs.

On August 12, 1947, our repatriation began with a first stop at Sudbury Camp 23 near Mildenhall for two weeks. We then made our way by train to Harwich on the east coast of England, and then across by ship to Hoek van Holland, Netherlands. Here we were loaded aboard boxcars to a transit camp at Dachau, Germany. The Americans had converted a portion of this former concentration camp into a POW discharge center. At Dachau, we underwent a medical exam to certify that we were free of vermin and contagious diseases. I also received my military discharge money, and more importantly my discharge certificate, on September 8,

1947. With that paper, I was again a free man after six years. The discharge money was paid in *Reichsmark* and had such little value that it was almost worthless. We departed from Dachau aboard a train that delivered us to the city nearest to our respective hometowns.

My hometown was in Saxony, but because our family residence had been destroyed and the area occupied by Russian troops, I told the American authorities at the discharge center that I lived in Deisenhofen, in the American zone. I was fortunate that my brother, who lived in Deisenhofen, was able to take me into his house. The destruction throughout Germany was so extensive—and with so many homeless refugees—the prospect of finding a room of your own was impossible and unthinkable.

HEINRICH KERSTING

I was in Camp Cooke from June 25, 1944, to March 10, 1946, when the POW camp began closing down. We were taken to the branch camp at Lemoore, California, to wait for transportation that would take us to the East Coast. After a few days of passing time playing sports, we traveled by train to Camp Shanks, New York. We then crossed the Atlantic Ocean aboard the Liberty ship *Los Angeles*, and steamed up the mouth of the Schelde River to Antwerp, Belgium. Immediately after leaving the ship, English soldiers took charge of us even though our American officer had assured us we would remain under his supervision all the way to Frankfurt, Germany. To our surprise and displeasure, we were put aboard a Danish vessel and proceeded up the Thames River in the direction of London.

A train then spirited us to a transit camp at Moreton-in-Marsh, where English soldiers confiscated practically everything we had bought in America with our hard-earned money. I was sent to POW Camp 294 (Fisher's Camp) at Alton, Hampshire. After well over a year of working in agriculture and then as a clerk in the camp, my journey back to Germany began. We passed through the English port of Hull in the direction of Hamburg to Munsterlager in the Lüneburger Heide. A few days' stay and then a train ride to the old police facility at Münster/Westfalia. Here, I received my discharge certificate and 40 *Reichsmark* in May 1947. Using my certificate, I received a free train ride from the discharge center to my hometown of Wattenscheid. This same certificate later entitled me to meal tickets that were available at the local city hall. Back at home, my parents were delirious with joy to have me in their arms again. In my heart, I felt the same for them.

WERNER GILBERT

On March 17, 1946, we departed Camp Cooke by train to Camp Shanks, New York. We next boarded a ship that docked at Rotterdam, Netherlands—and upon arrival were placed in the custody of the English. They promptly put us aboard railroad cars and transported us to a POW camp in Brussels, Belgium. Shortly thereafter we were shipped to England and were moved around to various camps, all the time working in agriculture. After about a year, we were returned to Germany, and at Münster/Westfalia I received my release documents on May 10, 1947. With a group of other POWs, I went by truck to my home at Altena/Westfalia. Having been away for six long years, I found my homecoming a very emotional experience.

HEINRICH SCHÜNEMANN

My transfer from Camp Lamont to Camp Lemoore on March 9, 1946, brought me one step closer to my return to Germany. During the five days we stayed at this camp, all sorts of preparations were made for our repatriation. We sorted and packed our belongings and received new black "PW" uniforms. With our packs heavily loaded, we rode to the railway station at Lemoore and began our homeward journey. Aboard the train we passed through Reno, Nevada; Ogden, Utah; the cornfields of Illinois; and Rochester, New York, before turning south toward New York City. By mid-afternoon of the fifth day, we arrived at Camp Shanks. This was a bustling camp with transports coming and going every day. On March 23, we were sent to the New York harbor and placed aboard a Liberty ship. With over one thousand other POWs packed aboard this vessel, we steamed out of the harbor the following day. As we departed New York and America, the Statue of Liberty seemed to wave its farewell to us.

Most POWs aboard our ship were happy to be going home, though all of us knew that awaiting us were deprivations and disappointments. That first afternoon at sea the ocean was calm, and many of us stood around on deck talking. Invariably the subject most often discussed was the destination of the ship. Meanwhile, from loudspeakers aboard the vessel came continuous news and music. Below deck in the mess hall so many men were playing cards and gambling that it looked like a casino.

On April 2, our ship docked at Antwerp, Belgium. With snappy commands we were loaded into troop transport trains that we hoped would take us to Frankfurt, Germany. After a few hours, we arrived at Camp 2221 near Brussels. Here we got our first experience of postwar conditions in Europe: hot pot stews, bread rationing, and poor housing. After about three weeks, we boarded a train to Camp 2225. As usual with POWs, rumors of every kind were not lacking. Although we were still unaware of our fate, most of us by now believed a return to Germany was not in our immediate future. We spent two days at Camp 2225 and then back to Antwerp for a Danish steamer that took us to Tilbury, England, on April 28. For the next seventeen months, I worked in agricultural jobs at various camps in England.

Finally, on September 12, 1947, I was sent with Group 152A to Harwich, England, and around noon we boarded a ship that took us to Hoek van Holland, Netherlands. We docked about midnight and were treated to a delicious meal. We then walked to a waiting train that traveled to Bentheim, Germany. Arriving at the station at about ten in the morning, we changed trains and continued our journey eastward. Throughout the day we rolled past the German countryside and waved to the people we saw. By this time our emotions were swelling with anticipation at the thought of going home. Toward evening we reached our destination: Munsterlager.

On September 15, I received my discharge certificate and 40 *Reichsmark*. Since Munsterlager is only about fifty miles from my hometown near Hamburg, a group of us were driven there in trucks. In Hamburg, I met a very kind Englishwoman who had her driver take me to my home at Ohlsdorf, a suburb about twelve miles north of the city. When I got to my house, I jumped over the garden gate and into the waiting arms of my mother. After three years, three months, and eight days of captivity, I was finally home again.

HELMUT WOLTER

The repatriation of POWs from Camp Cooke to Europe began in the early part of 1946 and continued for about four months. We were moved out in large groups, but didn't know how the selection was made. Before departing from the camp, we had to dye our clothing black.

About April 1946, we left Camp Cooke by train and headed to a POW camp in Montana. We worked at this camp thinning sugar beets in fields that seemed to stretch as far as the eye could see. After a few weeks, we were put aboard a train and moved to Camp Shanks, New York. From there we were trucked to the port and boarded a ship bound for Europe.

Instead of arriving in Germany as we all hoped, the ship docked at Le Havre, France. It was July 1946. We were immediately taken to a nearby POW camp at Bolbec. Some of the guards at this camp were French. They were constantly trying to move POWs into French labor camps, and sometimes they succeeded. I was lucky the Americans got me out of there by train to Marburg. Marburg was one of the discharge centers for German POWs in the American occupation zone. Here we received our release certificate from captivity and several sandwiches for our journey home.

Although my hometown of Bremen was an American enclave located within the British zone, it was very difficult to get a train to that city. I fudged a little and told the American authorities at Marburg that my hometown was Heidelberg. I was quickly put aboard the next available train. From Heidelberg I was able to arrange a ride the next day to Bremen, where I began to rebuild my life. I arrived home in August 1946.

ADOLF KELMER

My last workday at Camp Cooke was in March 1946. Shortly thereafter, I was transferred with a large group of other POWs to a camp at Stockton, California. While in Stockton we lived in tents outside the base camp, but took all our meals in the camp's mess hall. Since none of us were obligated to work, we watched movies, played cards, exercised, and generally did whatever we could to pass the time. After about four weeks, we went by train to the port in New York City. During this ride we received those practical and tasty Army K rations.

At the harbor in New York, we boarded a Liberty or Victory class vessel called the *Coaldale*. A short time later we raised anchor, passed the Statue of Liberty, and were out on the high seas with a good wind behind us. As America receded into the distance, we waved goodbye to a democratic land where all people are free regardless of social class.

The next morning only half the number of POWs appeared at breakfast. The others were in their bunks or in the toilets trying to cope with the rough seas that plagued us throughout much of the crossing. To avoid getting seasick, I would remain on deck for several hours at a time. On one of these occasions the ship was tossed so severely that I slid from the bulkhead all the way to the ship's railing and then back again. Not until we reached the Azores did the weather finally quiet down. Meanwhile, along the way we were sometimes entertained by dolphins that swam circles around our ship.

The meals aboard our ship were good, but in no way comparable to the menu at Camp Cooke. It would be a long time before I would sit at a table that measured up to the fare we received in America.

We arrived at the mouth of the Schelde River in Belgium sometime in April 1946. Here we were finally told that our destination was not Germany, but Belgium. All of us were deeply disappointed. That night, while the ship remained in port, we stayed aboard and contemplated our future. The next day the gangway was dropped and off the ship we went. One of the English soldiers used the butt of his rifle and words of anger to move us along more quickly. Fortunately, this sort of behavior was an isolated experience. All the other British people I would later meet were very warm and kind.

The first few weeks, we stayed at a camp in Belgium where the conditions were unpleasant. We were then transported to Britain to help in agriculture. I was sent to South Wales.

The trip home finally began in December 1947. We were taken to a collection camp and then to Harwich, England. From the port at Harwich, we crossed the North Sea to Hoek van Holland, Netherlands, and then traveled by train to Germany. We rode to Munsterlager for initial separation and then to Münster/Westfalia to receive our discharge papers, separation pay, and a train ticket home. I had wondered if Munster suffered under the bombings as had so many other cities, large and small. Many towns were not much more than immense fields of rubble. Occasionally there stood the remains of structures, and a few buildings that survived the storm. Strange as it may seem, much of the rubble had been pushed into tidy piles for removal, giving the streets an impression of cleanliness.

Despite the enormous war damage, the trains of the former *Reichsbahn* (today the *Deutsche Bundesbahn*) were already being repaired. Connections between cities were reasonably good.

I was thrilled to be going home after being away for such a long time. But I also thought about the countless other people who had been affected by the war, and who had no such possibility of going home. The entire eastern part of Europe, not just the East German lands, had been turned upside down, and millions knew nothing about the fate of their family and relatives. It was a terrible time with years of suffering for those people.

A few miles from my parents' house the train stopped because of a signal problem. I remained patient until I could wait no longer. I got off the train and started walking home. I soon met a neighbor pushing his bicycle. He loaded my bag onto his bike and asked how I was doing. I told him everything.

A half hour later I was home, but only the cat was there to greet me. A few minutes later my sisters and mother walked in, and with tears in our eyes we embraced for a long time. (My dad had passed away in 1940.) My homecoming occurred a few days before Christmas, and despite our impoverishment we celebrated by singing Christmas songs and decorating our tree with homemade white paper stars.

GEORG KROEMER

After my third escape from Camp Cooke and recapture, I was sent to Camp Rupert, Idaho, in June 1945, and remained at this penal camp until the start of our repatriation at the end of January 1946. We were put on trains and sent to San Francisco. From there, we boarded a ship bound for Europe. We passed under the famed Golden Gate Bridge and through the Panama Canal into the Atlantic Ocean. During the first part of the journey, we sunned ourselves on deck, played cards, and were in excellent humor. We also watched the dolphins that followed our ship part of the way. We thought we were going to Germany. After we had crossed into the Atlantic, however, we found out through a translator that our destination was England. Our morale plummeted.

We arrived in Liverpool and were promptly whisked away to Camp Cattistock, north of Dorchester. When we got to the camp, we had to empty the contents of our duffel bags under the watchful eyes of English guards. Personal possessions we were allowed to keep, but all other items that we had bought, such as cigarettes, coffee, and chocolate, were confiscated. The English took these things to the camp canteen and redistributed a small portion free of charge to every POW in the camp.

During the next thirteen months, I worked in agriculture at several branch camps near Cattistock. By the end of March 1947, so many of my comrades had been repatriated that I decided to do something I hoped would get me back home. One day I wandered away from the branch camp and hid in a haystack until I was found. I was taken to Cattistock and put into the calaboose. I vowed a hunger strike and began a masquerade of paranoia. I didn't actually go hungry because a good friend of mine who worked in the camp bakery slipped me bread. The highlight of my charade came on Sunday when the English guard brought me a piece of cake, nicely decorated with colored icing on top. I flung the cake at his feet, and while pointing to the icing, I shouted, "It's a rattlesnake, it's poisonous."

After a couple more days in jail, I was taken to a woman psychologist in Exeter. We conversed at length in German. She asked me several questions, which I answered in a normal manner. I never found out what she wrote in the report that she gave to the guard, but that same day I was brought back to Camp Cattistock and a week later was put aboard a transport heading home.

Our ship took us to Bremerhaven, Germany. We then went by train to the former Wehrmacht training area at Munsterlager, which was now a staging camp for dispatching POWs to the various occupation zones. Not wanting to return to my hometown, now in the occupied Russian zone, I showed the American authorities letters mailed to me by my brother in the American zone and convinced them to send me to Dachau in the American sector for final processing. At Dachau, we were housed in barracks of the former concentration camp. During the week that I was at this camp we were shown holocaust films and were led through the camp where scenes of unspeakable atrocities were committed.

Shortly before our release, the Americans allowed us to take from a storehouse as much clothing as we could possibly carry in our bags. All the clothing was dyed black. We took full advantage of this generous offer and even fashioned additional soles on our shoes because there was nothing to buy in any of the stores.[10] All my civilian clothes were in my hometown in Silesia. I dared not go back because the Poles who were now occupying the area had seized everything and driven out the entire German population. It was a repeat of what Hitler did to the Polish people in 1939 after the Polish campaign.

I received my discharge certificate and discharge money at Dachau on April 25, 1947. With my heavy baggage in hand, I walked to the main train station at Munich where I got a free pass to my brother's house at Schorndorf. Waiting for me were my mother, brother, and his family. It was a tearful reunion.

LEONHARD REUL

In February 1946, we left Tagus Ranch and were sent to a camp at Sacramento, California. Around April, we headed for Camp Shanks, New York, where we boarded a ship to Great Britain. Until the autumn of 1947, I spent most of my time at Camp 101 in Newtown, Wales. Almost every month while at this camp, we listened to thought-provoking lectures conducted by university professors from nearby Aberystwyth and from other cities. Most of these lectures were about history and politics.

In October 1947, I was returned to Germany, and received my discharge certificate from the release center at Münster/Westfalia, on October 24. I also received my military discharge money of 40 *Reichsmark*.

KLAUS HEBEL

Our return to Europe was announced on the camp public address system. Notices posted on the camp's main bulletin board gave the names of individuals who would be leaving on the next truck caravan. The process was repeated with each subsequent group that departed from Camp Delano. I left Delano in February or March 1946 and went to Oakland, where we boarded the *Sea Partridge* with POWs from other camps. The ship had a displacement of between 20,000 and 25,000 tons. Since the weather was warm in the Pacific, we were allowed to sleep on deck. After we crossed into the Caribbean Sea the weather became increasingly stormy. From then on, we spent most of our time in the cabins. We were all immensely joyful to be going home and occupied our time speculating and spreading rumors about the ship's destination. When we later learned that the vessel was headed to England and not to Germany, a cloud of despair settled over us POWs. There were even a few suicide attempts. After several days at sea, our ship docked at Liverpool, England.

In Liverpool, we were trucked to a transit camp where we were questioned individually about our political affinities and sent to various camps. I went to two different camps near Norwich. After about a year of agricultural work, I was moved to Camp Bodesford between Perth and Dundee in Scotland. At this camp I worked at the nearby air base, cleaning barracks, making beds, and folding blankets.

About May or June 1948, we were taken to Hull, England, where we boarded a boat to Hoek van Holland, Netherlands. We then traveled by train to a former troop training center at Munsterlager, south of Hamburg, Germany. After a few days, I went by train to Bretzenheim in the French occupation zone. Here I received 40 *Deutschemark*, my discharge certificate, and a train ride to my hometown of Lieser.

• *Parting Thoughts* •

WERNER BLANCK
If I could have stayed in California when Camp Cooke was closing in 1946, I would have done so. Many of my friends would have also stayed on. I liked the country and the people. Looking back on my military service and my time as a prisoner of war in America, I learned there can be no justification to use force against another. I see no reason why disagreements between nations cannot be settled peacefully.

HANS-JOACHIM BÖTTCHER
I never wanted to be a soldier and fortunately never had to shoot anyone. I was lucky to have survived the war as a prisoner of the Americans. In France, we were part of the occupation forces and could move about freely. I never encountered the so-called resistance, but perhaps I was too young to worry. During the last weeks before my capture, I witnessed a lot of bombing and destruction, but was never directly involved. I don't think I have to elaborate on my opinion of wars.

WERNER GILBERT
As POWs we all had one thought: Get back to the homeland. We were much too young for the tragedy of World War II. For me the past is forgotten, and it had no influence on my later life.

Father FRANZ GÖDDE
I lost nearly six years of my life in the *Reichsarbeitsdienst*, the Wehrmacht, and as a prisoner of war. During my confinement in America, I enjoyed a very humane treatment. I think of the United States as a people of all races, religions, and colors held together by the basic thoughts of freedom and justice.

KLAUS HEBEL
One day when my grandchildren ask me about World War II, I will have to explain to them the history leading up to the war and what it meant to live under a dictatorship. They will of course then ask me, "*Opa* [grandfather], how could you have possibly allowed Hitler to come to power and start such a terrible war?"

RUDOLF HINKELMANN
I was in many POW camps in America, but Camp Cooke was clearly one of the best. Everything was in proper form: the meals,

the barracks, and the guards. I would like to end my story by thanking the American people for their exceedingly humane treatment during my captivity. My sincere gratitude.

ADOLF KELMER

I am very glad to have survived the war. The world today is a much different place than it was fifty years ago. Although some things are better now, there are new dangers in the world that must be watched.

HEINRICH KERSTING

Thank God that as a radioman in the Wehrmacht I never had to fire my rifle. We were brainwashed by the Nazis who had stolen our youth, the most beautiful time of our lives. For the "little" people like myself, there was not much that we could have done to change the situation.

Despite the hostile propaganda drummed into us by our officers, my views about America remained uncorrupted. For all its remoteness to us, one always spoke of America as a land of unlimited possibilities, and that's how it appeared to me. For myself and the vast majority of my fellow POWs, our time in America had been the most agreeable period in our lives.

As I look forward, my wish for all times is that the world be at peace and that the people of all nations live together in harmony.

GEORG KROEMER

Looking back to the period of World War II, I can honestly say that "He who sows the wind reaps the storm." The raping of women, the plundering of towns, and the elimination of entire populations by German troops was repaid by the Poles and the Russians, who, with the same vehemence, drove out all German residents from East Prussia, Pomerania, and Silesia after the war. Such injustices against mankind should never be allowed to happen again.

LEONHARD REUL

During the campaign in North Africa, not a single shot ever left my rifle. For this, I am thankful to God. At this point, I must express my highest respect to Captain [Claude L.] Curtis and to Major Whitechurch for their pleasant courtesies at Tagus Ranch, and last but not least to all the GIs who treated us German busters fairly well. Thank you again.

HERBERT SCHAFFRATH
Only by a remarkable stroke of fate was I able to find myself out of the war and in America. Having experienced the war, the cruelty of the French camps, and later the overall generosity of the Americans, I learned in a short time a great deal about human nature. At Camp Cooke I discovered the importance of democracy, which helped me a great deal in my later years. Reflecting back, I sometimes find it difficult to believe all the things that I experienced and saw as a young man. My wish for today is that Germany will never again be embroiled in another war.

ALFRED SCHMUCKER
As a prisoner of the Americans I was treated much better than I could ever have imagined. Many times after the war I thought how fortunate I was that destiny had guided me into American custody back in July 1944. A great number of my German friends with whom I spent time in French camps never returned home.

Since the end of World War II, we in Germany have struggled with what we call "Vergangenheitsbewältigung" (coming to terms with the past). Even today there is a minority of incorrigible so-called "yesterday people" who deny the existence of concentration camps and the Nazi terror. However, the majority of the population right after the war began building a democratic society that is now recognized by others as stable, dependable, and peaceful. The irreparable injustices committed by the Nazis during their twelve-year rule brought immeasurable suffering and misery that cannot be excused. Every victim of the Holocaust, as well as every soldier on both sides, and every civilian who paid with their lives, their homes, and their possessions was one victim too many. The injustices exercised over others should never be forgotten and should be prevented from ever happening again.

HEINRICH SCHÜNEMANN
In all respects, we POWs were treated very fairly while in America. Compared to the standard of living in Germany and the German army during the war, we had everything we needed. We did not have to worry about injury or death in combat, or live with the fear of being transferred to the Russian Front. We never had any problems with food, clothing, shelter, or anything else that could distract us from concentrating on our own little "fenced-in" world. Every POW had the opportunity to improve his education and to think about his future career after the war.

In fact, behind barbed wire one had time to think beyond the daily events and to reflect on the important questions affecting humanity. We looked at our lives, and indeed at the whole world, with a totally different understanding. I knew that we [Germans] must use our experiences to show the world that we are diligent, peace-loving human beings. Then, and only then, could we stand before the world in honor.

HELMUT WOLTER
The events of the Second World War influenced the life views of all the participants. First, of course, we were deliriously happy to have survived, which was not easy considering the enormous losses we had suffered. Those of us who were prisoners of the Americans or English could expect to receive humane treatment and had the prospect of seeing the homeland again. This was not the case with the millions who were captured by the Russians. Although fifty years have passed since those events, I often think of those experiences and especially of how senseless the war actually was.

CHAPTER 9

Epilogue

• *The Camps* •

IN THE fifty years since the main German prisoner of war camp and its sixteen branch camps were established under the jurisdiction of Camp Cooke, virtually all site evidence of their existence has vanished. Camp Cooke itself closed in June 1946, but reopened during the Korean War. In June 1957, the camp was transferred to the Air Force, and the following year was renamed Vandenberg Air Force Base. By this time, many of the buildings that comprised the former POW compound had already been taken down or sold off by the Army as surplus. In January 1958, the few remaining barracks were removed, clearing the way for new military family housing later that year. Streets in the area of the former prison camp were redesigned, thereby erasing the original boundaries of the stockade where some 1,200 or more enemy soldiers were housed. A short distance from the stockade stood the POW hospital, buildings 12300 and 12301. In the 1960s, the Air Force modified both buildings and used them for elementary school classrooms. Building 12301 was torn down in August 1971. Building 12300 remained standing until October 1972.[1]

Shortly after the POW branch camps were closed, the properties on which they were built reverted to private or municipal use. Nearly half these sites, those at Tagus Ranch, Edwards Ranch, Boswell Ranch, Lamont, Lakeland, Tipton, Old River, Buttonwillow, the former Tachi Farms, and Lemoore, are again used for agricultural purposes or are vacant lots.

Edwards Ranch, part of which was occupied by the prisoner of war camp, was sold to the Doheny family in the mid-1960s. By that time all the camp barracks had been removed, and today only the lower portion of the camp's water tower remains. The tower is visible along the south side of Highway 101, about seven miles west of Goleta.[2]

When the Army deactivated the camp at Tipton in February 1946, farmers in the local area purchased the surplus buildings and carted them away to their ranches. Manuel Faria Sr. bought

Epilogue

The Air Force demolished the former POW camp at Camp Cooke and built new military family housing in the area. The cleared section in the lower center portion of the picture was the site of the POW camp, April 1958. (Courtesy of U.S. Air Force)

the dining hall barrack and later modified it into a garage. Sheldon Rising bought at least two buildings and two outhouses and moved them to his ranch in Woodville, about nine miles northeast of Tipton. Sometime after 1990, the structures were removed from Sheldon's ranch. The POW campsite was east of Highway 99 near exit 77. It is now partly occupied by the Lower Tule River and Pixley Irrigation District Office.[3]

When the POW camp closed at Lemoore Army Air Field (LAAF), the property that made up part of LAAF, and which the federal government had leased from the city of Lemoore, was returned to the municipality. Private buyers snapped up the remaining airfield land as well as many of the buildings for repurposing at other locations. Today, all that remains at the site is one hangar and a few small structures. The runway and everything else is gone. Much of the land is used for agriculture. In 1961, the U.S. Navy commissioned Naval Air Station (NAS) Lemoore approximately three miles northeast of the former LAAF. Although NAS Lemoore is often mistaken for what used to be Lemoore Army Air Field, the two are not connected in any way.[4]

The remaining branch campsites found renewed usage for a variety of nonagricultural purposes. The POW camp at Chino was replaced by Brinderson Hall, a large banquet facility constructed in 1983 that makes up part of the Chino Fairgrounds. It is located off Edison Avenue between Central Avenue and 12th Street. The property is owned by the Chino Fair Association.[5]

At Rankin Field in Tulare, the administration building and one hangar are still in place, but it is doubtful the POW camp contingent ever used these structures. Several small retail businesses operate near the former campsite. The Tulare County Fairgrounds are still in existence, but modern structures have replaced the old wood-frame buildings that once made up the POW camp. The 24th Agricultural District Association of Tulare County owns the property.[6]

At Shafter, the campsite is now the Sierra Vista Mobile Home Estates at South Shafter and Los Angeles Avenues.[7] The campsite in Saticoy is occupied by private homes along Central Avenue between Rose Road and Vineyard Avenue.[8] Finally, nothing remains of the POW camp in Delano. Shortly after the war, the Army returned the camp and airfield property to Kern County. In the late 1960s, most of the land was transferred to the city of Delano, which operates a municipal airport at the site of the former Army airfield. The POW camp that was nearby at Lexington Street and Garces Highway, was replaced by the Delano Historical Society building, a park (the Heritage Park and Museum), and private homes.[9]

• *The Men* •

The former POWs from Camp Cooke returned to a devastated and occupied homeland, racked by widespread housing and food shortages, the rationing of just about everything, and a thriving black market. At first, many of these men struggled with personal deprivations and a myriad of postwar readjustment problems in their attempt to rebuild a civilian life. They eventually overcame these difficulties and, in their own ways, established satisfying and prosperous lives.

Werner Blanck worked as an apprentice hairdresser from 1934 to 1938. When he returned home in April 1947, he resumed his career in his father's hairdressing shop in Hamburg. A year later, they established a business partnership. Later on, and for the next several years, Werner owned a chain of three hair salons. In 1984, at the age of sixty-five, he retired from the business.

Epilogue

Hans-Joachim Böttcher held a string of jobs after his return to Germany. In March 1952, he entered a career position as a sales representative for Riedel-de Haen AG, a chemical firm in Seelze. He remained with the company until his retirement in September 1988. Hans passed away on May 19, 2006.

———

Shortly after returning home, Werner Gilbert opened a shoe repair business. In 1952, he expanded the business to include a shoe sales store. In 1982, at the age of sixty-four, Werner sold the business and in retirement spent much of his time with his hobbies—gardening and shoe repair. He died on December 13, 2004.

———

In 1947, Father Gödde began his studies for the Catholic priesthood in Münster/Westfalia. Six years later, in 1953, he was ordained a priest and served as a curate in the Ruhr area. Entering federal civil service in 1958, Father Gödde ministered as a military chaplain in the Bundeswehr (German army). After nine years of service, he accepted a position as parish priest in Harsewinkel, where he served until his retirement in September 1991. The reasons for his commitment to the clergy are clear:

> The awfulness of the war and more importantly my time in captivity were the primary reasons for my decision to become a priest after returning to Germany. As a POW I developed a better understanding of the complexities and anxieties of human nature. I witnessed the aimlessness and the disorientation of my comrades. From their superficiality and disinterest in all matters of religion came my calling to the priesthood. My desire was to bring mankind closer to God, and to bring man closer to himself and his fellow human being. After four decades of service I have no regrets over my decision.

Father Gödde passed away on June 3, 1993.

———

After returning to Lieser in 1948, Klaus Hebel continued his apprenticeship in business. In 1951, he was hired as a sales representative for a firm that manufactures commercial cleaning products, and remained with this company until his retirement. On January 9, 2003, Klaus passed away. He was seventy-four years old.

In September 1944, Rudolf Hinkelmann was transferred from Tagus Ranch to Camp Clark in Missouri. He was subsequently relocated to several other camps. In April 1946, he was transferred to Camp Shanks in New York and placed on a convoy headed for Le Havre, France. On April 17, he was released from American custody near Munich, Germany. Unable to return to his native Czechoslovakia, because of the anti-German sentiment, he found work as a farm laborer in several Bavarian towns. With the assistance of an American Army officer, Rudolph obtained an administrative position with the police department near Kassel. He remained with this job until his retirement on April 1, 1978. Rudolf died on December 10, 1991.

In 1948, Adolf Kelmer returned to his prewar employment in a textile factory. Struggling with postwar readjustment issues, he left his job near the end of 1950 and shifted between several laborer jobs and periods of unemployment. With professional help, he eventually overcame his difficulties and in 1962 began working for the Deutsche Tiefbohr AG (German Deep Drilling Company). He remained with this firm until his retirement in 1982.

Following his release by the British, Heinrich Kersting returned to his job at the federal finance administration in Gelsenkirchen, Germany. During the early 1950s, Heinrich also played professional soccer with the FC Schalke 04 club. He retired from his federal job as senior tax administrator on August 1, 1988. During the next several years, He worked as a tax instructor at various schools throughout Germany. Heinrich died from cancer on March 22, 2007.

In May 1947, two weeks after his release, Georg Kroemer was hired by the U.S. Army as a supply clerk at its ordnance rebuilding shop at Schwäbisch-Gmünd. In October 1947, he began working for the Daimler-Benz automobile company in Stuttgart. Five years later, Georg returned to his prewar profession as a beer brewer and worked for Beck and Company until his retirement in 1976. He died at the age of ninety-two on October 20, 2005.

Unable to find employment in his profession as a bank clerk, Leonhard Reul began working for the German railway police in February 1948. Through a series of examinations, he was promoted to the rank of inspector of the state rail system, and remained at this job until his retirement. Leonard passed away on September 2, 2000.

Two weeks after his release in Germany, Herbert Schaffrath found employment in Deisenhofen, working in a factory that manufactured office machines. He remained with this firm for the next forty years, and at the time of his retirement on April 30, 1988, Herbert was head of the administration department. He passed away on August 10, 2005 at the age of eighty-one.

Shortly after his release from POW status, Alfred Schmucker was employed by the U.S. Third Army in Heidelberg, as a cashier in the finance office. In 1951, he was promoted to budget analyst. He retired from that position on December 1, 1983 with thirty-seven years of government service. Alfred passed away on July 7, 1998.

Soon after his return to Hamburg, on September 15, 1947, Heinrich Schünemann returned to his father's automotive repair shop. In September 1949, he left the business and joined a small lighting fixture company that was later known as Ott International. Four years later, he was hired by the lighting firm of Kinkeldey-Leuchten and remained with this company until his retirement in December 1984. Heinrich died on May 13, 2000.

Happy to be back in Bremen, Helmut Wolter returned to his former occupation as tallyman at the export shipping company of F. Naumann Sr. He remained with this firm until his retirement in 1983.

APPENDIX A
Biographical Data

Werner Blanck
Military Rank: Obergefreiter
POW Serial No: 7WG-35061
Date of Birth: November 3, 1919
Place of Birth: Hamburg, Germany

Hans-Joachim Böttcher
Military Rank: Gefreiter
POW Serial No: 9WG-7202
Date of Birth: September 8, 1925
Place of Birth: Lüdersdorf, Germany

Werner Gilbert
Military Rank: Obergefreiter
POW Serial No: 7WG-35664
Date of Birth: September 18, 1918
Place of Birth: Altena, Germany

Father Franz Gödde
Military Rank: Gefreiter
POW Serial No: 7WG-25399
Date of Birth: July 19, 1922
Place of Birth: Flaesheim, Germany

Klaus Hebel
Military Rank: Soldat
POW Serial No: 31G-846424
Date of Birth: December 5, 1928
Place of Birth: Bernkastel-Kues, Germany

Rudolf Hinkelmann
Military Rank: Feldwebel
POW Serial No: 7WG-27047
Date of Birth: March 29, 1918
Place of Birth: Mokrau, Sudetenland
 (today in the Czech Republic)

Adolf Kelmer
Military Rank: Soldat
POW Serial No: 9WG-23026
Date of Birth: May 23, 1925
Place of Birth: Bremen, Germany

Heinrich Kersting
Military Rank: Gefreiter
POW Serial No: 31G-2426
Date of Birth: July 9, 1923
Place of Birth: Wattenscheid
 (now Bochum), Germany

Georg Kroemer
Military Rank: Obergefreiter
POW Serial No: 81G-3589884
Date of Birth: April 12, 1913
Place of Birth: Komeise,* Germany

Leonhard Reul
Military Rank: Gefreiter
POW Serial No: 7WG-25030
Date of Birth: December 30, 1923
Place of Birth: Krummennaab, Germany

Herbert Schaffrath
Military Rank: Gefreiter
POW Serial No: 81G-365494
Date of Birth: April 3, 1924
Place of Birth: Neustadt in Sachsen, Germany

Alfred Schmucker
Military Rank: Gefreiter
POW Serial No: 81G-307546
Date of Birth: November 3, 1923
Place of Birth: Heidelberg, Germany

Heinrich Schünemann
Military Rank: Obergefreiter
POW Serial No: 31G-212165
Date of Birth: November 29, 1922
Place of Birth: Hamburg, Germany

Helmut Wolter
Military Rank: Obergefreiter
POW Serial No: 81G-365584
Date of Birth: August 8, 1920
Place of Birth: Bremen, Germany

A small village near the county seat of Leobschütz (today Glubczyce, Poland).

APPENDIX B
Survey

(See pages 123-24 for background information)

Survey [of] Camp Cooke—4 Companies—1000 PWs.
(First line is number of PWs. Second line is percentage)

By 1st Lt. John T. Harris and Sgt. Manfred Lewinnek.

TOTAL 4 Cps—1000 PWs			With Names 2 Cps—500 PWs			Without Names 2 Cps—500 PWs		
Right	Wrong	No Answer	Right	Wrong	No Answer	Right	Wrong	No Answer
I. Nazi Hierarchy								
Adolf Hitler was a great idealist?								
304	556	140	111	317	72	193	239	68
30	56	14	22	63	15	38	48	14
Adolf Hitler was an insane criminal?								
648	202	150	305	34	81	263	168	69
65	20	15	77	7	16	53	33	14
The small unimportant Nazis are to blame for Germany's crimes also?								
112	740	148	42	365	93	70	375	55
11	74	15	8	73	19	14	75	11
The Nazi leaders now in Allied hands should be shot without trial?								
421	368	211	235	146	119	186	222	92
42	37	21	47	29	24	37	45	18
The Nazi hierarchy had no personal ambitions?								
172	643	175	82	343	75	90	310	100
18	64	18	16	69	15	18	62	20
Hitler told the truth always?								
78	834	88	1	467	32	77	367	56
7	84	9	0	93	7	15	74	11
The SS Troops were the greatest soldiers of all times?								
171	672	157	60	371	69	111	301	88
17	67	16	12	74	14	22	61	17

	TOTAL 4 Cps—1000 PWs			With Names 2 Cps—500 PWs			Without Names 2 Cps—500 PWs		
	Right	Wrong	No Answer	Right	Wrong	No Answer	Right	Wrong	No Answer
II. Nazi Policies									
Guns are more important for the existence of a nation than butter?									
	47	873	80	10	461	29	37	412	51
	4	88	8	2	92	6	7	83	10
Labor unions flourish in a fascist country?									
	16	895	89	5	451	44	11	444	45
	1	90	9	1	90	9	2	89	9
Freedom of the press is harmful to each nation?									
	85	826	89	14	457	29	71	369	60
	8	83	9	3	91	6	14	74	12
It was justified to institute concentration camps?									
	80	796	124	7	444	49	73	352	75
	8	80	12	1	89	10	14	71	15
Mercy-death is justifiable?									
	13	879	108	0	468	32	13	411	76
	1	89	10	0	94	6	2	83	15
No tortures have taken place in concentration camps?									
	26	697	257	7	378	115	19	319	162
	2	70	28	1	76	23	4	64	32
All boys and girls in Germany between the [ages] of 10 and 20 are the lost generation?									
	41	846	113	16	432	52	25	414	61
	4	85	11	3	86	11	5	83	12
Hitlerism was a better religion than Christianity?									
	16	879	105	3	467	30	13	412	75
	1	88	11	1	93	6	2	83	15
The Catholic church put up with National Socialism?									
	70	767	163	16	414	70	54	353	93
	7	77	16	3	83	14	11	71	18
Women should not be allowed to vote?									
	119	762	119	42	397	61	77	365	58
	11	76	13	8	79	13	15	73	12

Appendix B: Survey

	TOTAL 4 Cps—1000 PWs			With Names 2 Cps—500 PWs			Without Names 2 Cps—500 PWs		
	Right	Wrong	No Answer	Right	Wrong	No Answer	Right	Wrong	No Answer
German women should occupy their time with children and housekeeping only?									
	370	549	81	191	269	40	179	280	41
	37	55	8	38	54	8	36	56	8
Soldiering is the greatest sport of all men?									
	31	913	36	6	475	19	25	438	37
	3	92	5	1	95	4	4	88	8
The Nazi Party only can bring order back to Germany?									
	76	824	100	3	461	36	73	363	64
	7	83	10	1	92	7	14	73	13
If you lie often enough to the people they will believe your lies eventually?									
	515	362	123	278	168	54	237	194	69
	52	36	12	56	33	11	48	39	13
A controlled press is better than a free press?									
	95	774	131	22	431	47	73	343	84
	9	78	13	4	86	10	15	68	17
German music and literature only have world importance?									
	100	824	76	28	441	31	72	383	45
	10	83	7	6	88	6	14	77	9
German moviemaking is superior to that of other nations?									
	231	538	231	81	316	103	150	222	128
	23	54	23	16	63	21	30	45	25

	TOTAL 4 Cps—1000 PWs			With Names 2 Cps—500 PWs			Without Names 2 Cps—500 PWs		
	Right	Wrong	No Answer	Right	Wrong	No Answer	Right	Wrong	No Answer
III. Racial Problems									
As a race the Chinese are of equal value to the Germans?									
	531	357	112	309	126	65	222	231	47
	54	35	11	62	25	13	45	46	9
Such a thing as a "Master Race" is non-existent?									
	801	121	78	432	41	27	369	80	51
	80	12	8	86	8	6	74	16	10

German Prisoners of War at Camp Cooke, California

	TOTAL 4 Cps—1000 PWs			With Names 2 Cps—500 PWs			Without Names 2 Cps—500 PWs		
	Right	Wrong	No Answer	Right	Wrong	No Answer	Right	Wrong	No Answer
I must not marry a Jewish girl because my children will be inferior?									
	123	783	94	19	444	37	104	339	57
	12	79	9	4	89	7	20	68	12
It makes no difference at all if I marry a Jewess?									
	732	161	107	430	27	43	302	134	64
	74	16	10	86	5	9	61	27	12
It makes no difference at all if I have Jewish ancestors?									
	739	149	112	432	27	41	307	122	71
	74	14	12	86	5	9	62	24	14
If I had a "pure Aryan" father and a Jewish mother then I am only half inferior?									
	92	804	104	21	440	39	71	364	65
	9	81	10	4	88	8	14	73	13
Converted Jews are not as bad as Orthodox Jews?									
	65	563	372	26	269	205	39	294	167
	6	57	37	5	54	41	8	59	33
Jesus Christ was an Aryan?									
	30	633	337	15	330	155	15	303	182
	3	64	33	3	66	31	3	61	36
The Jews brought Germany's downfall?									
	99	756	123	5	428	67	94	328	78
	10	76	14	1	86	13	19	66	15
Mendolsohn's music belongs to German music?									
	656	108	236	351	28	121	305	80	115
	66	11	23	70	6	24	61	16	23
Heinrich Heine was a German poet?									
	706	56	238	378	14	108	328	42	130
	71	5	24	76	3	21	66	8	26
Albert Einstein and Thomas Mann could never be called Germans?									
	68	725	207	23	390	87	45	335	120
	7	73	20	5	78	17	9	67	24

Appendix B: Survey

	TOTAL 4 Cps—1000 PWs			With Names 2 Cps—500 PWs			Without Names 2 Cps—500 PWs		
	Right	Wrong	No Answer	Right	Wrong	No Answer	Right	Wrong	No Answer
IV. Political Events									
The Reichstag was set on fire by Communists?									
	124	527	349	23	279	198	101	248	151
	12	53	35	4	56	40	20	50	30
Poland attacked Germany?									
	131	730	139	30	403	67	101	527	72
	13	74	13	6	81	13	20	66	14
Italy was a valuable ally for Germany?									
	29	854	117	13	432	55	16	422	62
	3	85	12	3	86	11	3	85	12
Germany would not have used the atom bombs if they would have found the secret in time?									
	113	566	321	23	294	183	90	272	138
	11	57	32	5	59	36	18	55	27
England is trying to organize a state-bloc against Russia?									
	331	252	417	132	119	249	199	133	168
	33	26	41	26	24	50	40	27	33
America and Russia can solve all European problems?									
	328	401	271	163	156	181	165	245	90
	33	40	27	33	31	36	33	49	18
The invention of the atom bomb makes another war an impossibility?									
	193	547	260	94	223	183	99	324	77
	19	55	26	19	45	36	20	66	14
The "United Nations Charter" made in San Francisco cannot keep peace forever?									
	444	269	287	182	136	182	262	133	105
	45	26	29	36	27	37	53	26	21
Prague is a German city?									
	446	395	159	221	186	93	225	209	66
	45	39	16	46	36	18	45	42	13

Notes

Chapter 1. From Wehrmacht to Captivity

1. Christopher Argyle, comp., *Chronology of World War II* (London: Marshall Cavendish Books, 1980), pp. 8, 11, 21.
2. Ibid., pp. 26–27, 31, 35.
3. Ibid., pp. 55, 56, 66, 78, 79.
4. Wesley F. Craven and James L. Cate, *The Army Air Forces in World War II*, vol. 3, *Europe: Argument to V-E Day January 1944 to May 1945* (Chicago: University of Chicago Press, 1951; reprint, Office of Air Force History, Washington, D.C., 1983), p. 437; George Lewis and John Mewha, *History of Prisoner of War Utilization by the United States Army, 1776–1945*, Pamphlet No. 20-213, Department of the Army (Washington, D.C.: Government Printing Office, 1955), p. 90.
5. A. J. P. Taylor, *The Second World War: An Illustrated History* (New York: G. P. Putnam's Sons, 1975), pp. 159, 172; Arnold Krammer, *Nazi Prisoners of War in America* (New York: Stein and Day, 1979; reprint, Chelsea, Mich.: Scarborough House, 1991), p. 15.
6. Kromer arrived on the Eastern Front during the Russian winter counteroffensive. I have chosen to conceal the names of the farmer and his daughter because collaboration with the enemy during the war might still be looked upon unfavorably in France, despite circumstances where the farmer had no recourse but to accept his uninvited "guests."
7. After the June 22, 1941 invasion of the Soviet Union, the German army divided the occupied areas into civil administrative districts and imposed draconian rule over the indigenous populations. The *Vernichtungskrieg*, or war of annihilation, began almost immediately and was carried out by Einsatzgruppen, SS units, the Wehrmacht, German police and security units, and local collaborators. Singled out for mass shootings were "Communist instigators" and Jews. The remaining Jews were crowded into ghettos sometimes numbering thousands of people and were eventually murdered or died from disease and starvation by deliberately withholding provisions. The Jews of Vitebsk and Velikiye Luki who did not flee east to the interior of Russia when the towns fell to German occupation in July 1941 were massacred a short time later. The remaining several thousand Jews in Vitebsk were placed in a ghetto and murdered between October and November 1941, a couple months before Georg Kromer arrived at Vitebsk. During this same time in Velizh, the remaining 1,500 Jews that were confined to a ghetto, and an additional few hundred housed in a pigpen, suffered a similar fate. As the Soviet army advanced toward the town in February 1942, hundreds perished when German soldiers and police units began burning buildings and shooting helpless Jews attempting to escape the flames. *See* Hannes Heer and Klaus Naumann, eds., *War of Extermination: The German Military in World War II, 1941-1944* (New York: Berghahn Books, 2000), pp. 57, 60-61 and 72-73; Yitzhak Arad, *The Holocaust in the Soviet Union* (Lincoln, Neb.: University of Nebraska Press, 2013), pp. 186, 200-201; and Shmuel Spector and Geoffrey Wigoder, eds., *The Encyclopedia of Jewish Life Before and During the Holocaust*, vol. 3 (New York: New York University Press, 2001), pp. 1381, 1382. For more disturbing details about the massacres at Vitebsk, see Alex J. Kay, *The Making of an SS Killer: The Life of Colonel Alfred Filbert, 1905-1990* (New York: Cambridge University Press, 2016).
8. For a concise summary of the fighting around Velikiye Luki, see *Operations of Encircled Forces: German Experiences in Russia*. This is a U.S. Department of the Army publication, Pamphlet No. 20-234, printed in 1952. It was written by German general officer Oldwig von Natzmer while in American custody. The monograph was republished by LuLu Press (www.lulu.com) in 2011 as a paperback in new typeset and given a modern book design.

Notes

9. Actually, after the pull back into Germany, the 33rd Infantry Division became the 15th Panzer Division. The confusion is understandable because the 15th Panzer retained the "33" designation for some of its subordinate units.

10. On April 16, 1942, the British ships *Janus, Jervis, Mohawk,* and *Nubian* of the 14th Destroyer Flotilla intercepted and completely destroyed the Axis convoy made up of four steamers from the German 20th Transport Squadron and the Italian freighter *Sabaudia,* bringing in soldiers, supplies, and equipment for the Afrika Korps. Two of the three Italian escort destroyers were sunk; the third grounded on Kerkennah Bank to keep from sinking. Of the 3,000 soldiers being transported, only 1,248 survived this first destroyer battle in the Mediterranean called the battle of the Tarigo convoy off Sfax. See Janusz Piekalkiewicz, *Sea War 1939–1945* (Poole, England: Blandford, 1987), p. 134, and Vincent P. O'Hara, *Struggle for the Middle Sea: The Great Navies at War in the Mediterranean Theater, 1940–1945* (Annapolis, Maryland: Naval Institute Press, 2009), pp. 109–110.

11. According to the Camp Cooke POW camp roster, Adolph Kelmer was captured on September 2, 1944. *See* Roster, "Army Service Forces, Ninth Service Command, Headquarters Prisoner of War Camp, Camp Cooke, California, April 11, 1945," Record Group 389, Provost Marshal General's Office, Enemy POW Information Bureau, inspection and field reports, Camp Cooke, California, Modern Military Branch of the National Archives, Washington D.C., hereafter cited as RG, PMGO, MMB-NA. RG 389, PMGO files have since been moved from Washington D.C. to the National Archives branch at College Park, Maryland.

Chapter 2. Journey to America

1. Helmut Hörner, *A German Odyssey: The Journal of a German Prisoner of War,* trans. and ed. Allen Kent Powell (Golden, Colo.: Fulcrum, 1991), p. 241; Krammer, *Nazi Prisoners of War,* pp. 10, 11, 24.

2. Krammer, *Nazi Prisoners of War,* pp. 24, 25.

3. This sounds like a corrupted version of the Morgenthau Plan and may have been heard by Hinkelmann during his return voyage to Germany in 1946. Named for its author, Henry Morgenthau Jr., U.S. Treasury secretary, the plan was titled, "Program to Prevent Germany from Starting World War III," and was promulgated on September 9, 1944. The plan outlined long-term policies concerning dismemberment, deindustrialization, and demilitarization of Germany. By turning Germany into an agrarian society, Morgenthau hoped to inhibit the tendency of an industrial nation to become militaristic. The plan later received widespread condemnation and was never adopted by the Allies. *See* Warren F. Kimball, *Swords or Ploughshares? The Morgenthau Plan for Defeated Nazi Germany, 1934 -1946* (Philadelphia: J. B. Lippincott, 1976).

4. Karl May (1842-1912) was a popular German novelist who wrote several books about the United States and American Indians.

Chapter 3. The First Weeks as POWs

1. In December 1945, the War Department directed that all clothing issued to prisoners be dyed black. *See* "German PW Clothes Will be Dyed Black," *Cooke Clarion,* December 14, 1945, p. 1.

2. United States War Department, Technical Manual, TM 19-500, *Enemy Prisoners of War,* October 5, 1944, supplement, April 25, 1945, p. 2.10. The basic document is dated October 5, 1944. The Army periodically revised the document with "supplements." "Die Seitenlager" ("The Side Camps"), *Der Lagerspiegel,* issue no. 4, July 15, 1945, p. 9.

3. TM 19-500, "Enemy Prisoners of War," supplement, April 25, 1945, p. 2.10; Father Franz Gödde and Alfred Schmucker, interview by author, Orcutt, California, October 18, 1991; Hörner, *A German Odyssey,* pp. 279–80.

4. TM 19-500, "Enemy Prisoners of War," supplement, April 25, 1945, pp. 2.4–2.5; "Office of the Provost Marshal General; World War II. A Brief History," Department of the Army, Washington, D.C., January 15, 1946, p. 390.

5. TM 19-500, "Enemy Prisoners of War," supplement, April 25, 1945, p. 2.5–2.6; Provost Marshal General: A Brief History," Department of the Army, p. 391.

6. TM 19-500, "Enemy Prisoners of War," supplement, April 25, 1945, pp. 2.5–2.6.

7. Krammer, *Nazi Prisoners of War*, pp. 16, 27; TM 19-500, "Enemy Prisoners of War," supplement, August 9, 1945, p. 1.1; Lewis and Mewha, *History of Prisoner of War Utilization*, p. 75.

8. Actually, during this time the camp commander was Captain Charles S. Fletcher Jr. Captain Almon F. Rockwell received command on April 18, 1945. Captain Royce L. Dixon held the post briefly in April before Rockwell. See Camp Chino in Chapter 7.

9. The only recorded tent camps in existence around Bakersfield were those administered from Camp Cooke at Old River and Buttonwillow, beginning in October 1945. There are no reports of any other tent camps in this area before that time. The prisoners were most likely taken to the branch camp at Boswell Ranch near Corcoran, some sixty miles north of Bakersfield, which was activated as a tent camp on December 1, 1944. See Boswell Ranch camp in Chapter 7.

10. It is highly improbable that American authorities would release an enemy prisoner of war on these grounds. This may have been a story camp officials deliberately leaked.

Chapter 4. Organization and Management at Camp Cooke

1. TM 19-500, "Enemy Prisoners of War," supplement, September 15, 1944, pp. 1.3–1.4; Lewis and Mewha, *History of Prisoner of War Utilization*, pp. 79–80; Krammer, *Nazi Prisoners of War*, p. 36; John D. Millett, *The Army Service Forces: The Organization and Role of the Army in World War II,* Office of the Chief of Military History, Department of the Army (Washington, D.C.: Government Printing Office, 1954), pp. 314–15; "Informational Directory of Personnel Engaged in Prisoner of War Activities," January 1945, RG 389, PMGO, Executive Division, box 20, entry 440, MMB-NA; "Camp Cooke to Celebrate 4th Anniversary October 5," *Cooke Clarion* September 28, 1945, pp. 1, 4; program booklet, "Christmas 1944," PW Detachment, SCU 1908, Camp Cooke, California, courtesy of George Foth.

2. Memo, Colonel Lee A. Denson, GSC, Headquarters, Army Service Forces to Chief of Engineers, subject: "Proposed Prisoner-of-War Camp at Camp Cooke, California," March 8, 1944, RG 389, PMGO, Operational Branch, Correspondence Files, box 1420, entry 457, MMB-NA.

3. Ibid.

4. "Thousand German War Prisoners Scheduled Soon for Camp Cooke," *Lompoc Record*, April 7, 1944, p. 1; historical briefs, A.G. Form 1-8, "Prisoner of War Camp, Camp Cooke, California," n.d., National Archives Branch Depository, Kansas City, Missouri.

5. Engineering drawings, "Building Location Plan," sheet 2, Camp Cooke Prisoner of War Camp U.S. Army Corps of Engineers, April 1944; engineering drawings, "Guard Towers," sheet 9, Camp Cooke Prisoner of War Camp, U.S. Army Corps of Engineers, April 1944, courtesy of Vandenberg Air Force Base.

6. Engineering drawings, "Building Location Plan," Camp Cooke. The American camp administration had intended for one of the buildings be used as a chapel, but approved a request from the POWs to allow them to modify it into theater.

7. Ibid.; engineering drawings, "General Plan & Schedule Sheet," sheet 1, Camp Cooke Prisoner of War Camp, U.S. Army, Corps of Engineers, April 1944, courtesy of Vandenberg Air Force Base; inspection report, "Camp Cooke, California," visited by Maurice E. Perret [Swiss Legation], September 23, 1944, RG 389, PMGO, MMB-NA.

8. TM 19-500, "Enemy Prisoners of War", supplement, September 15, 1944, pp. 1.3–1.4.

9. Special Orders Number 146, Army Service Forces, Ninth Service Command, Camp Cooke, California, June 17, 1944, courtesy of John Pellew; program booklet, "Christmas 1944."

10. Special Order Number 146, Army Service Forces, Ninth Service Command, Camp Cooke, California, June 17, 1944; Special Order Number 110, Army Service Forces, Ninth Service Command, Camp Cooke, California, May 7, 1945; Special Order Number 266, Army Service Forces, Ninth Service Command, Camp Cooke, California, November 5, 1945, courtesy of John Pellew; "Lt. Col. F. Fuller Now Commands All PW Camps," *Cooke Clarion*, August 3, 1945, p. 1; "Lt. Col. Foster New PW CO," *Cooke Clarion*, February 8, 1946, p. 1.

11. Special Orders Number 146, Camp Cooke, June 17, 1944; program booklet, "Christmas 1944"; Special Orders Number 181, Army Service Forces, Ninth Service Command, Camp Cooke, California, July 28, 1944, courtesy of John Pellew.

12. Program booklet, "Christmas 1944"; Special Orders Number 234, Army Service Forces, Ninth Service Command, Camp Cooke, California, September 28, 1944, courtesy of Raymond Feinberg; Stockade Order No. 6, "Guard Orders," Prisoner of War Camp, Camp Cooke, California, June 20, 1944, courtesy of John Pellew; "Standard Operating Procedure and Security Regulations," Prisoner of War Camp, Camp Cooke, California, July 1, 1944, courtesy of John Pellew.

13. Stockade Order No. 6, "Guard Orders," June 20, 1944; "Standard Operating Procedure and Security Regulations," July 1, 1944.

14. Memo, Major Paul A. Neuland, chief, Field Service Branch, to Director, Prisoner of War Special Projects Division, subject: "Field Service Report on Visit to Prisoner of War Camp, Camp Cooke, California, 6–8 May 1945, by Captain Alexander Lakes," May 15, 1945, RG 389, PMGO, inspection and field reports, Camp Cooke, box 2659. MMB-NA; "Mira Loma Colonel Assigned to PW Camp," *Cooke Clarion*, February 9, 1945, p. 1; Special Orders Number 7, Army Service Forces, Ninth Service Command, Camp Cooke, California, January 8, 1945, courtesy of John Pellew.

15. "Nazi War Prisoners Confined at Cooke," *Cooke Clarion* July 23, 1944, p. 1; report, "Camp Cooke, California," visited by Maurice E. Perret, September 23, 1944.

16. "Allgemeines" (Miscellaneous), *Der Lagerspiegel*, issue no. 8, September 16, 1945, p. 22. For the period October to November 15, 1945, the U.S. Army reported 2,044 prisoners at Camp Cooke, "Strength Reports, October to November 15, 1945," RG 389, PMGO, Enemy POW Information Bureau, box 2707, MMB-NA. A slightly different set of numbers were reported in Wesley W. Purkiss, comp., "A History of Camp Cooke, 1941 to 1946," April 27, 1946, p. 68. It is difficult to know which of the Army's figures, or those appearing in *Der Lagerspiegel*, are more accurate. In any case, to accommodate the increase in the number of prisoners at the base camp, the Army replaced the single-frame beds in all the housing barracks with bunk beds. Schmucker, interview, October 18, 1991.

17. "How PWs Live and Work at Cooke," *Cooke Clarion*, October 13, 1944, p. 4.

18. Charles I. Bevans, comp., *Treaties and Other International Agreements of the United States of America 1776–1949*, vol. 2, Department of State (Washington, D.C.: Government Printing Office, 1969), p. 948; Krammer, *Nazi Prisoners of War*, pp. 37–38; inspection report, "Camp Cooke, California," visited by Maurice E. Perret, September 23, 1944; inspection report, "German Prisoner of War Camp, Camp Cooke, California," visited by Paul Schnyder, International Red Cross, and Louis S. N. Phillipp, Special War Problems Division, U.S. Department of State, June 9–17, 1945, confidential, RG 389, PMGO, Operations Branch, Correspondence Files, box 1420, entry 457, MMB-NA; Alfred Schmucker, interview, October 18, 1991; "How PWs Live and Work at Cooke," *Cooke Clairon*, October 13, 1944, p. 4.

19. Schmucker, interview, October 18, 1991.

Chapter 5. Prisoner of War Labor Program

1. U.S. Bureau of Census, *Historical Statistics of the United States: Colonial Time to 1970*, Part 2 (Washington, D.C.: Government Printing Office, 1975), p. 1141; Krammer, *Nazi Prisoners of War*, p. 79; TM 19-500, "Enemy Prisoners of War," supplement, June 25, 1945, p. 5.1; Bevans, *Treaties*, p. 932.
2. Bevans, *Treaties*, pp. 944–46.
3. Tony Armas, interview by author, Lompoc, California, February 16, 1989; "Combined Shops Will Fix Anything," *Cooke Clarion*, February 16, 1945, pp. 1, 3; report, Colonel Sumner Everingham, Medical Corps, post surgeon, to the commanding officer, Camp Cooke, subject: "Sanitation Report for the Month of May 1945," June 1, 1945, RG 112, SGO, Geographic Series 1945–46, box 1329, National Records Center of the National Archives, Suitland, Maryland, hereafter cited as NRC-NA; "War Prisoners Prepare Plot for Truck Garden," *Cooke Clarion*, May 4, 1945, p. 1; Alfred Schmucker, letter to author, March 29, 1990.
4. Lewis and Mewha, *History of Prisoner of War Utilization*, p. 77; TM 19-500, "Enemy Prisoners of War," supplement, April 20, 1945, pp. 5.8–5.9; Krammer, *Nazi Prisoners of War*, p. 83.
5. TM 19-500, "Enemy Prisoners of War," supplement, August 27, 1945, p. 4.4.
6. TM 19-500, "Enemy Prisoners of War," supplement, April 20, 1945, pp. 4.1, 4.2; "Individual Pay Data Record," WD PMG Form No. 20 for Werner Blanck, June 18, 1943 to August 1944; "Individual Pay Data Record," WD AGO Form 19-13 for Werner Blanck, August 1945 to March 15, 1946.
7. TM 19-500, "Enemy Prisoners of War," supplement, April 20, 1945, p. 4.1; Krammer, *Nazi Prisoners of War*, p. 83.
8. Lewis and Mewha, *History of Prisoner of War Utilization*, pp. 101–2, 123; TM 19-500, "Enemy Prisoners of War," supplement, June 30, 1945, p. 5.1; Krammer, *Nazi Prisoners of War*, p. 86; "War Prisoners May Assist in Coast Harvests," *Santa Barbara News-Press*, September 20, 1944, pp. 1, A-2; "County Farms May Get 400 War Prisoners," *Santa Barbara News-Press* September 26, 1944, p. B-1.
9. Krammer, *Nazi Prisoners of War*, p. 89; TM 19-500, "Enemy Prisoners of War," supplement, June 30, 1945, pp. 5.17, 5.18, 5.18a, and supplement of May 31, 1945, pp. 5.19–5.20, 5.21.
10. "German POWs Give Aid in Local Fields," *Lompoc Record*, September 29, 1944, p. 8; "250 War Prisoners Here to Aid Farmers," *Santa Barbara News-Press*, October 28, 1944, p. B-1; "Sign Contract Today for POWs at Rankin Field," *Visalia (Calif.) Times-Delta*, November 17, 1945, p. 1; "Prisoner of War Camp Opens," *Advance-Register*, December 12, 1944, p. 1; A. E. Panetta, interview by author, Tipton, California, November 8, 1990.
11. Guayule is a plant grown in the southwest United States and Mexico. It has a sap from which natural rubber is sometimes processed. During World War II the federal government operated an experimental guayule rubber program in the southwest, including a $450,000 plant near Bakersfield, California. Guayule was harvested by prisoners at the Lamont POW branch camp. See "Nation's Second Guayule Mill Opens Here April 15," *The Bakersfield Californian*, April 5, 1945, pp. 11, 19; "Rubber Mills Set for Kern," *The Bakersfield Californian*, May 16, 1945, p. 9.
12. Inspection report, "German Prisoner of War Camp, Camp Cooke, California," visited by Paul Schnyder and Louis S. N. Phillipp, June 9–17, 1945.
13. TM 19-500, "Enemy Prisoners of War," supplement, August 23, 1945, p. 5.9; Lewis and Mewha, *History of Prisoner of War Utilization*, p. 120.
14. Krammer, *Nazi Prisoners of War*, p. 87; report, 1st Lieutenant John T. Pellew, CMP, "Statement of John T. Pellew, 0-1288608, Taken by Post Inspector," November 21, 1944, courtesy of John Pellew; "400 Prisoners of War Here to Pick Cotton," *Corcoran Journal*, December 8, 1944, p. 1.

15. "Two More PW Side Camps Opened; Crop Harvest Figures High," *Cooke Clarion*, June 1, 1945, p. 3.

16. Krammer, *Nazi Prisoners of War*, pp. 106–7; Lewis and Mewha, *History of Prisoner of War Utilization*, pp. 128–29, 131; "Poor Labor Done by German Help in Local Fields," *Lompoc Record*, October 6, 1944, pp. 1, 5; leaflet, "Wie Man Baumwolle Pflücken Muss," co-operative extension work in agriculture and home economics, University of California, and United States Department of Agriculture, co-operating, October 1944, courtesy of Heinrich Schünemann; "PW Labor Supervisor Training Announced," *Cooke Clarion*, April 20, 1945, p. 1; report, "Statement of John T. Pellew," November 21, 1944.

17. Bevans, *Treaties*, pp. 948–51.

18. TM 19-500, "Enemy Prisoners of War," supplement, April 25, 1945, p. 2.31; Lewis and Mewha, *History of Prisoner of War Utilization*, pp. 150–52.

19. TM 19-500, "Enemy Prisoners of War," supplement, April 25, 1945, pp. 2.31–2.32; Lewis and Mewha, *History of Prisoner of War Utilization*, pp. 152, 154–55.

20. TM 19-500, "Enemy Prisoners of War," supplement, April 25, 1945, pp. 2.31–2.32; Lewis and Mewha, *History of Prisoner of War Utilization*, pp. 154–55; Krammer, *Nazi Prisoners of War*, p. 143.

21. Inspection report, "Prisoner of War Camp, Camp Cooke, California," visited by Verner Tobler, Swiss Legation, and Carl Marcy, U.S. Department of State, April 19–20, 1945, RG 389, PMGO, confidential, POW Special Projects Division, Administration Branch, Decimal File 1943–46, box 255, MMB-NA; inspection report, "German Prisoner of War Camp, Camp Cooke, California," visited by Paul Schnyder and Louis S. N. Phillipp, June 9–17, 1945.

22. Raymond Feinberg, letter to author, November 4, 1990.

23. Transcript, "Telephone Conversation Between Colonel Hanover, HQ 9th Service Command, and Captain LeMire of This Office," ca. December 29, 1944, RG 389, PMGO, Executive Division, box 26, entry 440, MMB-NA; transcript (partial), "Telephone Report by Captain Albrecht at 1550, 27 December 1944," with Major Nolan, Emergency Protection Branch, RG 389, PMGO, Executive Division, box 26, entry 440, MMB-NA; Gödde, interview, October 18, 1991.

24. Transcript, "Telephone Conversation Between Colonel Hanover and Captain LeMire," ca. December 29, 1944; C. A. Carlson, telephone conversation with author, January 24, 1989.

25. "German PWs in One-Day Sit-Down Sympathy Strike," *Cooke Clarion*, January 5, 1945, p. 6; "Hun Prisoners Return to Work at J-M Plant," *Lompoc Record*, January 5, 1945, p. 1; C. A. Carlson, letter to author, February 1, 1989; Gödde, interview, October 18, 1991.

26. "German PWs in One-Day Sit-Down Sympathy Strike," January 5, 1945, p. 6.

27. Transcript, "Telephone Conversation Between Colonel Hanover and Captain LeMire," ca. December 29, 1944.

28. Gödde and Schmucker, interview, October 18, 1991.

29. The first two companies of Italian Service Units arrived at Camp Cooke in May 1944. They were housed in two-story barracks on the main post, separate from the German POW camp. See "Camp Cooke Receives Italian Soldier Group," *Cooke Clarion*, May 12, 1944, p. 1, and "Second Italian Service Company Arrives in Camp," *Cooke Clarion*, October 27, 1944, p. 1.

30. Mr. Kelmer is almost certainly referring to the Army's rock quarry at Point Sal on the northern edge of Camp Cooke.

31. The U.S. Navy operated a blimp base in Lompoc from November 1942 to about August 1945. See "Navy May Settle Soon for Blimp Base Property," *Lompoc Record*, March 31, 1944, p. 1; and "Local Blimp Base Sale Is Scheduled Rumor Indicates," *Lompoc Record*, November 2, 1945, p. 1.

Chapter 6. Everyday Life in the Camp

1. Krammer, *Nazi Prisoners of War*, pp. 39–40.
2. Memo, Captain Lyle T. Dawson, CMP, Labor and Liaison Branch, to Colonel C. S. Urwiller, chief of labor and liaison, subject: "Report on Visit to Camp Cooke, California, 12, 13 April 1945," April 23, 1945, RG 389, PMGO, Executive Division, box 26, entry 440, MMB-NA; memo, Major Paul A. Neuland, "Field Service Report," May 15, 1945.
3. Rudolf Hinkelmann, letter to author, June 21, 1990; Werner Gilbert, letter to author, July 13, 1990; Ray and Doris Bailey, letter to author, July 18, 1993.
4. "Admits Guilt in Relations with Nazi PW," *Santa Maria Daily Times*, June 9, 1945, p. 2.
5. Bevans, *Treaties*, p. 942. See Krammer, *Nazi Prisoners of War*, for an excellent discussion of the reeducation and diversion programs.
6. Krammer, *Nazi Prisoners of War*, pp. 196–97, 199, 200–2. The Special Projects Division established a special secret camp at Fort Philip Kearney in the middle of Rhode Island's Narragansett Bay where the assembled staff, including selected prisoners, could develop the program and publish the periodical, *Der Ruf*.
7. Ibid., pp. 198, 199.
8. The POWs' biweekly newspaper, *Der Lagerspiegel*, at Camp Cooke devoted an entire section to these activities in each issue.
9. "Allgemeines," (Miscellaneous), *Der Lagerspiegel*, issue no. 8, September 16, 1945, p. 22; "Unterhaltung" (Entertainment), *Der Lagerspiegel*, issue no. 10, October 15, 1945, p. 16; Armas, interview, February 16, 1989; Stan Tulledo, "The Prisoners of WW II at Camp Cooke," part 1 of a three-part series, *Lompoc Record*, February 27, 1974, p. 14A; TM 19-500, "Enemy Prisoners of War," supplement, May 31, 1945, p. 5.14.
10. Inspection report, "German Prisoner of War Camp, Camp Cooke, California," visited by Paul Schnyder and Louis S. N. Phillipp, June 9–17, 1945; inspection report, "Camp Cooke, California," visited by Maurice E. Perret, September 23, 1944; inspection report, "Report on Visit to Prisoner of War Camp Cooke, California, and Side Camps," visited by Luis Hortal, January 16–20, 1945, RG 389, PMGO, POW Special Projects Division, Administration Branch, Decimal File 1943–46, box 255, MMB-NA.
11. Inspection report, "Camp Cooke, California," visited by Maurice E. Perret, September 23, 1944; Schmucker, interview, October 18, 1991.
12. "How PWs Live and Work at Cooke," *Cooke Clarion*, October 13, 1944, p. 4; inspection report, "Camp Cooke, California," visited by Maurice E. Perret, September 23, 1944; Werner Blanck, letter to author, July 10, 1989.
13. "Unterhaltung" ("Entertainment"), *Der Lagerspiegel*, issue no. 9, n.d., p. 19.
14. Memo, Major Paul A. Neuland, "Field Service Report," May 15, 1945. See the various issues of *Der Lagerspiegel*, for a complete listing of first-run movies shown in the POW camp.
15. "How PWs Live and Work at Cooke," October 13, 1944, p. 4; inspection report, "Prisoner of War Camp, Camp Cooke, California," visited by Verner Tobler and Carl Marcy, April 19–20, 1945; Werner Blanck, letter to author, July 10, 1989.
16. Inspection report, "Report on Visit to Prisoner of War Camp Cooke, California, and Side Camps," visited by Luis Hortal, January 16–20, 1945; inspection report, "Camp Cooke California," visited by Maurice E. Perret, September 23, 1944; Special Orders Number 7, Camp Cooke, January 8, 1945.
17. Chart, "Überblick Über Ausgegebene Gelder aus dem POW fueür die Zeit von Jan–Jun 1945" ("Overview of Expended Monies from the POW Trust Fund for the Time January–June 1945,") *Der Lagerspiegel*, issue no. 5, August 1, 1945, p. 10.
18. Memo, Major Paul A. Neuland, "Field Service Report," May 15, 1945; inspection report, "Prisoner of War Camp, Camp Cooke, California," visited by Verner Tobler and Carl Marcy, April 19–20, 1945; Alfred Schmucker, letter to author, September

24, 1990; report, "Analysis and Findings to German Prisoner of War Re-Education Survey," Manfred Lewinnek, n.d., courtesy of Anne Hurwitz; letter of recommendation from Captain John T. Harris, assistant executive officer, HQ Prisoner of War Camp, Camp Cooke, California, for Sergeant Manfred Lewinnek, November 24, 1945, courtesy of Anne Hurwitz; letter, Captain Floyd T. Smith, CMP Adjutant, HQ Prisoner of War Camp, Camp Cooke, California, to all branch P/W camp commanders, subject: "Interviews," May 26, 1945, courtesy of Anne Hurwitz; "Schulwesen" ("School Matters"), *Der Lagerspiegel*, issue no. 4, July 15, 1945, p. 13; "Schulwesen" ("School Matters"), *Der Lagerspiegel*, issue no. 1, June 1, 1945, n.p.

19. Inspection report, "Report of Visit to POW Camp, Camp Cooke, California," Luis Hortal, July 30, 1944, RG 389, PMGO, POW Special Projects Division, Administration Branch, Decimal File 1943–46, box 255, MMB-NA; inspection report, "Camp Cooke, California," visited by Maurice E. Perret, September 23, 1944; inspection report, "Corcoran, California (Annex to Camp Cook)" [sic], visited by Paul Schnyder, June 11, 1945, RG 389, PMGO, POW Special Projects Division, Administration Branch, Decimal File 1943–46, box 255, MMB-NA; inspection report, "German Prisoner of War Camp, Camp Cooke, California," visited by Paul Schnyder and Louis S. N. Phillipp, June 9–17, 1945; "List of Running Courses at Camp Cooke," n.d., RG 389, PMGO, POW Special Projects Division Administration Branch, Decimal File 1943–46, box 255, MMB-NA.

20. List of correspondence courses from the University of California at Berkeley, Army Services Forces, Ninth Service Command, Headquarters Prisoner of War Camp, Camp Cooke, California, n.d., RG 389, PMGO, POW Special Projects Division Administration Branch, Decimal File 1943–46, box 255, MMB-NA.

21. Inspection report, "German Prisoner of War Camp, Camp Cooke, California," visited by Paul N. Phillipp, June 9–17, 1945; inspection report, "Report of Visit to POW Camp, Camp Cooke, California," Luis Hortal, July 30, 1944; Purchase Order, Lt. J. T. Harris to Thomas Mann, August 5, 1945, courtesy of Anne Hurwitz; "Zeitungsstimmen" ("Newspaper Excerpts"), *Der Lagerspiegel*, issue no. 8, September 15, 1945, p. 4.

22. "List of German Language Publication[s] Sold in [the] Canteen at Camp Cooke," n.d., RG 389, PMGO, POW Special Projects Division Administration Branch, Decimal File 1943–46, box 255, MMB-NA. In his May 15, 1945, memo to the director, prisoner of war special projects, Major Paul A. Neuland put the number at 38 approved German language publications on sale in the canteen at Camp Cooke.

23. "News of the Transmitter C.P.C.P.W.," *Der Lagerspiegel*, issue no. 11, November 1, 1945, p. 15; "Shafter PW Camp Boasts Own Station," *Cooke Clarion*, August 17, 1945, p. 3; *Der Lagerspiegel*, issue no. 7, September 1, 1945, p. 11.

24. *Der Lagerspiegel*, issues 1–14, June 1 to December 1945.

25. "Das Erwachen" ("The Awakening"), *Der Lagerspiegel*, issue no. 9, n.d., p. 3; Otto Heinze, "Die Schuldigen!" ("The Guilty Ones!") *Der Lagerspiegel*, issue no. 10, October 15, 1945, p. 12.

26. Memo, Major Paul A. Neuland, "Field Service Report," May 15, 1945; survey results, "Survey Camp Cooke–4 Companies–1000 PWs," 1st Lieutenant John T. Harris and Sergeant Manfred Lewinnek, n.d., courtesy of Anne Hurwitz. A copy of the survey appears in the appendix of this history. Similar surveys were conducted at other camps in the U.S. See John Hammond Moore, *The Faustball Tunnel* (New York: Random House, 1978), pp. 238–40.

27. According to the theater program booklet for the comedy "Petermann fährt nacht Madeira" performed at Camp Cooke, the costumes were obtained from Western Costume Company in Los Angeles, California. Author's collection.

28. Mr. Böttcher may be referring to the Benny Fox "Star Spangled Circus," which opened a one-week engagement at Camp Cooke on December 10, 1944. See "Star Spangled Circus to Open One Week Run in Arena Sunday," *Cooke Clarion*, December 8, 1944, pp. 1 and 6; and "Star Spangled Circus in Final Saturday Night," *Cooke Clarion*, December 15, 1944, pp. 1 and 3.

29. "War Prisoners Here Must See Films of European Horrors," *Advance-Register*, May 14, 1945, p. 1; "PW Reactions Toward Atrocity Film Vary," *Santa Maria Daily Times*, June 9, 1945, p. 3; "Camp Cooke POWs Believe Atrocity Films, Study Shows," *Santa Barbara News-Press*, June 15, 1945, p. 1; "Prisoners of War Are De-Nazified," photo and caption, the *Visalia (Calif.) Times-Delta*, June 28, 1945, p. 12; inspection report, "German Prisoner of War Camp, Camp Cooke, California," visited by Paul Schnyder and Louis S. N. Phillipp, June 9–17, 1945. The U.S. Army did not consider all Germans to be guilty of offenses. But it did want to instill in them a sense of responsibility for Nazism, and initially went along with the government policy of collective guilt. By October 1946, with the start of the International Military Tribunal in Nuremberg of major war criminals, American authorities had shifted their focus from blanket culpability to the punishment of culpable individuals responsible for the offenses.

30. "Unsere Meinung," ("Our Opinion"), *Der Lagerspiegel*, issue no. 7, September 1, 1945, p. 12; "German PW's at Camp Cooke Give to Red Cross," *Lompoc Record*, January 17, 1946, p. 4.

31. There were concentration camps and extermination camps in Nazi-occupied Europe. The latter, located outside of Germany, had facilities (gas chambers) for the express purpose of murdering people, primarily Jews, on an industrial level. While there were no extermination camps in Germany, there were many concentration camps in which multitudes died from slave labor, disease, starvation, beatings, and torture. See Deborah E. Lipstadt, *Denying the Holocaust: The Growing Assault on Truth and Memory*. (New York: Free Press, 1993), p. 78. The former POWs interviewed in this history are commenting on the atrocity films. It should also be mentioned here that in the occupied territories, especially in Eastern Europe, the Nazis and their willing collaborators carried out localized mass massacres of men, women, and children. The victims were again mostly Jews, as well as Roma and Sinti, popularly referred to as Gypsies. They were taken from their homes, brutalized, shot in unmarked mass graves, murdered in mobile gas vans, or herded into buildings that were then set ablaze.

32. Raymond Feinberg, letters to author, November 4, 1990, and January 15, 1991.

33. Memo, Major Paul A. Neuland, "Field Service Report," May 15, 1945.

34. Report, "Analysis and Findings to German Prisoner of War Re-Education Survey," Manfred Lewinnek, n.d.; letter from Horst Schneider. Both documents courtesy of Anne Hurwitz.

35. On October 4, 1944, *The Advance-Register* reported a simpler take on the incident that a prisoner of war was shot in the leg during an attempted escape on September 22, 1944, at 10:45 p.m. See "Prisoner Shot at Tagus Ranch," p. 3.

36. Inspection report, "Camp Cooke California," September 23, 1944; Richard Grunberger, *The 12-Year Reich, A Social History of Nazi Germany 1933–1945* (New York: Holt, Rinehart and Winston, 1971), p. 452.

37. "Gottesdienst" ("Religious Services"), *Der Lagerspiegel*, issue no. 2, June 25, 1945, p. 23; "Gottesdienst" ("Religious Services")," *Der Lagerspiegel*, issue no. 1, June 1, 1945, n.p.; memo, Major Paul A. Neuland, "Field Service Report," May 15, 1945; inspection report, "Report of Visit to Prisoner of War Camp, Camp Cooke, California," Karl Gustaf Almquist, July 25–26, 1945, RG 389, PMGO, POW Special Projects Division, Administration Branch, Decimal File 1943–46, box 255, MMB-NA.

38. Helene De Groodt, letter to author, June 24, 1990.

39. Protestant churches in Germany were largely sympathetic to Nazism. German Catholics, on the other hand, during the early days of the Nazi movement, were generally politically united in the Catholic Center Party, which opposed National Socialism. To help remove opposition to his leadership role in Germany, Adolph Hitler sought a concordat with the Vatican. By the time it was signed in 1933, the Center Party had dissolved itself after coming under pressure to vote for the Enabling Act, the legislation that gave Hitler dictatorial powers. Among other things, the Concordat gave Hitler a free hand to pursue his political and social agenda without criticisms or meddling from the Church, and required bishops to take an oath of loyalty to the Reich. In

exchange for its deference to the State, the Vatican received a guarantee from the Reich that it would preserve the institutional integrity of the Church, though this promise was subjected to frequent violations. Despite misgivings and even secret or overt opposition to National Socialism by some individual Catholic clergy and nuns, notably Father Bernhard Lichtenberg of Germany, on the whole the Church went along with the Nazi dictatorship and remained passive on the greater moral issues of racism, genocide, and the war itself. See Robert Gellately, *Backing Hitler: Consent and Coercion in Nazi Germany* (New York: Oxford University Press, 2001), pp. 14, 26; Anthony Read, *The Devil's Disciples: Hitler's Inner Circle* (New York: W.W. Norton & Company, 2004), p. 323; and Ian Kershaw, *To Hell and Back: Europe 1914 – 1949* (New York: Viking, 2015), pp. 438–40.

40. Krammer, *Nazi Prisoners of War*, p. 114; TM 19-500, "Enemy Prisoners of War" (complete document); "PW Camp Gets Sentry Dogs to Assist Guards," *Cooke Clarion*, January 26, 1945, p. 3.

41. Krammer, *Nazi Prisoners of War*, p. 115; Father Franz Gödde, letter to author, July 26, 1991; Rudolf Hinkelmann, letter to author, March 23, 1990.

42. Georg Kroemer, letter to author, February 2, 1990.

43. John Hammond Moore, *The Faustball Tunnel*, (New York: Random House, 1978), pp. 70–71; Werner Gilbert, letter to author, March 21, 1990.

44 "Two Escaped PWs Returned to Stockade," *Cooke Clarion*, February 1, 1946, p. 3. The names of the POWs and the newspaper accounts of their escapes from Camp Cooke are as follows: Ferdinand Hofbauer and Mappias Becker, "Two Prisoners Escape Camp Cooke," *Santa Maria Daily Times*, August 14, 1944, p. 1; Helmut Hahn and Gerhard Hennig, "F.B.I. Requests Help in Search for Two War Prisoners Escaped From Camp Cooke," *Santa Barbara News-Press*, September 23, 1944, p. 1; Gustav Apel, Joseph (or Josef) Kuhner, and Kurt Meier, "Three Prisoners of War Escape, FBI Reports," *Santa Barbara News-Press*, March 6, 1945, p. 1; Georg Kroemer, "F.B.I. Hunting German Escapee From Camp Cooke," *Lompoc Record*, May 11, 1945, p. 1; Adolf Kelmer and Horst Stellbrand, "Two German PWs Escaped from Camp," *Cooke Clarion* November 23, 1945, p. 3; Walter Just and Herbert Kahlert, "Prisoners Escape," *Lompoc Record*, February 28, 1946, p. 2; Rolph Gantent, "German Prisoner Escapes at Cooke," *Lompoc Record*, March 21, 1946, p. 4, (this was Gantent's second escape from Cooke); Bertram Ronner, Christian Zwilling, and Manfred Thome, "Three Prisoners Escape at Cooke," *Lompoc Record*, May 2, 1946, p. 8.

45. "Four PWs on Short 'Vacation,' Get Caught," *Cooke Clarion*, November 9, 1945, p. 3; letter, Captain John T. Pellew, CMP, and 1st Lieutenant Harold W. Wolff, CMP, to commanding officer, prisoner of war camp, Camp Cooke, California, subject: "Report of Investigation," November 13, 1945.

46. "Three Prisoners of War Escape, FBI Reports," *Santa Barbara News-Press*, March 6, 1945, p. 1; "Recaptured Nazi Prisoners Say Hitler Will Rule World," *Los Angeles Times*, March 9, 1945, p. A2; "Third Escaped Nazi Nabbed," *Santa Barbara News-Press*, March 16, 1945, p. B-1.

47. "Nazis Escape Corcoran Camp," *Fresno Bee*, January 14, 1945, p. 4-B; "3 Escaped Kings War Prisoners Give Selves Up," *Fresno Bee*, January 15, 1945, p. 1-B; "War Prisoner Makes Escape," *Santa Maria Daily Times*, May 12, 1945, p. 1; "Nazi in P.O.W. Uniform Tours City 10 Days," *Los Angeles Times*, May 16, 1945, p. A1.

48. Adolf Kelmer, letters to author, October 13, 1993 and November 10, 1993; "Officers Catch War Prisoners," *San Diego Union*, December 12, 1945, p. 12B; "Escaped PWs Nabbed Near Border," *Cooke Clarion*, December 14, 1945, p. 6. These newspaper accounts vary from each other and conflict with the recollections of Mr. Kelmer.

49. Raymond Feinberg, letter to author, November 4, 1990.

50. Moore, *The Faustball Tunnel*, p. 226; Lewis and Mewha, *History of Prisoner of War Utilization*, pp. 154–55; Raymond Feinberg, letter to author, November 4, 1990; Special Orders Number 249, Army Service Forces, Ninth Service Command, Camp Cooke, California, October 16, 1944, courtesy of Raymond Feinberg. Special Order

249 was issued to transfer the 67 prisoners to Camp Clark. Lt. Raymond Feinberg was the train commander for this transfer that included ten Army guards and one medic.

51. Krammer, *Nazi Prisoners of War*, p. 140.

52. According to the following articles in the *Santa Barbara News-Press*, Georg Kroemer and Oskar Köhnlein escaped while on a "work detail" on April 20, 1945, "2 Escaped German Prisoners Hunted," April 23, 1945, p. B-1. They were recaptured on May 2, "Escaped German Prisoners Nailed," May 2, 1945, p. 1. Kroemer's third escape was on May 5, "German Prisoners Escapes From Cooke," May 6, 1945, p. A-2. His recapture on May 15 was reported as "Escaped Nazi Caught 2nd Time," May 15, 1945, p. B-1.

53. *The Fresno Bee* reported that Werner Blanck escaped on January 12, 1945, the same day that Georg Kroemer and Richard Martin also escaped from the camp at Corcoran. See "Nazis Escape Corcoran Camp," January 14, 1945, p. 4-B. Blanck did not know the other two men. *The Fresno Bee* reported on the capture of all three men. See "3 Escaped Kings War Prisoners Give Selves Up," January 15, 1945, p. 1-B. The newspaper account alleges that Blanck surrendered in Lost Hills where he appeared at a restaurant asking for food and suggesting that the authorities be called. Werner Blanck insists that except for possibly the name of the town, the restaurant portion of the story is incorrect.

54. The Sunday "head count" was probably discontinued after the capitulation of Germany in May 1945.

55. The newspaper accounts about the recapture of Kelmer and Stellbrand differ from the way it is remembered by Mr. Kelmer. According to a captioned photograph of the two prisoners that appeared in the San Diego Union, Adolf Kellmer [sic] and Horst Stellbrink [sic] were hiding in a stable in the Tijuana River bottoms near the Mexican border when they were apprehended by U.S. Customs Inspectors Jack Carter and James McVicar. "Officers Catch War Prisoners," *San Diego Union*, December 12, 1945, p. 12B.

56. Helmut Hahn and Gerhard Hennig were discovered missing from Camp Cooke during the morning roll call at the stockade on September 16, 1944. For more than a week they roamed the countryside as far south as Ventura. Tired and hungry, the pair made their way back to Camp Cooke on September 25. See "F.B.I. Requests Help in Search for Two War Prisoners Escaped From Camp Cooke," *Santa Barbara News-Press*," September 23, 1944, p. 1; "Two Escaped Nazis Return to Stockade," *Santa Barbara News-Press*," September 25, 1944, p. 1.

57. Bevans, *Treaties*, p. 941; TM 19-500, "Enemy Prisoners of War," supplement, April 25, 1945, pp. 2.24–2.25, and Appendix A, "Items Which May be Sold in Prisoner of War Canteens"; inspection report, "Camp Cooke, California," visited by Maurice E. Perret, September 23, 1944.

58. TM 19-500, "Enemy Prisoners of War," supplement, August 27, 1945, p. 4.6.

59. Ibid.; Schmucker, interview, October 18, 1991.

60. TM 19-500, "Enemy Prisoners of War," supplement, August 27, 1945, pp. 4.7, 4.8, and 4.9.

61. TM 19-500, "Enemy Prisoners of War," supplement, April 25, 1945, p. 2.15; Curtis E. Fahnert Jr., letter to author, September 11, 1990.

62. TM 19-500, "Enemy Prisoners of War," supplement, April 25, 1945, pp. 2.15, 2.17–2.19; "How PWs Live and Work at Cooke," October 13, 1944, p. 4.

63. TM 19-500, "Enemy Prisoners of War," supplement, April 25, 1945, p. 2.18l; Drew Pearson, "Prisoner-Coddling Still Bothers Senate," *Ventura County Star-Free Press*, April 16, 1945, p. 10.

64. "Nazis' Prisoners Reported Suffering," *Los Angeles Times*, February 22, 1945, p. 2; "71 Californians Home from Nazi Prison Camps," *Ventura County Star-Free Press*, April 21, 1945, p. 3. Dwight D. Eisenhower, *Crusade in Europe* (Baltimore: Johns Hopkins University Press, 1997), pp. 408-09. In his autobiography, Gen. Eisenhower describes his revulsion and that of his visiting party after touring the horrible scenes that awaited them at the Ohrdruf concentration camp near Gotha, Germany. Extensive

documentation exists concerning the reluctance of the Roosevelt administration and Congress to save European Jewry from certain death at the hands of the Nazis—when they knew as early as November 1942 that Jews were being annihilated by the Nazis. Two works on this subject are David S. Wyman, *The Abandonment of the Jews: America and the Holocaust, 1941–1945* (New York: Pantheon Books, 1984) and Martin Gilbert, *Auschwitz and the Allies* (New York: Holt, Reinhart and Winston), 1981.

65. Krammer, *Nazi Prisoners of War*, p. 240; letter from Robert P. Patterson, under secretary of war, to Walter Winchell, March 27, 1945, RG 389, PMGO, Executive Division, box 26, entry 440, MMB-NA; "Menus for German Prisoners Here Are Cut Because of Food Shortage," *New York Times*, April 25, 1945, pp. 1, 5; Gödde and Schmucker, interview, October 18, 1991.

66. Krammer, *Nazi Prisoners of War*, p. 241; inspection report, "German Prisoner of War Camp, Camp Cooke, California," visited by Paul Schnyder and Louis S. N. Phillipp, June 9–17, 1945; Gödde and Schmucker, interview, October 18, 1991.

67. Bevans, *Treaties*, Articles 13, 14, and 15, pp. 941–42; TM 19-500, "Enemy Prisoners of War," supplement, April 25, 1945, p. 2.22.

68. Inspection report, "Camp Cooke, California," visited by Maurice E. Perret, September 23, 1944; inspection report, "German Prisoner of War Camp, Camp Cooke, California," visited by Paul Schnyder and Louis S. N. Phillipp, June 9–17, 1945.

69. John H. Galgiani, "Coccidioidomycosis," in *Cecil Textbook of Medicine*, ed. James B. Wyngaarden, Lloyd H. Smith, and J. Claude Bennett, vol. 2, (Philadelphia: W.B. Saunders, 1992), pp. 1890–92.

70. Letter from Lieutenant Colonel Robert D. Smith, MC, post surgeon, 1908 SCU, station hospital, Camp Cooke, to surgeon general, Washington, D.C., August 24, 1945, RG 112, SGO, Geographic Series 1945–46, box 1329, NRC-NA; letter, Captain Floyd T. Smith, executive officer, to surgeon general, Washington, D.C., August 21, 1945, with attached letter from Charles E. Smith, MD, Stanford University School of Medicine, to Colonel Wilson C. Von Kessler, camp surgeon, Camp Cooke, February 19, 1945, RG 112, SGO, Geographic Series 1945–46, Box 1329, NRC-NA; *Medical Department of the United States Army in World War II, Clinical Series*: vol. IV, *Preventive Medicine in World War II; Communicable Diseases Transmitted Chiefly Through Respiratory and Alimentary Tracts*, chapter XVI, Coccidioidomycosis, (Washington, D.C.: Office of the Surgeon General, Department of the Army, 1958), p. 298, http://history.amedd.army.mil/booksdocs/wwii/PM4/default.htm (accessed June 30, 2016).

71. Letter from Lieutenant Colonel Arthur P. Long, director of epidemiology, preventive medicine service, surgeon general's office, Washington, D.C., to commanding officer, Camp Cooke POW camp, August 7, 1945, RG 112, SGO, Geographic Series 1945–46, box 1329, NRC-NA.

72. Inspection report, "Prisoner of War Camp, Camp Cooke, California," visited by Verner Tobler and Carl Marcy, April 19–20, 1945.

73. Herbert Schaffrath, letter to author, May 6, 1993.

74. Raymond Feinberg, letter to author, June 7, 1991; report, Colonel Wilson C. von Kessler, camp surgeon, to commanding officer of Camp Cooke, subject: "Sanitary Report for the Month of February 1945," March 6, 1945, RG 112, SGO, Geographic Series 1943-44, box 490, NRC-NA. The prisoners and American staff moved to the new camp, also on J. G. Boswell property, in April 1945. The sanitary report may have hastened the move and ensured that the new camp would provide better living conditions. See "War Prisoners to Be Used to Chop Cotton," *Corcoran Journal*, April 13, 1945, p. 1.

75. Report, Colonel Wilson C. von Kessler, to commanding officer of Camp Cooke, subject: "Sanitary Report for the Month of February 1945," March 6, 1945.

76. Report, Colonel Sumner Everingham, to commanding officer of Camp Cooke, subject: "Sanitary Report for the Month of May 1945," June 1, 1945.

77. Ibid.
78. Ibid.
79. Ibid.

80. Letter from Major D. L. Turpin, AGD, adjutant, Camp Cooke, to commanding general Ninth Service Command, n.d., RG 389, PMGO, unclassified decimal file, Decimal 255, box 1267, MMB-NA; memo, AG 687, Camp Cooke, January 13, 1945, RG 407, Army AGO, Military Posts and Reservations, box 4422, MMB-NA. RG 407, Army AGO files were moved from Washington D.C. to the National Archives branch at College Park, Maryland. Graves Registration Office, Golden Gate National Cemetery, San Bruno, California; death certificates, Department of Health Services, Office of the State Registrar of Vital Statistics, Sacramento, California. Death certificates are unavailable for POWs Ernst Hupe and Ernst Krafthofer.

81. "Nazi Prisoner Found Hanged at Lamont," *Bakersfield Californian*, February 9, 1945, p. 9; "Nazi Prisoner Is Found Hanged," *Fresno Bee*, February 12, 1945, p. 4A; Golden Gate National Cemetery; Department of Health Services, Sacramento, California.

82. "Carl Sands Remembers Ribier Prisoner-of-War Camp," *Arvin Tiller*, August 10, 1977, p. 7-A. Carl and Helen Sands, interview by the author, Lamont, California, October 28, 1992.

83. *Arvin Tiller*, August 10, 1977, p. 7-A. Carl and Helen Sands, interview, October 28, 1992.

84. "Nachruf," ("Obituary"), *Der Lagerspiegel*, issue no. 2, June 25, 1945, p. 23.

85. The bodies of fourteen prisoners of war, ten German and four Italians, who were interred at Camp Cooke, were moved from Camp Cooke on November 25, 1947 and reburied the following day at the Golden Gate National Cemetery in San Bruno, California. "14 POW Bodies Being Sent to San Bruno," *Santa Maria Daily Times*, November 25, 1947.

86. Graves Registration Office, Golden Gate National Cemetery, San Bruno, California; death certificates, Department of Health Services, Office of the State Registrar of Vital Statistics, Sacramento, California; "Nazi Prisoner Found Hanged at Lamont," *Bakersfield Californian*, February 9, 1945, p. 9; "Nazi Prisoner Is Found Hanged," *Fresno Bee*, February 12, 1945, p. 4A; "Nachruf" ("Obituary"), *Der Lagerspiegel*, issue no. 2, June 25, 1945, p. 23; "Camp Cooke Prisoner of War Dies," *Lompoc Record*, March 7, 1946, p. 4; "German War Prisoner Killed in Truck on Way to Groves," *Los Angeles Times*, August 22, 1945, p. A1; "Second Prisoner of War Dies of Traffic Injuries," *The Van Nuys News and Valley Green Sheet*, August 27, 1945, p. 1.

Chapter 7. The Branch Camps

1. Krammer, *Nazi Prisoners of War*, p. xiv; TM 19-500, "Enemy Prisoners of War," supplement, April 25, 1945, pp. 2.1–2.2.

2. TM 19-500, "Enemy Prisoners of War," supplement, April 25, 1945, pp. 2.1–2.3; Bevans, *Treaties*, p. 940.

3. TM 19-500, "Enemy Prisoners of War," supplement, April 25, 1945, pp. 2.2, 2.3.

4. "Head of War Prisoner Camp Talks at Rotary Meeting," *Corcoran Journal*, January 19, 1945, p.1; *Der Lagerspiegel*, issues 1–14, June 1 to December 1945; inspection report, "Goleta, California (Annex to Camp Cook)" [sic], visited by [Paul] Schnyder [International Red Cross], June 16, 1945, RG 389, PMGO, POW Special Projects Division, Administration Branch, Decimal File, 1943–46, box 255, MMB-NA.

5. Historical briefs, A.G. Form 1-8, "Prisoner of War Camp, Camp Cooke, California," n.d., National Archives Branch, Kansas City, Missouri; inspection report, "German Prisoner of War Camp, Camp Cooke, California," visited by Paul Schnyder and Louis S. N. Phillipp, June 9–17, 1945.

6. Inspection report, "German Prisoner of War Camp, Camp Cooke, California," visited by Paul Schnyder and Louis S. N. Phillipp, June 9–17, 1945; Camp Cooke POW "Strength Reports, October–November 15, 1945."

7. "Seek Six Month Extension of P.W. Contract," *Shafter Press*, March 8, 1945, p. 1; "Coastal War Prisoner Camp Closed by Operating Association," *Santa Barbara News-Press*, December 3, 1945, p. B-3.

8. "War Prisoners to Help in Cotton Harvest, Far Behind Schedule—To be Opened Soon," *Advance-Register*, November 29, 1944, p. 1; "Prisoner of War Camp Opens," *Advance-Register*, December 12, 1944, p. 1; Panetta, interview, November 8, 1990; "Coastal War Prisoner Camp Closed," *Santa Barbara News-Press*, December 3, 1945, p. B. 3.

9. "POW Camp Here Closes," *Advance-Register*, January 28, 1946, p. 1; "German War Prisoners Have Cotton Sack in One Hand, Geneva Rules in Other," *Fresno Bee*, April 2, 1945, pp. 1, 10; "Care and Treatment of Prisoners of War Rotary Topic," *Chino Champion*, December 15, 1944, p. 8.

10. "German War Prisoners Have Cotton Sack in One Hand," *Fresno Bee*, April 2, 1945, pp. 1, 10; "Head of War Prison Camp Talks at Rotary Meeting," *Corcoran Journal*, January 19, 1945, p. 1; Bevans, *Treaties*, p. 945; Helene De Groodt, letter to author, June 24, 1990; Spencer B. Stallings, letter to author, November 16, 1992.

11. Inspection report, "German Prisoner of War Camp, Camp Cooke, California," visited by Paul Schnyder and Louis S. N. Phillipp, June 9–17, 1945.

12. Spencer B. Stallings, letter to author, November 16, 1992.

13. "Prisoners Will Not Aid Farmers in 1946," *Fresno Bee*, August 15, 1945, p. 17; "German PWs Out of Country by April '46," *Cooke Clarion*, December 7, 1945, p. 4; "German PWs to Start Home Jan. 26," *Cooke Clarion*, January 5, 1946, p. 2; "PW Camp at Tipton Winds Up Last Week," *Cooke Clarion*, February 15, 1946, p. 1; historical briefs, A. G. Form 1-8, "Prisoner of War Camp, Camp Cooke, California."

14. Historical briefs, A.G. Form 1-8, "Prisoner of War Camp, Camp Cooke, California"; "German War Prisoners Arrive Here," *Advance-Register*, August 2, 1944, p. 1.

15. "Nazi Prisoners to Be Used Here," *Advance-Register*, June 6, 1944, p. 8; "Construction Under Way on Local Camp for German War Prisoners; to Help Harvest Crops," *Advance-Register*, June 21, 1944, p. 1; "German Prisoner Unit Now Here Building Labor Camp," *Advance-Register*, July 5, 1944, p. 1; "Prisoner of War Quarters Finished at Tagus Ranch," *Visalia (Calif.) Times-Delta*, July 28, 1944, p. 2; "Journey Through Local German Prisoners of War Camp," *Advance-Register*, September 13, 1944, pp. 1, 7.

16. Inspection report, "Tagus Ranch Labor Detachment, California (Annex to Camp Cook)" [sic], visited by Maurice E. Perret, September 24, 1944, RG 389, PMGO, POW Special Projects Division, Administration Branch, Decimal File, 1943–46, box 255, MMB-NA.

17. Inspection report, "Tagus Ranch Labor Detachment, California (Annex to Camp Cook)" [sic], visited by Maurice E. Perret, September 24, 1944; "German War Prisoners Arrive Here," *Advance-Register*, August 2, 1944, p. 1; Special Orders Number 183, Army Service Forces, Ninth Service Command, Camp Cooke, California, July 31, 1944, courtesy of John Pellew; inspection report, "German Prisoner of War Camp, Camp Cooke, California," visited by Paul Schnyder and Louis S. N. Phillipp, June 9–17, 1945; "Journey Through Local German Prisoners of War Camp," *Advance-Register*, September 13, 1944, pp. 1, 7.

18. Inspection report, "Tagus Ranch Labor Detachment," California (Annex to Camp Cook)" [sic], visited by Maurice E. Perret, September 24, 1944.

19. "Journey Through Local German Prisoners of War Camp," *Advance-Register*, September 13, 1944, pp. 1, 7.

20. Special Orders Number 268, Army Service Forces, Ninth Service Command, Camp Cooke, California, November 7, 1944, courtesy of George Foth; report, Maj Ralph J. Schuetz, CMP, prisoner of war special projects division, PMGO, to Commanding Officer, Prisoner of War Camp, Camp Cooke, subject: "Report of Field Service Visit," November 6, 1945, courtesy of John Pellew; historical briefs, A.G. Form 1-8, "Prisoner of War Camp."

21. "German War Prisoners Coming Here," *Chino Champion*, September 29, 1944, p. 1.

22. "German War Prisoners Coming Here," *Chino Champion*, p. 1; Schmucker, interview, October 18, 1991; "More German Prisoners of War Expected at Camp Ayers," *Chino Champion*, December 22, 1944, p. 1.

23. "German 'PW' Contingent at Camp Ayers," *Chino Champion*, October 13, 1944, p. 1; "Three Nazis Escape Work Crew in Upland Citrus Grove," *Chino Champion*, February 23, 1945, p. 1.

24. "German 'PW' Contingent," *Chino Champion*, p. 1; "Care and Treatment of Prisoners of War Rotary Topic," *Chino Champion*, p. 8.

25. "More German Prisoners of War Expected at Camp Ayers," *Chino Champion*, p. 1.

26. "P.O.W. Commandant at Ayers Asks Loan of Music Instruments," *Chino Champion*, November 3, 1944, p. 1.

27. Historical briefs, A.G. Form 1-8, "Prisoner of War Camp, Camp Cooke, California"; inspection report, "Prisoner of War Camp, Camp Cooke, California," visited by Verner Tobler and Carl Marcy, April 19–20, 1945; Camp Cooke POW Camp "Strength Reports, October to November 15, 1945"; roster, "Army Service Forces, Ninth Service Command, Headquarters Prisoner of War Camp, Camp Cooke, California," April 11, 1945," RG 389, PMGO, Enemy POW Information Bureau, inspection and field reports, Camp Cooke, California, MMB-NA; letter, Phyllis Outhier, Chino Valley Historical Society, November 6, 1993.

28. Memo, Captain Lyle T. Dawson, CMP, Labor and Liaison Branch, to Colonel C. S. Urwiller, chief of labor and liaison, subject: "Visit to Chino POW Camp, California," April 23, 1945, RG 389, PMGO, Executive Division, box 26, entry 440, MMB-NA.

29. Inspection report, "German Prisoner of War Camp, Camp Cooke, California," visited by Paul Schnyder and Louis S. N. Phillipp, June 9–17, 1945; "First Prisoners of War Due at Camp Next Week," *Santa Barbara News-Press*, October 13, 1944, p. B-1.

30. Inspection report, "German Prisoner of War Camp, Camp Cooke, California," visited by Paul Schnyder and Louis S. N. Phillipp, June 9–17, 1945; inspection report, "Goleta, California (Annex to Camp Cook)" [sic], visited by [Paul] Schnyder, June 16, 1945.

31. Inspection report, "Goleta, California (Annex to Camp Cook)" [sic], visited by [Paul] Schnyder, June 16, 1945; "Die Seitenlager" ("The Side Camps"), *Der Lagerspiegel*, issue no. 10, October 15, 1945, p. 19.

32. Inspection report, "Goleta, California (Annex to Camp Cook)" [sic], visited by [Paul] Schnyder, June 16, 1945; "250 War Prisoners Here to Aid Farmers," *Santa Barbara News-Press*, October 28, 1944, p. B-1.

33. Inspection report, "Goleta, California (Annex to Camp Cook)" [sic], visited by [Paul] Schnyder [International Red Cross], June 16, 1945.

34. Ibid.

35. "Lemon Growers Reassured on Citrus Decline," *Santa Barbara News-Press*, January 6, 1945, p. B-1; "Hoff Officially Made 'Surplus,'" *Santa Barbara News-Press*, November 11, 1945, p. 1; "German Prisoners from Camp Cooke Dismantle Hospital," *Lompoc Record*, November 30, 1945, p. 1.

36. Special Orders Number 268, Camp Cooke, November 7, 1944; Special Orders Number 131, Army Service Forces, Ninth Service Command, Camp Cooke, California, May 31, 1945, courtesy of John Pellew; inspection report, "Goleta, California (Annex to Camp Cook)" [sic], visited by [Paul] Schnyder, June 16, 1945; historical briefs, A.G. Form 1-8, "Prisoner of War Camp, Camp Cooke, California."

37. Historical briefs, A.G. Form 1-8, "Prisoner of War Camp, Camp Cooke, California"; "400 Prisoners of War Here to Pick Cotton" and "Civic Groups Are Joining in Plans for Entertainment of Soldiers Stationed Here," *Corcoran Journal*, December 8, 1944, p. 1; "Head of War Prison Camp Talks at Rotary Meeting," *Corcoran Journal*, January 19, 1945, p. 1. James G. Boswell was the patriarch of a cotton business that grew into an empire under the leadership of his nephew, James G. Boswell II. See Mark Arax and Rick Wartzman, *The King of California: J. G. Boswell and the Making of a Secret American Empire* (New York: Public Affairs, 2003).

38. "War Prisoners to Be Used to Chop Cotton," *Corcoran Journal*, April 13, 1945, p. 1; inspection report, "German Prisoner of War Camp, Camp Cooke, California," visited by Paul Schnyder and Louis S. N. Phillipp, June 9–17, 1945; "Unterhaltung" ("Entertainment"), *Der Lagerspiegel*, issue no. 9, n.d., p. 19; Special Orders Number 153, Army Service Forces, Ninth Service Command, Camp Cooke, California, June 26, 1945, courtesy of John Pellew.

39. Newspaper accounts of escapes from the Corcoran camp are sometimes conflicting. Names of escaped prisoners also sometimes appear with different spellings. Therefore, more than one source is provided and the spelling variations appear in brackets. The escapes are as follows: Hermann Kuehne, "Escaped Prisoner of War Picked Up by Corcoran Police," *Corcoran Journal*, January 5, 1945, p. 1; unidentified prisoner, "Escaped Prisoner of War Is Captured After Struggle With Two Local Ranchers," *Corcoran Journal*, January 5, 1945, p. 1; Wilhelm Ruh, Rich Dedough and Carl [probably Karl] Aemmler, "3 Nazis Escape Corcoran Camp," *Santa Barbara News-Press*, January 5, 1945, p. A-2, also "4 Nazi Escapees Give Selves Up," *Santa Barbara News-Press*, January 8, 1945, p. A-5, and "Four Escaped Prisoners of War Captured," *Corcoran Journal*, January 12, 1945, p. 1; Werner Blanck, Georg Kroemer, and Richard Martin, "Nazis Escape Corcoran Camp," *Fresno Bee*, January 14, 1945, p. 4-B; Otto Arendt, Herbert Friede [or Friebe], Kurt Maslowski, and Georg Meilandt [or Merlandt], "Four Nazis Escape From Corcoran Camp," *Bakersfield Californian*, January 16, 1945, p. 9, "Four Escaped Nazis Give Up to Rancher," *Bakersfield Californian*, January 17, 1945, p. 7, and "7 Prisoners Escape, Give Up in One Week," *Corcoran Journal*, January 19, 1945, p. 1; Erwin Lenke and Alfred Shict [Schicte?], "2 Nazi Fugitives Are Recaptured," *Fresno Bee*, February 26, 1945, n.p.; Otto Arendt and Erwin Lamke, "Two 'Critical' Nazis in Jail at Hanford," *Bakersfield Californian*, March 6, 1945, p. 7; "Nazi Prisoner Flees Corcoran Camp Third Time," *Bakersfield Californian*, March 10, 1945, p. 7; Johann Joachim and Wenzel Kuenzel, "Nazis Are Caught by Kings Sheriff," *Fresno Bee*, May 8, 1945, p. 11.

40. Historical briefs, A.G. Form 1-8, "Prisoner of War Camp, Camp Cooke, California"; "Jap PWs Move into German Camps," *Cooke Clarion*, October 6, 1945, p. 3.

41. Historical briefs, A.G. Form 1-8, "Prisoner of War Camp, Camp Cooke, California"; "Jap Prisoners to Arrive Here Today," *Corcoran Journal*, October 5, 1945, p. 1; "Jap PWs Move into German Camps," *Cooke Clarion*, October 6, 1945, p. 3; "Germans Replacing Japs in Valley Camps," *Cooke Clarion*, January 4, 1946, p. 4.

42. "Gins Contract 800 German Prisoners to Harvest Cotton," *Shafter Press*, November 23, 1944, p. 1; "600 German Prisoners Due Here," *Shafter Press*, December 7, 1944, p. 1; "Potato Pickers, Cotton Choppers Badly Needed," *Delano Record*, June 2, 1944, p. 1; "Prisoners Build Camp at Shafter," *Wasco News*, December 8, 1944, p. 1.

43. "Prisoners Build Camp at Shafter *Wasco News*, December 8, 1944, p. 1; "Prisoners Harvest Cotton," *Shafter Press*, December 21, 1944, p. 1; "Extension of Nazi Camps Sought Here," *Bakersfield Californian*, March 10, 1945, p. 7; Mae Saunders, "Prisoner Labor Aids Kern Crops," part 4 of a 4-part series, *Bakersfield Californian*, October 2, 1945, pp. 7, 13.

44. "Prisoners Build Camp at Shafter," *Wasco News*, December 8, 1944, p. 1; Special Orders Number 289, Army Service Forces, Ninth Service Command, Camp Cooke, California, December 1, 1944, courtesy of Raymond Feinberg; "Gins Contract 800 German Prisoners to Harvest Cotton," *Shafter Press*, November 23, 1944, p. 1; Spencer B. Stallings, letter to author, November 25, 1992.

45. Inspection report, "Prisoner of War Camp, Camp Cooke, California," visited by Verner Tobler and Carl Marcy, April 19–20, 1945; inspection report, "German Prisoner of War Camp, Camp Cooke, California," visited by Paul Schnyder and Louis S. N. Phillipp, June 9–17, 1945; "Capt. Brown Gives Details Regarding Shafter POW Camp at Exchange Meeting," *Wasco News*, March 2, 1945, pp. 1, 8.

46. Historical briefs, A.G. Form 1-8, "Prisoner of War Camp, Camp Cooke, California"; inspection report, "German Prisoner of War Camp, Camp Cooke, California," visited by Paul Schnyder and Louis S. N. Phillipp, June 9–17, 1945; Spencer B. Stallings,

letter to author, November 16, 1992; "War Prisoners Sing Marching Thru Shafter," *Shafter Press*, December 14, 1944, p. 1.

47. "Prisoners Harvest Cotton," *Shafter Press*, December 21, 1944, p. 1; "War Prisoners Average 90 Pound Pick," *Shafter Press*, January 11, 1945, p. 1; "Capt. Brown Gives Details Regarding Shafter POW Camp at Exchange Meeting," *Wasco News*, March 2, 1945, pp. 1, 8; "Seek Six Month Extension of P.W. Contract," *Shafter Press*, March 8, 1945, p. 1.

48. Spencer B. Stallings, letter to author, November 16, 1992; Spencer B. Stallings, telephone conversation with author, December 7, 1992.

49. "Shafter PW Camp Boasts Own Station," *Cooke Clarion*, August 17, 1945, p. 3; Spencer B. Stallings, letter to author, November 16, 1992.

50. "Die Seitenlager" ("The Side Camps"), *Der Lagerspiegel*, September 15, 1945, p. 11.

51. "Capt. Brown Gives Details," *Wasco News*, March 2, 1945, pp. 1, 8.

52. Inspection report, "German Prisoner of War Camp, Camp Cooke, California," visited by Paul Schnyder and Louis S. N. Phillipp, June 9–17, 1945.

53. Spencer B. Stallings, letters to author, November 16, 1992 and November 25, 1992.

54. Spencer B. Stallings, letters to author, November 25, 1992, and January 6, 1993.

55. Spencer B. Stallings, letter to author, November 25, 1992.

56. Spencer B. Stallings, letter to author, January 6, 1993.

57. Ibid.

58. Ibid.

59. Helene De Groodt, letter to author, undated, circa April 1990.

60. Historical briefs, A.G. Form 1-8, "Prisoner of War Camp, Camp Cooke, California."

61. Historical briefs, A.G. Form 1-8, "Prisoner of War Camp, Camp Cooke, California"; "Prisoner of War Camp Opens," *Advance-Register*, December 12, 1944, p. 1; inspection report, "German Prisoner of War Camp, Camp Cooke, California," visited by Paul Schnyder and Louis S. N. Phillipp, June 9–17, 1945.

62. Historical briefs, A.G. Form 1-8, "Prisoner of War Camp, Camp Cooke, California"; "Tulare Ranch Camp Locked Up," *Cooke Clarion*, January 25, 1946, p. 1; "P.O.W. Buildings to Be Auctioned Off," *Visalia (Calif.) Times-Delta*, March 27, 1946, p. 1.

63. Historical briefs, A.G. Form 1-8, "Prisoner of War Camp, Camp Cooke, California"; Inspection report, "German Prisoner of War Camp, Camp Cooke, California," visited by Paul Schnyder and Louis S. N. Phillipp, June 9–17, 1945; Carl and Helen Sands, interview, October 28, 1992.

64. Inspection report, "German Prisoner of War Camp, Camp Cooke, California," visited by Paul Schnyder and Louis S. N. Phillipp, June 9–17, 1945; inspection report by Maj. D. L. Schwieger and Capt. Robert W. Mess (Office of the Provost Marshal General), of POW Camp, Camp Cooke, to Commanding Officer, Camp Cooke, July 24, 1945, attached labor report for branch camp Lamont, July 21, 1945, PMGO, POW Special Projects Division, Administration Branch, Decimal File, 1943–46, box 255, MMB-NA.

65. Carl and Helen Sands, interview, October 28, 1992.

66. Inspection report, "German Prisoner of War Camp, Camp Cooke, California," visited by Paul Schnyder and Louis S. N. Phillipp, June 9–17, 1945; Special Orders Number 6, Army Service Forces, Ninth Service Command, Camp Cooke, California, January 6, 1945, courtesy of John Pellew; Mae Saunders, "Prisoner Labor Aids Kern Crops," part four of a four-part series, *Bakersfield Californian*, October 2, 1945, pp. 7, 13.

67. Mae Saunders, "Camp Life of P.O.W.s Here Told," part 3 of a 4-part series, *Bakersfield Californian*, September 27, 1945, p. 9; "Schulwesen" ("School Matters"), *Der Lagerspiegel*, issue no. 4, July 15, 1945, p. 13.

68. "Lt. Col. Griffin Is Post Chaplain," *Cooke Clarion*, July 6, 1945, p. 3; Mae Saunders, "Nazis Held Here Work on Farms," part 2 of a 4-part series, *Bakersfield Californian*, September 11, 1945, pp. 7, 11.

69. Historical briefs, A.G. Form 1-8, "Prisoner of War Camp, Camp Cooke, California"; Jap PWs Move into German Camps," *Cooke Clarion*, October 6, 1945, p. 3; "Germans Replacing Japs in Valley Camps," *Cooke Clarion*, January 4, 1946, p. 4.

70. "Von Glahn Plans Huge Farm 'Hotel'," *Advance-Register*, September 15, 1944, p. 1; "War Prisoners to Be Used to Chop Cotton," *Corcoran Journal*, April 13, 1945, p. 1; "Lakeland PW Camp Commander Commended for Success of von Glahn Ranch Program," *Cooke Clarion*, June 29, 1945, p. 1.

71. "War Prisoners to Be Used to Chop Cotton," *Corcoran Journal*, September 15, 1944, p. 1; "Free Labor to Get First Call for Picking," *Corcoran Journal*, August 3, 1945, p. 1; "Potato Pickers, Cotton Choppers Badly Needed," *Delano Record*, June 2, 1944, p. 1; historical briefs, A.G. Form 1-8, "Prisoner of War Camp, Camp Cooke, California"; "175 Prisoners to Be Left Here for Work This Summer," *Corcoran Journal*, June 22, 1945, p. 1; "Lakeland PW Camp Commander Commended for Success of von Glahn Ranch Program," *Cooke Clarion*, June 29, 1945, p. 1.

72. Historical briefs, A.G. Form 1-8, "Prisoner of War Camp, Camp Cooke, California"; "Jap PWs Move into German Camps," *Cooke Clarion*, October 6, 1945, p. 3; "Germans Replacing Japs in Valley Camps," *Cooke Clarion*, January 4, 1946, p. 4.

73. Inspection report, "German Prisoner of War Camp, Camp Cooke, California," visited by Paul Schnyder and Louis S. N. Phillipp, June 9–17, 1945; Panetta, interview, November 8, 1990; historical briefs, A.G. Form 1-8, "Prisoner of War Camp, Camp Cooke, California."

74. Manuel Faria Jr., telephone conversation with author, May 21, 1995.

75. Inspection report, "German Prisoner of War Camp, Camp Cooke, California," visited by Paul Schnyder and Louis S. N. Phillipp, June 9–17, 1945; historical briefs, A.G. Form 1-8, "Prisoner of War Camp, Camp Cooke, California"; "PW Camp at Tipton Winds Up Last Week," *Cooke Clarion*, February 15, 1946, p. 1; "Die Seitenlager," ("The Side Camps"), *Der Lagerspiegel*, June 15, 1945, p. 11; T/4 Nathan N. Willinsky, "Tipton Branch Camp," *Cooke Clarion*, July 6, 1945, p. 4.

76. Lee Hafkin, "German Labor: In Ventura County It Returns Rich Dividends to the Government, Makes the Citrus Growers Happy," *Ventura County Star-Free Press*, September 5, 1945, pp. 1, 3.

77. "Opposition Forms on Prison Camp," *Santa Barbara News-Press*, January 13, 1945, p. B-1; "Establishment of Prisoner of War Camp in Ventura's Seaside Park Thought Blocked," *Santa Barbara News-Press*, January 19, 1945, p. A-8; "War Prisoner Site Selected," *Los Angeles Times*, February 23, 1945, Part II, p. 2.

78. Hafkin, "German Labor In Ventura County It Returns Rich Dividends to the Government, Makes the Citrus Growers Happy," *Ventura County Star-Free Press*, September 5, 1945, pp. 1, 3; Special Orders Number 131, Camp Cooke, May 31, 1945; historical briefs, A.G. Form 1-8, "Prisoner of War Camp," "New Prisoner Camp Commander on Job," *Ventura County Star-Free Press*, August 31, 1945, p. 3.

79. Hafkin, "German Labor In Ventura County It Returns Rich Dividends to the Government, Makes the Citrus Growers Happy," *Ventura County Star-Free Press*, September 5, 1945, pp. 1, 3; "German Captives at Work," *Ventura County Star-Free Press*, May 28, 1945, p. 1.

80. Hafkin, "German Labor In Ventura County It Returns Rich Dividends to the Government, Makes the Citrus Growers Happy," *Ventura County Star-Free Press*, September 5, 1945, pp. 1, 3.

81. Historical briefs, A.G. Form 1-8, "Prisoner of War Camp, Camp Cooke, California."

82. "500 German Sent to New Prison Camp South of City," *Bakersfield Californian*, October 20, 1945, p. 7; "Two More Camp Activated next Week," *Cooke Clarion*, October 12, 1945, p. 4; historical briefs, A.G. Form 1-8, "Prisoner of War Camp, Camp Cooke, California."

83. Diary of Heinrich Schünemann, 1944–1947; "500 Germans Sent to New Prison Camp South of City," *Bakersfield Californian,* October 20, 1945, p. 7.

84. Historical briefs, A.G. Form 1-8, "Prisoner of War Camp, Camp Cooke, California."

85. "Cotton Picking War Prisoners Due at Air Base," *Delano Record,* October 26, 1945, p. 1; William J. Taylor Jr., telephone conversation with author, December 20, 1993. During the war, the Delano airfield served as an emergency and practice landing field for Army Air Force planes, and housed P-61 Black Widow aircraft crews from Hammer Field at Fresno, California. These crews were completing their last leg of flight training at Delano before going overseas. See "German Prisoners Housed in Delano Airport Barracks," *Bakersfield Californian,* October 30, 1945, p. 9.

86. "500 Germans at Delano Air Base Help in Cotton," *Delano Record,* November 2, 1945, p. 6.

87. "PW Base Will Be Run From Here," *Cooke Clarion,* November 9, 1945, p. 3.

88. "German Prisoners of War Answer They're Democrats, Not Nazis Now," *Delano Record,* January 18, 1946, p. 1; "Last German War Prisoners Leave Delano," *Delano Record,* March 26, 1946, p. 1.

89. Historical briefs, A.G. Form 1-8, "Prisoner of War Camp, Camp Cooke, California"; "Camps Inactivated– 9th Service Command, Camp Buttonwillow," January 1946, RG 389, PMGO, Enemy POW Information Bureau, box 2511, entry 461, MMB-NA.

90. Historical briefs, A.G. Form 1-8, "Prisoner of War Camp, Camp Cooke, California"; "PW Base Will Be Run From Here," *Cooke Clarion,* November 9, 1945, p. 3.

91. "History of Air Corps Training Detachment Tulare, California, 5 February 1941 to 7 December 1941" and "Final Installment of History of Rankin Academy and 3050th AAF Base Unit, 1 May 1945 to 27 June 1945," roll no. A2501, call no. 234.703, station histories, Rankin, Air Force Historical Research Agency, Maxwell AFB, Alabama; Walt Bohrer, *Black Cats and Outside Loops* (Oregon City, Oreg.: Plere Publishers, 1989), p. 174.

92. "Sign Contract Today for POW at Rankin Field," *Visalia (Calif.) Times-Delta,* November 17, 1945, p. 1; "German Prisoners at Rankin Field," *Visalia (Calif.) Times-Delta,* December 3, 1945, p. 1.

93. "German Prisoners at Rankin Field," *Visalia (Calif.) Times-Delta,* December 3, 1945, p. 1; historical briefs, A.G. Form 1-8, "Prisoner of War Camp, Camp Cooke, California."

94. "Summarization History of Lemoore Army Air Field, 3 Feb. 1941–22 Sept. 1945," roll no. B2331, call no. 285.65-1A, station histories, Lemoore, Air Force Historical Research Agency, Maxwell AFB, Alabama; "Lemoore Field Becomes Sub-base of Pinedale," *Casual Observer,* Lemoore Army Air Field, Lemoore, California, October 6, 1945, p. 3; "Army Officer Clarifies Question Over Surplus Property at Lemoore Army Air Field," *Hanford Daily Sentinel,* January 9, 1946, pp. 1, 8; "3 More Camps Activated Next Week," *Cooke Clarion,* November 23, 1945, p. 1; historical briefs, A.G. Form 1-8, "Prisoner of War Camp, Camp Cooke, California."

95. "Army Officer Clarifies Question Over Surplus Property at Lemoore Army Air Field," *Hanford Daily Sentinel,* January 9, 1946, pp. 1, 8; historical briefs, A.G. Form 1-8, "Prisoner of War Camp, Camp Cooke, California"; "German PWs to Start Home Jan. 26," *Cooke Clarion,* January 25, 1946, p. 2.

Chapter 8. Auf Wiedersehen

1. "Employers Urged to Replace POWs," *Palisades,* August 15, 1945, p. 2; "War Captives in the U.S. to Be Gone by Spring; Total of Prisoners Here Is Put at 417,034," *New York Times,* September 13, 1945, p. 5.

2. Krammer, *Nazi Prisoners of War,* pp. 231–32; "War's End Will Not Rob Farmers of Prisoner Aid," *Fresno Bee,* May 8, 1945, p. 8; "Paroling of Prisoners for Farms Proposed," *Visalia (Calif.) Times-Delta,* December 20, 1945, p. 1.

Notes

3. "Coastal War Prisoner Camp Closed by Operating Association," *Santa Barbara News-Press*, December 3, 1945, p. B-3; Krammer, *Nazi Prisoners of War*, pp. 234–35.

4. The ship's namesake, Frances Y. Slanger, was a Jewish Army nurse killed in a German artillery bombardment in Elsenborn, Belgium, on October 21, 1944. On the night before her unit was attacked, Slanger wrote a letter to the military newspaper *Stars and Stripes*, lauding the American soldier that fought the war while downplaying her own contribution. The letter was published posthumously and elicited a tremendous response for this nurse who cared so deeply for others. In honor of her service, a cruise ship, converted into a hospital ship to return wounded American soldiers from Europe, was commissioned in June 1945 as the *Frances Y. Slanger*. See Bob Welch, *American Nightingale: The Story of Frances Slanger, Forgotten Heroine of Normandy* (New York: Atria Books, 2004).

5. "Camp Shanks Ends War Missions As Last German PW's Start Home," *New York Times*, July 23, 1946, p. 27; Alfred Schmucker, letter to author, March 29, 1990; Helmut Wolter, letter to author, January 28, 1993; Leonhard Reul, letter to author, May 28, 1991; Krammer, *Nazi Prisoners of War*, pp. 221–22.

6. "1,975 German PW's Leave for Reich," *New York Times*, December 8, 1945, p. 9; memorandum, Gerald R. Murphy, Major AGD, adjutant, HQ PW Camp, Camp Cooke, March 6, 1946.

7. Wesley W. Purkiss, comp. "A History of Camp Cooke, 1941 to 1946," April 27, 1946, p. 68; "German PWs to Start Home Jan. 26," *Cooke Clarion*, January 5, 1946, p. 2; "German Prisoners Being Shipped," *Lompoc Record*, March 21, 1946, n.p.; "Three Prisoners Escape at Cooke," *Lompoc Record*, May 2, 1946, p. 8; historical briefs, A.G. Form 1-8, "Prisoner of War Camp, Camp Cooke, California."

8. "Camp Shanks Ends War Missions As Last German PW's Start Home," *New York Times*, July 23, 1946, p. 27; Lewis and Mewha, *Prisoner of War Utilization*, p. 91; Krammer, *Nazi Prisoners of War*, p. 255.

9. Krammer, *Nazi Prisoners of War*, pp. 247, 249–50; Alfred Schmucker, letters to author, June 17, 1990, and February 20, 1993; Werner Blanck, letter to author, October 20, 1989.

10. The garments and shoes most likely belonged to the former inmates at the concentration camp. After its liberation on April 29, 1945, Dachau temporarily housed displaced persons. From July 1945 through August 1948, the U.S. Army's Counterintelligence Corps used much of the camp to detain captured SS members from the region, and was the scene of the Dachau trials for Nazi war criminals.

Chapter 9. Epilogue

1. Historical vignette, "The Heritage of Vandenberg Air Force Base," Jeffrey Geiger, 30th Space Wing History Office, November 1993; real property accountable records for buildings 12300 and 123001, 30th Space Wing Real Estate Office, Vandenberg AFB, California.

2. Elizabeth Hvolboll, telephone conversation with author, September 12, 1993; Leslie Freeman, interview by author, Goleta, California, September 21, 1993.

3. Don MacMillan, interview by author, Tipton, California, November 8, 1990; Don MacMillan, telephone conversation with author, May 16, 1991; Mary Ann Faria-Silva, telephone conversation with author, August 10, 1993.

4. Candy Harper, Public Affairs Office, Lemoore Naval Air Station, Lemoore, California, letter to author, November 7, 1990; Dave Fraker, Public Affairs Office, Lemoore Naval Air Station, Lemoore, California, telephone conversation with author, December 2, 1993; Dave Fraker, "Navy's First 2,000 Acres a Token Good Will Gesture," *Golden Eagle*, July 15, 1988.

5. http://www.chinofairgrounds.com/index.php (accessed June 28, 2016); Alice Reher, Chino Historical Society, Chino, California, letter to author, October 21, 1993; Phyllis Outhier, Chino Historical Society, Chino, California, letter to author, November 6, 1993.

6. Tom Hennion, Tulare Historical Society, Tulare, California, letter to author, August 14, 1990; Tom Hennion, telephone conversation with author, September 10, 1993.

7. Spencer B. Stallings, telephone conversation with author, December 7, 1992.

8. William Schneider, telephone conversation with author, October 10, 1993; Robert Steele, telephone conversation with author, October 10, 1993.

9. William J. Taylor Jr., telephone conversation with author, December 20, 1993.

Abbreviations and Glossary

Afrika Korps. *See* **DAK.**

Afrikaner. A member of the Deutsche Afrika Korps (DAK).

AGO. Adjutant General's Office.

ASF. Army Service Forces.

Bundeswehr. The German army after World War II.

C Ration. A U.S. Army field ration consisting of three B (bread) and three M (meat) components for meals arranged into six combinations, two each for breakfast, dinner, and supper. The ration also included an accessory packet comprised of nine cigarettes, halazone water purification tablets, book matches, toilet paper, chewing gum, and an opener for the meat cans.

DAF. Deutsche Arbeitsfront. German Labor Front. The sole and compulsory labor organization permitted in Nazi Germany.

DAK. Deutsches Afrika Korps. The German Africa Corps motorized part of Field Marshal Erwin Rommel's forces in North Africa, 1941-43.

Der Lagerspiegel. *The Camp Mirror.* The officially sanctioned POW newspaper published at Camp Cooke.

Der Ruf. *The Call.* The German POW newspaper, part of the War Department's reeducation program, published at Fort Philip Kearney, Rhode Island.

Deutsche Jungvolk. German Young People. A wing of the Hitlerjugend for younger boys 10 to 14 years old.

Deutschemark. German monetary unit after 1948.

Ersatz Abteilung. Replacement Unit.

Fallschirmjäger Regiment. Parachute Regiment.

FBI. Federal Bureau of Investigation.

Feldwebel. German army rank, roughly equivalent to a staff sergeant in the U.S. Army.

Flak. Abbreviation for Flugabwehrkanone. Antiaircraft gun. In English, Flak refers to the gunfire.

Führerhauptquartier. Adolf Hitler's field headquarters, known to the world as the Wolfschanze (Wolf's Lair).

G-2. The intelligence section of the American Army.

Gefreiter. German army rank, roughly equivalent to private first class in the U.S. Army.

Gestapo. Geheime Staatspolizei. The secret state police. A well-publicized enforcement agency closely intertwined with the SS.

GI. Government Issue. The nickname given to American soldiers during World War II.

Goums. North African (Moroccan) tribesmen recruited as soldiers under French command.

Halma. A board game.

Hitlerjugend. Hitler Youth. A league for teenage boys aged 14 to 18, and one of many different state-sponsored youth organizations indoctrinated with National Socialism.

Infanterie Sturmabzeichen. Infantry Assault Badge.

Ju. Junker. From the aircraft factory by the same name that produced the Ju 52 three-engine transport aircraft.

Kampfstaffel des Oberbefehlshabers. Battle Staff of the Commander in Chief.

Kettenhunde. Lit. "Chain dogs." Pejorative term for the German military police who wore metal crescent gorgets around their necks suspended by a chain.

Kompaniesprecher. Company spokesman.

KP. Kitchen Police.

Kraderkunderzug. Motorcycle Reconnaissance Platoon.

K Ration. A more compact and improved packaging variation of the C ration that evolved into the one-package breakfast-dinner-supper combination used first by U.S. paratroopers. The three-meal combination included meat products, biscuits, various confections, and beverage components.

Lagerpolizei. Camp Police.

Lagersprecher. Camp Spokesman.

Landesschützen-Regiment der Luftwaffe. Luftwaffe Ground Defense Regiment.

Leichte Flakabteilung. Light Antiaircraft Unit.

Luftwaffe. Air Weapon. The German Air Force.

Marschbataillon z.b.V. [zur besonderen Verfügung]. March Battalion for Special Details.

Me 109. Messerschmitt aircraft.

Medaille Winterschlacht im Osten, 1941-42. Medal for the Winter Battle in the East, 1941-42. Known to German soldiers as the "Cold Cuts Order" or the "Frozen Flesh Medal" for the brutal winter conditions on the Eastern Front.

MMB–NA. Modern Military Branch–National Archives.

Munich Agreement. The agreement signed between Great Britain, France, Italy, and Germany that surrendered the Czechoslovakian Sudetenland to Germany in September 1938.

Nachrichtendienst. Communications Service.

USDStB. Nationalsozialistischer Deutscher Studentenbund. National Socialist German Students' League.

NSKK. Nationalsozialistisches Kraftfahrkorps. National Socialist Motor Corps.

Nazi. A member of the Nationalsozialistiche Deutsche Arbeiterpartei (NSDAP). National Socialist German Workers' Party.

NCO. Noncommissioned Officer.

Obergefreiter. German army rank roughly equivalent to corporal in the U.S. Army.

Panzer. Abbreviation for Panzerwagen. Tank vehicle.

Panzergräben. Tank trap.

Panzerjäger-Ersatz-Abteilung. Antitank Replacement Unit.

Panzernachrichten Abteilung. Tank Communications Unit.

Panzersperren. Antitank obstacles, typically large concrete blocks.

Plattdeutsch. The collective term for German dialect.

PMGO. Provost Marshal General's Office.

POW. Prisoner of war.

PW. A variation of the abbreviation for Prisoner of war.

Regiment Grossdeutschland. A regiment of the SS or Schutzstaffel.

RAD. Reichsarbeitsdienst. National Labor Service. Service usually performed following time in the Hitlerjugend and before entering full military service.

Reichsmark. The monetary unit of Germany from 1924 to 1948.

SA. Sturmabteilung. Assault Unit/Storm Unit. They were a paramilitary wing of the Nazi Party.

Sanitätskraftwagen. An ambulance.

Schlägertruppen. Military thugs, usually Nazi stalwarts.

Schnaps. Alcoholic spirits.

Schwere Flak-Ersatz-Abteilung. Heavy Antiaircraft Replacement Unit.

SCU. Service Command Unit. In commenting on the quality of personnel assigned to SCU units, American servicemen sarcastically referred to them as the "Sick, Crippled, and Useless."

SGO. Surgeon General's Office.

Skat. A German card game.

Soldat. German army rank, roughly equivalent to a buck private in the U.S. Army.

SS. Schutzstaffel. The so-called Nazi elite corps and originally the protective guard of the Nazi Party. It carried out special police duties, controlled concentration and extermination camps, and had its own military formations. Heinrich Himmler was chief of the SS.

Sturmbataillon. Assault Battalion.

Unterfeldwebel. German army rank, roughly equivalent to a sergeant in the U.S. Army.

UvD. Unteroffzier vom Dienst. Noncommissioned Officer of the Day.

VE Day. Victory in Europe Day.

Vergangenheitsbewältigung. Coming to terms with the past.

Volkssturm. People's Storm. The German Home Guard drawn from conscripts of young boys and older men, established in October 1944.

WAC. Women's Army Corps.

WD. War Department.

Waffen SS. The military wing of the SS or Schutzstaffel.

Wehrmacht. The German Armed Forces.

Bibliography

Archival Sources

Records of the Provost Marshal General's Office, Prisoner of War Division, 1941–1946. Special Projects Division, 1943–1946. RG 389. MMB-NA.
Records of the Army Adjutant General's Office, Operations Branch. Classified Decimal File, Decimal File 1940–1945. RG 407. MMB-NA.
Records of the Surgeon General's Office, Geographic Series 1943–1944 and 1944–1946. RG 112. NRC-NA.
Index to "Prisoner of War Camp, Camp Cooke, California," National Archives Branch, Kansas City, Missouri.
U.S. Army Military History Institute, Carlisle Barracks, Pennsylvania.
Golden Gate National Cemetery, San Bruno, California.
Department of Health Services, Office of the State Registrar of Vital Statistics, Sacramento, California.
Air Force Historical Research Agency, Maxwell AFB, Alabama.

Unpublished Manuscripts

"History of Air Corps Training Detachment Tulare, California, 5 February 1941 to 7 December 1941" and "Final Installment of History of Rankin Academy and 3050th AAF Base Unit, 1 May 1945 to 27 June 1945." Air Force Historical Research Agency, Maxwell AFB, Alabama.
Koehler, Franz A. *Special Rations for the Armed Forces*. QMC Historical Studies, series 2, no. 6. Historical Branch, Office of the Quartermaster General, Washington, D.C., 1958.
"Office of the Provost Marshal General; World War II. A Brief History." Provost Marshal General's Office. Department of the Army. Washington, D.C., January 15, 1946.
Purkiss, Wesley W., comp. "A History of Camp Cooke, 1941 to 1946." April 27, 1946.
"Summarization History of Lemoore Army Air Field, 3 Feb. 1941 – 2 Sept. 1945." Air Force Historical Research Agency. Maxwell AFB, Alabama.
Technical Manual, TM 19-500. "Enemy Prisoners of War." United States War Department. Washington, D.C., October 5, 1944.

Newspapers

Advance-Register [Tulare, California]
Arvin [California] *Tiller*
Bakersfield Californian
Casual Observer [Lemoore, California]
Chino [California] *Champion*
Cooke [California] *Clarion*
Corcoran [California] *Journal*
Delano [California] *Record*
Der Lagerspiegel [Camp Cooke, California]
Fresno [California] *Bee*

Golden Eagle [Lemoore, California]
Hanford [California] *Daily Sentinel*
Lompoc [California] *Record*
Los Angeles Times
New York Times
Palisades [Camp Shanks, New York]
San Diego Union
Santa Barbara [California] *News-Press*
Santa Maria [California] *Daily Times*
Shafter [California] *Press*
Van Nuys [California] *News and Valley Green Sheet*
Ventura County [California] Star-Free Press
Visalia (Calif.) Times-Delta
Wasco [California] *News*

Miscellaneous Documents

"Building Location Plan," sheet 2. Camp Cooke Prisoner of War Camp, April 1944, U.S. Army, Corps of Engineers.
"Christmas 1944." Program Booklet, PW Detachment, SCU 1908, Camp Cooke, California.
Diary of Hans-Joachim Böttcher, 1944–1948.
Diary of Heinrich Schünemann, 1944–1947.
First Lieutenant John T. Pellew, CMP. "Statement of John T. Pellew, 0-1288608, Taken by Post Inspector." November 21, 1944.
"General Plan and Schedule Sheet," sheet 1. Camp Cooke Prisoner of War Camp, April 1944, U.S. Army, Corps of Engineers.
"Guard Orders." Stockade Order No. 6, Prisoner of War Camp, Camp Cooke, California, June 20, 1944.
"Guard Towers," sheet 9. Camp Cooke Prisoner of War Camp April 1944, U.S. Army, Corps of Engineers.
"Individual Pay Data Record." WD AGO Form 19-13, Werner Blanck, August 1945 to March 15, 1946.
"Individual Pay Data Record." WD PMG Form No. 20, Werner Blanck, June 18, 1943 to August 1944.
Memorandum. Gerald R. Murphy, major AGD, adjutant, HQ PW Camp, Camp Cooke, March 6, 1946.
Special Orders. Army Service Forces, Ninth Service Command, Camp Cooke, California, incomplete set 1944–1946.
"Standard Operating Procedure and Security Regulations." Prisoner of War Camp, Camp Cooke, California, July 1, 1944.
"Wie Man Baumwolle Pflücken Muss." Leaflet, Co-operative Extension Work in Agriculture and Home Economics, University of California, and United States Department of Agriculture Co-operating, October 1944.

Books

Angolia, John R. *For Führer and Fatherland: Military Awards of the Third Reich*. 3rd ed. San Jose, Calif.: R. James Bender, 1987.
Arad, Yitzhak. *The Holocaust in the Soviet Union*. Translated by Ora Cummings. Lincoln, Neb.: University of Nebraska Press, 2013.

Arax, Mark, and Rick Wartzman. *The King of California: J. G. Boswell and the Making of a Secret American Empire,* New York: Public Affairs, 2003.
Argyle, Christopher, comp. *Chronology of World War II.* London: Marshall Cavendish Books, 1980.
Bevans, Charles I., comp. *Treaties and Other Agreements of the United States of America 1776–1949.* Vol. 2. Department of State. Washington, D.C.: Government Printing Office, 1969.
Bohrer, Walt. *Black Cats and Outside Loops.* Oregon City, Oreg.: Plere, 1989.
Craven, Wesley F., and James L. Cate, eds. *The Army Air Forces in World War II.* Vol. 3, *Europe: Argument to V-E Day, January 1944 to May 1945.* Chicago: University of Chicago Press, 1951. Reprint. Office of Air Force History, Washington, D.C., 1983.
Eisenhower, Dwight D. *Crusade in Europe.* Baltimore: Johns Hopkins University Press, 1997.
Espenshade, Edward B. Jr., ed. *Goode's World Atlas.* 17th ed. Chicago: Rand McNally, 1987.
Galgiani, John H. "Coccidioidomycosis." In *Cecil Textbook of Medicine,* edited by James B. Wyngaarden, Lloyd H. Smith, and J. Claude Bennett. Philadelphia: W. B. Saunders, 1992.
Gansberg, Judith M. *Stalag: U.S.A.* New York: Crowell, 1977.
Gellately, Robert. *Backing Hitler: Consent and Coercion in Nazi Germany.* New York: Oxford University Press, 2001.
Gilbert, Martin. *Auschwitz and the Allies.* New York: Holt, Reinhart, and Winston, 1981.
Goure, Leon. *The Siege of Leningrad.* Stanford, Calif.: Stanford University Press, 1962.
Grunberger, Richard. *The 12-Year Reich: A Social History of Nazi Germany 1933–1945,* New York: Holt, Rinehart and Winston, 1971.
Gutiérrez, David G. ed. *Between Two Worlds: Mexican Immigration in the United States,* 4th ed., Wilmington, Del.: Scholarly Resources, 2001.
Heckmann, Wolff. *Rommel's War in Africa.* Garden City, New York: Doubleday, 1981.
Heer, Hannes and Klaus Naumann, eds. *War of Extermination: The German Military in World War II, 1941-1944.* New York: Berghahn Books, 2000.
Hörner, Helmut. *A German Odyssey: The Journal of a German Prisoner of War.* Translated and edited by Allen Kent Powell. Golden, Colo.: Fulcrum, 1991.
Kay, Alex J. *The Making of an SS Killer: The Life of Colonel Alfred Filbert, 1905-1990.* New York: Cambridge University Press, 2016.
Kimball, Warren F. *Swords or Ploughshares? The Morgenthau Plan for Defeated Nazi Germany, 1943–1946.* Philadelphia: J. B. Lippincott, 1976.
Kershaw, Ian. *To Hell and Back: Europe 1914 – 1949.* New York: Viking, 2015.
Krammer, Arnold. *Nazi Prisoners of War in America.* Reprint. Chelsea, Mich.: Scarborough House, 1991.
Lewis, George, and John Mewha. *History of Prisoner of War Utilization by the United States Army, 1776–1945.* Pamphlet No. 20-213. Washington, D.C.: Department of the Army, 1955.
Lipstadt, Deborah E. *Denying the Holocaust: The Growing Assault on Truth and Memory.* New York: Free Press, 1993.

Lumsden, Robin. *The Collector's Guide to Third Reich Militaria.* New York: Hippocrene Books, 1987.

MacDonald, Charles B. *A Time For Trumpets.* New York: William Morrow, 1985.

Medical Department of the United States Army in World War II, Clinical Series: vol. IV, *Preventive Medicine in World War II; Communicable Diseases Transmitted Chiefly Through Respiratory and Alimentary Tracts,* chapter XVI, Coccidioidomycosis. Washington, D.C.: Office of the Surgeon General, Department of the Army, 1958.

Millett, John D. *The Army Service Forces: The Organization and Role of the Army in World War II.* Washington, D.C.: Office of the Chief of Military History, Department of the Army, 1954.

Moore, John Hammond. *The Faustball Tunnel.* New York: Random House, 1978.

Munro, David, ed. *Chambers World Gazetteer.* Cambridge: Cambridge University Press, 1988.

O'Hara, Vincent P. *Struggle for the Middle Sea: The Great Navies at War in the Mediterranean Theater, 1940–1945.* Annapolis, Maryland: Naval Institute Press, 2009.

Piekalkiewicz, Janusz. *Sea War 1939–1945.* Poole, England: Blandford, 1987.

Read, Anthony. *The Devil's Disciples: Hitler's Inner Circle.* New York: W.W. Norton & Company, 2004.

Seltzer, Leon E. *The Columbia Lippincott Gazetteer of the World.* New York: Columbia University Press, 1962.

Simpson, J. A., and E. S. C. Weiner, *The Oxford English Dictionary.* 2nd ed. Oxford: Clarendon Press, 1989.

Spector, Shmuel and Geoffrey Wigoder, eds. *Encyclopedia of Jewish Life Before and During the Holocaust.* Vol. 3, New York: New York University Press, 2001.

Taylor, A. J. P. *The Second World War: An Illustrated History.* New York: G. P. Putnam's Sons, 1975.

The New International Atlas. Chicago: Rand McNally, 1981.

U.S. Bureau of Census. *Historical Statistics of the United States: Colonial Time* to 1970. Part 2. Washington, D.C.: Government Printing Office, 1975.

Welch, Bob. *American Nightingale: The Story of Frances Slanger, Forgotten Heroine of Normandy.* New York: Atria Books, 2004.

Wyman, David S. *The Abandonment of the Jews: America and the Holocaust, 1941–1945.* New York: Pantheon Books, 1984.

Internet Sites

Chino POW camp. http://www.chinofairgrounds.com

Medical Department of the United States Army in World War II. http://history.amedd.army.mil/booksdocs/wwii/PM4/default.htm

Index

Note: Names listed in **bold** are the primary interviewees. Page numbers listed in **bold** refer to illustrations. Page numbers listed in *italics* refer to tables. The letter "n" following a page number refers to an endnote and is followed by a note number. For instance, 241n28 means page 241, note 28.

Abbeville, France, 26
Abbott and Costello, 119
Abe Lincoln in Illinois (film), 119
Achmer, Germany, 20
Adana (ship), 16
Aemmler, Karl, 187
Afrika Korps. *See* Germany military
Agina (ship), 17
Alex, Pfc. Leon, 190
Alexander, Mrs., 92
Algiers, Algeria, 9, 17, 32
Allison, June, 125
"Alte Kameraden" (song), 59
American military: 4
    II Army Corps, 19
    Third Army, 227
    Fourth Air Force, 200
    Ninth Service Command, 46, 62, 63, 178, 187, 196, 200
    101st Airborne Division, 27
    1021st Engineers Treadway Bridge Company, 198
    Army Service Forces, 62
    Service Command Unit 1908, 62
    Service Command Unit 1909, 183
    Service Command Unit 1946, 187, 195, 196
    WAC (Women's Army Corps), 39
    Western Flying Training Command, 200
American Red Cross, 133
Anti-Semitism, 123, 137, **138**
Apel, Gustav, 145
Arab Legion, 18
Arabs, 18, 24
Argentina, 145
Argentina (ship), 36
Ariana, Tunisia, 17
Arnold, Jim, 112
Arta (ship), 17
Articles of War (U.S.), 90
Arvin Tiller, 173
Aryan, 15, 179
Athens, Greece, 13

Athrops, Rev. E., 198

Bad Aibling, Germany, **205**, 208
Bailey, Doris, 108-9, **109**, 125
Bailey, Cpl. Ray A., 97, 125, 161
Bakersfield Californian, 173
Bankrath, Walter, 81
Barbian, Robert, 187
Baumholder, Germany, 16
Bear, M/Sgt. Jack, 93
Belgium, 8, 9, 16, 26, 136, 206, 209, 210, 211, 212, 214
"Bell Bottom Trousers" (song), 124
Belorussia, 10
Bendoski, Lawrence H., 199
Benny Fox circus, 241n28
Bensburg, W. J., 187
Berbers, 12
Berck-sur-Mer, France, 20
Bergman, Ingrid, 124
Berkemer, Willie, 174, *174*
Berlin, Irving, 116, 125
Berlin Symphonic Orchestra, 18
Bernkastel-Kues, Germany, 28
Bieber Mr., 94
Bir M'cherga, Tunisia, 24
Bishop, Sgt., 112
Bizerte, Tunisia, 24
Blacky, 111
Blanck, Werner, 13, 35, 56-57, 72, **72**, 85, 92, **117**, 125-26, 134, 149, 207-8, 218, 224
Bleckert, Jürgen, 127
Blenheim bombers (aircraft), 10
Bong, Maj. Richard I., 200
Borna, Germany, 22
Boston, Massachusetts, 32, 40
Boswell Ranch, J. G. *See* Camp Boswell
Böttcher, Hans-Joachim, 25-26, 40, 49-50, 77, **77**, 78, 92-95, 111-12, **117**, 126-27, 134-35, 139-40, 142, 166-67, 206-7, 218, 225
Bou Arfa, Morocco, 22
Boyer, Capt. Ralph G., 94

263

Bracero Program, 86, 201. *See also*
  Mexican farm laborers
Bremen, Germany, 13, 27, 204, 213, 227
Bretzenheim, Germany, 217
British military: 4, 8, 9, 10, 13, 16, 20
  Eighth Army, 20
  14th Destroyer Flotilla, 235n10
Brooke, Sgt. Milton, 102
Brown, Capt. Dan W., 179, 190, 192
Brown, Capt. Robert J., 186
Buchner, "Peppi," 127
Büdingen, Germany, 18
Bueltmann, Rev. A. J., 198
Bützow, Germany, 25

C rations, 37, 38
California, 3, 4, 35, 47, 50, 51, 58, 80,
  121, 187, 201, 213, 216, 218
California Agricultural Extension Service,
  89, 187, 197
California Department of Agriculture, 181
California Packing Corporation
  (Wisconsin), 61
Camp 101, Wales, 216-17
Camp 131, Algeria, 25
Camp 210, Algeria, 17, 32
Camp 294 (Fisher's Camp), England, 210
Camp 2218, Belgium, 206, 209
Camp 2221, Belgium, 206, 212
Camp 2225, Belgium, 209, 212
Camp 2228, Belgium, 209
Camp Ayers, California. *See* Camp Chino
Camp Bodesford, Scotland, 217
Camp Bolbec, France, 204, 208, 213
Camp Boswell (Corcoran), California, 87,
  119, 145, 146, 149, 170, 171, 172,
  177, 186-87, 222, 248n 37
Camp Bury, England, 26
Camp Buttonwillow, California, 3, *177,*
  199, 222
Camp Cattistock, England, 215, 216
Camp Chino, California, 3, 47, 51, 52,
  132, 135, 143, *177,* 182-84, 223-
  24, 236n8
Camp Clarinda, Iowa, 187
Camp Clark, Missouri, 140, 146, 226
Camp Concordia, Kansas, 33, 58
Camp Cooke military installation, 3
Camp Cooke POW camp:
  activation of, 3
  branch camps assigned to, 3, 4, 177-200
  canteen coupons, 49, 78, 85, 87, 92,
    124, 162, **162**, 163, 206
  canteen for, 48, 49, 53, 57, 92, 106,
    119, 124, 161-62

closure of, 3, 203, 222, **223**
design and construction of, 62-63, **65**,
  66
first German POWs at, 63, 66
guards and camp personnel, 64-66,
  108, 110
  commanding officers, *64*
  excesses by guards, 102, 108, 147,
    179
  fraternization with POWs, 5, 51, 98,
    99-100, 106, 108-9, 110-11, 112-
    13, 126, 179, 193.
  See under Labor Program by POWs
POW hospital at, 62, 63, **65**, 74, 102,
  170, 222
POW organization at, 67-69, 73-74
POW population at, 3, 4, 66-67
Camp Cranwich, England, 209
Camp Custer, Michigan, 37, 60
Camp Delano, California, 3, 107, 132,
  141-42, *177,* 198-99, 217, 224
Camp Edwards Ranch (Goleta) California,
  3, 82, 96, 106-7, 119, 123, 132,
  135, 145, 147, 169, 171, *177,* 178,
  184, **184**, 185, **185**, 186, 222
Camp Ellis, Illinois, 60-61
Camp Eloy II, Arizona, 49-50
Camp Eureka, Illinois, 60
Camp Florence, Arizona, 2, 38, 39, 40,
  43, 46, 47, 49, 50, 51, 76, 78
Camp Goleta, California. *See* Camp
  Edwards Ranch
Camp Grant, Wisconsin, 61
Camp Hearne, Texas, 2
Camp Lakeland (Corcoran), California,
  119, 170, 171, 172, *177,* 187,
  195-96, 222
Camp Lamont, California, 3, 91, 119,
  131-32, 141, 170, 171, 172, 173-
  74, *174, 177,* 178, 179, 187, 194-
  95, 198, 211, 222, 238n11
Camp Lemoore, California, 3, *177,* 179,
  196, 198, 200, 206, 210, 211, 222,
  223
Camp Lodi, Wisconsin, 61, 198
Camp McCoy, Wisconsin, 187
Camp Old River, California, 3, 81, 106,
  131, 140-41, 143, 144-45, *177,*
  198, 222, 236n9
Camp Oldham, England, 32
Camp Phillips, Kansas, 18, 33, 58-59
Camp Pinedale, California, 200
Camp Pomona, California, 52, 183, 195,
  196. *See also* Pomona Ordnance
  Depot

264

Index

Camp Rankin (Tulare), California, *177,* 178, 199, 200, 224
Camp Rupert, Idaho, 53, 95, 103, 146, 149, 189, 215
Camp Saticoy, California, 3, 119, 169, 171, 172, *177,* 197-98, 224
Camp Shafter, California, 3, 87, 92, 97, 119, 123, 170, 171, 172, *177,* 179, 187, 188, **188**, 189, **189**, 190, **191**, 192-93
Camp Shanks, New York, 201, 204, 206, 207, 208, 209, 210, 211, 212, 216, 226,
Camp Sudbury 23, England, 209
Camp Tachi Farms (Corcoran), California, *177,* 178, 199, 222
Camp Tagus Ranch (Tulare), California, 35, 66, 87, 96, 104, 105, 113, 119, 131, 132, 133, 140, 166, 169, 170, 171, *177,* 179, **180**, 181, **181**, 182, 193, 222
Camp Tipton, California, 3, 52, 87, 119, 170, 171, 172, *177,* 178, 193, 196, 222, 223
Camp Tooele, Utah. See Camp Warner
Camp Trinidad, Colorado, 35, 56-57
Camp Tulare County Fairgrounds (Tulare), California, 3, 87, 119, 171, *177,* 178, 193, 224
Camp Warner, Utah, 35, 57, 58, 59-60, 66, 71, 73, 75, 133
Camp-West-Lowe Farms Co., 187
Canadian Ace beer, 60-61
Canadian military, 28, 40
Cap Bon, Tunisia, 10, 24
Carentan, France, 27
Casablanca, Morocco, 9, 33, 35
Caserta, Italy, 20
Chansy, Algeria, 20
Chapel Hill Victory (ship), 206
Chappell, Capt. C. W., 194
Cherbourg, France, 31
Chino Fair Association, 224
Christiansen, Karl, 74
Civilian Conservation Corps, 186
Clifford, Col. Charles L., *64,* 111
Coaldale (ship), 213
Coast Farm Labor Association, 178
Coberly West Ginning Co., 187
Coccidioidomycosis, 170
concentration camps, 133, 134, 135, 136, 143, 164, 167, 209, 216, 220, 242n10, 244n64, 253n10
Concordat of 1933, 242n39
Constantine, Algeria, 10, 12, 19, 20, 22, 35

Cooke Clarion, 144
Co-Operative Gin Co., 187
Crete, 23
Crosby, Bing, 37, 123, 125
Curtis, Capt. Claude L., 105, 182, 219

D. C. Moore Gin Co., 187
Dachau, Germany, 209, 210, 216, 253n10
Dahlmann, Alfred, 68
Daley, Capt. Rudolph J., 193
Dammel, Lt. Theodore, 64
Davis, Mr. 94
Dawson, Capt. Lyle T., 183
De Groodt, Capt. Franklin T., 141, 142, 186, 190, **191**, 193, 199
De Groodt, Helene, 141, 142, 193
Dedow, Richard, 187
Delano Army Air Field, 198, 224. *See also* Camp Delano
Delano Historical Society, 224
Denmark, 13
Der Bibliothekar (musical play), 116
Der Lagerspiegel (newspaper), 5, 67, 103, 120, 123, 141, 174, 190
Der Ruf (newspaper), 114, 123, 124, 127, 240n6
Derna, Libya, 10
Deul, Georg, *174*
Dieppe, France, 9, 28
Dixon, Capt. Royce L., 183, 236n8
Djelfa, Algeria, 14, 24
Doheny, family the, 222
"Don't Fence Me In" (song), 123, 124, 128
Dunkirk evacuation (1940), 8
Durbin, Deanna, 124

Eisenhower, Gen. Dwight D., 96, 244n64
El Alamein, Egypt, 10, 13
Empress of Japan (ship), 32
Everett, Capt. Robert L., 111, 130, 160, 167, 193

Fahnert, Capt. Curtis E., Jr., 186
Faria, Manuel, Jr., 196
Faria, Manuel, Sr., 222
Farm Production Council, 182, 183
FC Schalke 04 soccer club, 226
Federal Bureau of Investigation (FBI), 145, 146, 147, 149
Feinberg, Lt. Raymond, 136, 188, 244n50
Filipino farm laborers, 101
Fischbach, Germany, 31
"Five Minutes More" (song), 124
Flaesheim, Germany, 19

265

Fletcher, Capt. Charles S., Jr., 182, 183, 236n8
Food Rations for German POWs, 14, 26, 31, 33, 35, 37, 38, 40, 42, 43, 46, 47, 56, 80, 163-64, 166, 167, 168, 169, 192, 213, 220
  reduced in spring 1945, 5, 108, 164, 166, 167, 168, 169
  smuggled into Camp Cooke stockade, 167, 168, 169
  tailored to national taste, 163-64
Fort Devens, Massachusetts, 120
Fort Douglas, Utah, 62
Fort Eustis, Virginia, 201, 208
Fort Ord, California, 58, 172, *174*
Fort Philip Kearney, 240n6
Fort Reno, Oklahoma, 90
Foster, Lt. Col. E. I., *64*
Foth, Lt. George W., 64
Foum Defla, Morocco, 12, 22
France, 3, 8
Frances Y. Slanger (ship), 202, 253n4
Frankenberger, Franz, 144
French Foreign Legion, 18, 19, 24
French military, 4, 8, 14, 22, 24, 37, 38, 220
Führerhauptquartier, 21
Fuller, Lt. Col. Francis S., *64*

Gardner, Ava, 125
Garland, Judy, 125
Gelnhausen, Germany, 18
Geneva Convention, 4, 46, 50, 64, 67, 71, 83-84, 86, 89, 90, 91, 95, 103, 104, 113, 161, 164, 169, 176, 178
Gent, Belgium, 26
German Labor Front (DAF), 6
German military:
  1st Panzer Regiment, 21
  4th Antitank Replacement Unit, 22
  6th Parachute Regiment, 26
  9th Antitank Replacement Unit, 18
  15th Panzer Division, 235n9
  16th Motorized Infantry Division, 19
  19th Flak Division, 20
  20th Transport Squadron, 235n10
  33rd Armored Communications Unit, 15, 17
  33rd Infantry Division, 15, 235n9
  33rd Panzer Division, 16
  36th Heavy Antiaircraft Replacement Unit, 20
  84th Infantry Division, 28
  189th Infantry Division, 28
  257th Infantry Regiment, 10
  269th Infantry Division, 13
  490th Infantry Regiment, 13
  605th Flak Battalion, 13
  612th Flak Battalion, 13
  841st Light Antiaircraft Regiment, 9
  999th Infantry Division, 18, 19
  Afrika Korps, 3, 4, 8, 12, 13, 14, 18, 19, 22, 23, 24, 95, 126, 130, 135, 139, 140, 235n10
  Air Fleet Communications School, 20
  Assault Battalion A27, 12
  General Göring Regiment, 21
  Herman Göring Division, 21
  Luftwaffe, 9, 18, 25, 26, 28, 32, 61, 78, 130
  Luftwaffe Ground Defense Regiment, 25
  March Battalion for Special Details, 14
  March Battalion 27, 14
  RAD (Reichsarbeitsdienst), 18, 19, 20, 22, 25, 28, 218
  Regiment Grossdeutschland, 25
  SA (Sturmabteilung), 136
  Volkssturm, 28, 29
  Waffen SS, 4, 6, 15, 25, 28, 105, 136, 139, 140, 141, 234n7
  Wehrmacht, 6, 10, 13, 19, 20, 22, 23, 27, 29, 39, 49, 56, 73, 136, 216
German POWs:
  age at Camp Cooke, 4
  alcohol (POW access to), 4, 49, 60-61, 94, 126, 127, 129, 130-31, 132
  allegations of coddling, 164
  anti-Nazis, 114, 123, 127
  ardent Nazis (Schlägertruppen), 4, 6, 60, 78, 95, 103, 105, 133, 136-37, 138, 139, 140, 141, 145, 146, 173, 183, 195
  atrocity films and POW reaction to, 133-36, 216
  attempts to segregate Nazis from non-Nazis, 4, 95, 136
  camp spokesman (Lagersprecher), 61, 67-68, 69, 76, 77, 78, 97, 109-10, 142
  clothing for, 38, 39, 44, 46, 49, 212, 216, 235n1
  Communist sympathizers, 140
  company spokesman (Kompaniesprecher), 68-69, 74, 160-61
  deaths and burials of, 172, 173, **173**, 174, *174*, **175**
  dental care for, 170-71, 193
  escapes and punishment, 57, 143-61, 186-87, 203, 215, 243n44, 244n53, 244n55, 244n56

Index

impressions of America, 32, 33, 35, 37, 39, 41-42, 42-43, 218, 219, 220
medical care for, 4, 38, 63, 74, 169-70, 182, 185, 189
Nazi salute, 137, 139, 145, 173
postwar readjustment of, 224-27 *passim*
pranks by, 48, 55, 59, 192
processing after capture, 44, 45-46
religious services and attitude toward, 126, 141-42, 143, 190, 195, 198
repatriation. *See* Repatriation of POWs
segregation of offices from enlisted men, 4
transport to America (reason for), 3
German Red Cross, 61, 121
German Young People (Deutsche Jungvolk), 27
Germany:
advance into Russia, 8, 10, 11-12, 13-14, 19
invasion of Western Europe, 8, 9
postwar denazification effort, 7
Gilbert, Werner, 9, **9**, 19, 35, 57-58, 78, 102, 112-13, 130-31, 135, 168, 211, 218, 225
Gilkey, Ralph, 186
Glahn, Elmer C. von, 171, 195
Glasgow, Scotland, 28, 41
Göbbels, Josef, 33
Gödde, Father Franz, 19-20, 32-33, 58, 75, **75**, 102-3, 130, 133, 137, 139, 143, 169, 208, 218, 225
Going My Way (film), 36-37
Gold Flake cigarettes, 17
Golden Gate National Cemetery, 174
Goldman, Dr., 140
Gould, Sgt., 93
Goums, 12
Grable, Betty, 125
Great Britain, 8, 9
Griffin, Lt. Col. Herschel R., 195
Grombalia, Tunisia, 20
Guayule plant, 87, 173, 188, 194, 238n11
Gulliver's Travels (film), 119

Hahn, Helmut, 161, 243n44, 244n56
Halifax, Canada, 13, 35, 40
Hamburg, Germany, 14, 26, 126, 207, 208, 212, 224, 227
Hammamet, Tunisia, 24
Hammond, Gordon, 187
Harris, Capt. John T., 66, **69**, 119, 121, 123, 133, 141

Haussler, Longin, *174*
Hebel, Klaus, 6, 28-29, 31, 42-43, 51, 82, **82**, 106-7, 132, 135, 169, 217, 218, 225
Hebestreit, Günter "Picco," 127
Heide, Germany, 14
Heidelberg, Germany, 15, 206, 213, 227
Heiligenhafen, Germany, 25
Heinz 57 Varieties, 40
Heinze, Georg, *174*
Helenenberg, Germany, 29
Hershey chocolates, 112
Heuberg, Germany, 18
Heydel, Lothar, 93
Hinkelmann, Rudolf, 15-18, 33, 59-60, **70**, 71, **71**, 104, 111, 132-33, 135, 140, 166, 218-19, 226
Hiroshima, Japan, 8
Hitler, Adolf (Führer), 4, 7, 8, 15, 59, 60, 133, 136, 137, 139, 145, 173, 216, 218, 242n39
Hitler Youth (Hitlerjugend) organization, 6, 26, 27
Hoff General Hospital, 186
Holocaust, 6, 133, 216, 220
Honeywell, Chaplain, 93, 94
Hood, Richard B., 145
Hooper Foundation, 172
Hoover, J. Edgar, 146
Hope, Bob, 125
Hoppstädten, Germany, 29
Horn, Kurt, 94
Hupe, Ernst, 173, *174*

"I'm Always Chasing Rainbows" (song), 124
Infanterie Sturmabzeichen (medal), 12
International Red Cross, 44, 61, 68, 71, 121, 125, 129-30, 133, 137, 166, 179, 185
Iserlohn (ship), 17
Italian military, 13, 16, 17, 22, 235n10
Italian POWs, 93, 94, 239n29, 246n85
Italy, 3

Jacobs, Msgr. Anthony, 198
James, Capt. John E., 196
Janus (ship), 235n10
Japan, 8
Japanese-American internment, 193
Japanese POWs, 187, 195, 196
Jarschky, Heinz, 102
Jervis (ship), 235n10
Jews, 6, 93, 119, 134, 135, 137, 234n7, 242n31, 244n64

Johns-Manville Corp., 91, 95, 99, 102, 145
Johnson, Al, 94
Ju 52 (Junker) aircraft, 12, 13, 23

K rations, 26, 37, 149, 213
Kaiserslautern, Germany, 23
Kelmer, Adolf, 27-28, 41-42, 53-56, 79, 80, **80**, 97-101, 129-30, 134, 146, 149-161, 168-69, 213-15, 219, 226
Kerkennah Islands, 17, 235n10
Kersting, Heinrich, 20, 35, 58-59, 73, **73**, 74, 103-4, 110-11, **115**, 125, 139, 143, 161, 168, 210, 219, 226
Kesselring, Field Marshal Albert, 18
Kessler, Col. Wilson C. von, 171
King, Admiral Ernest J., 91
Klouser, Lt. Harold J., 196
Knorr, Lawrence, 1
Köhnlein, Oskar, 145, 147
Komeise, Germany, 10
Krafthofer, Ernst, *174*
Kroemer, Georg, 10, 11, **11**, 12, 38, 50-51, 77, 101, 131, 134, 143, 145-46, 146-49, 215-16, 219, 226
Krummennaab, Germany 18
Kuhner, Josef, 145
Kusserow, Hannes, 94
Kuster, Sgt. 94

Labor Program by POWs:
  farm and government work, 4, 47-48, 49-50, 51, 52, 53, 54, 55, 58-59, 60, 61, 76, 81, 83-107 *passim*, 178-79, 182, 185-86, 189, **189**, 193, 194, 195, 196, 197, 198, 199, 200
  parole plan, 201
  POW relationships with farmers, 48, 51, 89, 101, 104, 105, 107, 194, 196
  skills training for, **88**, 89, **89**, 197
  strikes and punishment, 4, 50, 52, 59, 60, 89, 90, 91-92, 102-3, 105, 183-84
  termination of, 179, 201
  union opposition to, 85, 201
  wages, 84, 87, 121
La Hacienda Ranch, 187
Ladoga, Lake, 14
Lamont Prisoner of War Labor Association, 194
Law for Liberation from National Socialism and Militarism, 7
Le Havre, France, 204, 208, 213, 226
Leipzig, Germany, 23

Lemoore Army Air Field, 170, 182, 200, 223. *See also* Camp Lemoore
Lemoore Naval Air Station (NAS), 223
Leningrad, Russia, 13, 14
Lewinnek, Sgt. Manfred, 119, 120, **120**, 121, 123, 137
Libby's Corp., 60
Lieser, Germany, 28, 29, 217, 225
Life Buoy soap, 38
Life magazine, 123, 124
Lisieux, France, 25
Lis-Sette, Lt. Anthony R., 64
Liverpool, England, 13, 20, 26, 32, 215, 217
Loewen, Hans, 127
Lompoc, California, 86, 91, 98, 99, 102, 104, 145
Lompoc Record, 63
Long, Lt. Col. Arthur P., 170
Los Angeles (ship), 210
Los Angeles County Fairgrounds, 183
Los Angeles Examiner, 47
Los Angeles Times, 145
Los Poso Ranch, 186
Lower Tule River and Pixley Irrigation District Office, 223
Lüdersdorf, Germany, 25
Luftwaffe. *See under* German military
Luga River, 14
Lux soap, 79

Maierhofer, Georg, *174*
Makarounis, Lt. Alexander G., 64
Mallory, Lt. Col. Frank N., 66
Malta, 16
Mangold, Richard, *174*
Mann, Thomas, 121
Marseille, Hans-Joachim, 9
Martin, Richard, 145, 147
Mattick, Walter, *174, 175*
May, Karl, 37, 235n4
McKeever, H. G., 187
Me 109 (Messerschmitt), aircraft, 57, 78
Me 110 (Messerschmitt), aircraft, 16
Me 262 (Messerschmitt), aircraft, 78
Medaille Winterschlacht (medal), 12
Medjez el Bab, Tunisia, 20
Meier, Kurt 145
Metzler, Rolf, 93, 94
Mexican farm laborers, 47, 51, 86, 101, 104, 106, 182, 184, 193, 195, 196.
  See also Bracero Program
Mexico, 86, 146, 147, 149, 158, 159, 160
Meyer, Kurt, 141
Michael, Lt. Glen E., 182
Migletta (or Miglietta), Nando, 51
Miller, Glenn, 116, 125

Index

Miller, Rudy, 112
Mims, Maj. Floyd C., *64*, 111-12
Minter Army Air Field, California, 170, 189
Mitchell, Lt. J. D., 186, 190, **191**
Mohawk (ship), 235n10
Mokrau, Sudetenland, 15
Monroe (ship), 33
Montford, Capt. William H., 194
Moreton-in-Marsh, England, 20, 210
Morgenthau Plan, 235n3
Morocco, 9, 12, 22
Muldoon, Harry, 92
Munich Agreement, 15
Munsterlager, Germany, 207, 208, 210, 212, 214, 216, 217
Murphy, Maj. Gerald, 96

Náchod, Czech Republic, 20
Nagasaki, Japan, 8
Naples, Italy, 13, 16, 19
National Socialism, 6, 7, 114, 121, 123, 141, 142, 242n29, 242n39
National Socialist German Students' League (USDStB), 7
National Socialist Motor Corps (NSKK), 6
National World War II Museum, 1
Nazi atrocities, 135, 137, 164, 216, 234n7, 242n29, 242n31, 244n64
Netherlands, 8
Neustadt an der Waldnaab, Germany, 20
Neustadt in Sachsen, Germany, 22
New Amsterdam (ship), 41
New York, 32, 35, 36, 41, 42-43, 211
New York Times, 123
New Zealand forces, 17
Newport News, Virginia, 33, 38
Newsweek magazine, 123
Niagara Falls, 37
Nicewanger, Capt. A. S., 186
Nigeria, 22
Nordhorn, Germany, 27
Norfolk, Virginia, 32, 33, 35, 38, 39
North Africa, 3, 5, 8, 9, 17, 18, 44, 46
Nubian (ship), 235n10
Nuremberg Tribunal, 242n29
Nussbaum, Rabbi Perry E., 93

O'Brien, Margaret, 124
Operation Torch, 9
Oran, Algeria, 9, 13, 18, 20, 25, 33, 37, 38, 39
Ortner, Lt. John H., 64

Palermo, Italy, 12, 22
Patterson, Undersecretary of War Robert P., 201

Pearl Harbor, Hawaii, 8, 182
Pearson, Drew, 164
Pellew, Capt. John T., 64, **69**, 144, 181, 182, 186
Pereira, Leah, 109
Perret, Maurice, 66, 141
pet animals, 124-25, 129, 132-33, 182, 190
Petersen, Pete, 92
Phillips, Maj. Earl E., 64, *64*
Phillips, Capt. Mark H., 197
Phillips, Capt. William H., 186
Plath, Kurt, 144
Plattdeutsch, 94, 159
Poland, 8, 136
Polish guards, 35
Pomona Ordnance Depot, 177, 183, 195
Pont du Fahs, Tunisia, 14
Porter, Cole, 116, 125
Procter & Gamble Corp., 112
Producers Cotton Oil Co., 199
Producers Gin Co., 187
Provost Marshal General's Office (PMGO), 4, 62, 90, 108, 114, 121, 123, 183

Qattara Depression, Egypt, 23

Rankin Aeronautical Academy, 199-200
Rankin Field, 199-200, 224. *See also* Camp Rankin
Rankin, John G. "Tex," 199-200
Rastenburg, Germany, 21
Reconstruction Finance Corporation, 200
Recreation Program for POWs, 4, 106, 113-19, 121-23, 124, 125, 126-27, 128, 129-30, 131, 132, 177, 183, 184, 185, 190, 194, 197
Reeducation Program for POWs, 4, 113-14, 121, **122**, 123-24, 127, 131, 141, 190, 195, 201-2, 206-7
  atrocity films (showing of), 133-36, 216
  hindrances to, 136
  staffing for, 66, 119-120
  survey to measure effectiveness of, 123-24, 229-33
  See also Der Lagerspiegel and *Der Ruf*
Remington, Lt. Lucius D., 64
Repatriation of POWs, 85, 163, 179, 195, 201, 202, **202**, 203-4, **205**, 206-15, 216-17
  Allied occupation zones, 203, 204, 207, 208, 209, 213
  discharge money and certificates received, 203-17 *passim*
  transfer to British and French custody, 203, 206-207, 208, 209, 210, 211, 212, 213, 214, 215-17

Reul, Leonhard, 18-19, 33, 35, 105, 113, **113**, 131, 169, 216-17, 219, 227
Ribier Market, 193
Rinso soap flakes, 79
Rising, Sheldon, 223
Road to Morocco (film), 119
Rockwell, Capt., Almon F., 51, 184, 236n8
Rommel, Field Marshal Erwin, 4, 8, 18
Ronchi, Sgt. John, 94, 112
Ronner, Bertram, 203
Roosevelt, President Franklin D., 167, 244n64
Rosenbaum, Mickey, 111
Rosenberger, Hurbert, *174*
Rowan, Maj., 94
Ruben, 92
Ruehling, Elmar, 111
Ruh, Wilhelm, 187
Russia, 8, 10, 11, 12, 13, 14, 18, 19, 127
Russo-German Non-Aggression Treaty, 8
Ryan, Lt. John, 193

Sabaudia (ship), 235n10
Sacramento, California, 216
Saint-Germain-des-Vaux, France, 10
Samos (ship), 17
San Joaquin Agricultural Labor Bureau, 86, 200
Sands, Carl, 173-74, 194
sanitary inspections of POW camps, 171-72
Santa Maria, California, 86, 92, 109, 145, 161
Saticoy Lemon Association, 197
Schaefer, Erich, 144
Schaffrath, Herbert, 22-25, 38-39, 49, 76, **76**, 77, 101-2, 112, 128-29, 134, 139, 142, 161, 167, 171, 208-10, 220, 227
Schatz, Maj. George, 112
Schermbach, Joachim, 68
Schmucker, Alfred, 20, **21**, 22, 37-38, 46-49, 78-79, 95-97, **96**, 109-10, **122**, 124-25, 135, 161, 167-68, 203-4, 206, 220, 227
schnaps. *See under* German POWs
Schneider, Horst, 136, 137, **138**
Schnyder, Paul, 185
Schofield, Capt. Robert P., 102
Schröder, Heinz, 127
Schubrow, Walter, 18
Schünemann, Heinrich, 26-27, 36-37, 60-61, 80-81, **81**, 106, 131-32, 136, 140-41, 143, 211-12, 220-21, 227

Scofield, Capt. David, 186
Sea Partridge (ship), 217
Selters, Germany 28
Senegalese troops, 12
Sétif, Algeria, 22
Seven Sinners (film), 119
Shafter Press, 189
Shafter Procurement Association, 188
"Shine On Harvest Moon" (song), 124
Sidi bel Abbès, Algeria, 19
Sierra Vista Mobile Home Estates, 224
Sleeth, Lt. Flem W., 65
Smith, Capt. Floyd T., 64, **68**
Smith, Marion, 109
Smith, William A., 145
Souk Ahras, Algeria, 20
Southampton, England, 28, 42, 207
Southern Grape Growers Association, 183
Southern Pacific Railroad, 145
Special Projects Division (of the PMGO), 114, 120, 240n6
Stalin, Joseph, 11
Stalingrad, Russia, 19
Stallings, Spencer B., 179, 189-90, 190, **191**, 192
Stanfel, Capt. Leland F., 199
Statue of Liberty, 35, 36, 43, 211, 213
Ste. Mère-Église, France, 26, 27
Stellbrand, Horst, 101, 146, 149, 150, 153, 154, 155, 156, 157, 158, 159, 160, 161, 243n44, 244n55
Stender, Juergen, 144
Stevens, E. M., 145
"Stille Nacht, heilige Nacht" (song), 128
Stockton, California, 187, 213
Stockton Ordnance Depot, 198
Strait, Chaplain Chester U., 93
Straits of Gibraltar, 33
Strasburg, Germany, 14
Sudetenland, 15
Sullivan, Frank, 112
Swiss intermediaries (Legation), 66, 68, 71, 90, 141, 166

Tagus Ranch Company, 181
The New Guide, 52
Thielemann, Gustav, 1, **189**
Third Reich, 15, 33, 49, 121, 123
Thirty Seconds Over Tokyo (film), 119
Thome, Manfred, 203
Time magazine, 123, 124
Tobruk, Libya, 10, 13, 23
Tolmachevo, Russia, 14
Toul, France, 25
Trapani, Sicily, 22
Trier, Germany, 31

Tripoli, Libya, 9, 10, 13, 17
Trottier, Capt. Edmund J., 196
Truman, President Harry S., 169
Trust Fund Accounts for POWs:
   camp and personal accounts, 66, 84,
      85, 119, 121, 162, 163, 194, 203
Tulare Procurement Association, 178, 196
Tunis, Tunisia, 12, 14
Tunisia, 8, 9, 10, 12, 13, 14, 18, 19, 20,
   21, 22, 24. *See also* by city name
Turpin, Maj. David, 93
24th Agricultural District Association,
   224

U-boats, 33, 39, 42
Uden, Netherlands, 20
United Nations, 124
University of California, 121, 172
U.S. Department of Agriculture, 86, 178,
   181
U.S. Department of State, 133
U.S. Department of the Treasury, 85, 87
U.S. Department of War, 3, 4, 46, 64, 84,
   86, 87, 113-14, 119, 143-44, 163,
   164, 176, 179, 200, 201, 235n1
U.S. Federal Reformatory, Oklahoma, 90
U.S. Forest Service, 173, 194
U.S. Navy, 223, 239n31
Utrecht, Netherlands, 20

Valley Fever, 170
Vandenberg Air Force Base, California, 3
Velikiye Luki, Russia, 11-12, 234n7, 234n8

Velizh, Russia, 10, 12, 234n7
Virginia, 32, 33, 38, 39, 201, 208
Vitebsk, Russia, 10, 234n7
Volkswagen, 23
von der Heydte, Col. Friedrich August
   Freiherr, 27

Wagner, Karl, 120-21, 131
War Manpower Commission, 86, 201
Weber's Bread Co., 153
Wehrmacht. *See under* German military
Welschbillig, Germany, 29
Westbrook, Lt. Col. Robert B., 200
Western Costume Co., 241n27
Whitechurch, Maj., 219
Williams Victory (ship), 209
Wimber, Capt. Raymond, 64
Winchell, Walter, 164
Wojnowski, Maj. Arthur J., 64, **68**, 197
Wolfenbüttel, Germany, 20
Wolff, Lt. Harold W., 64, **69**, 103, 144
Wolff, Sgt. James, 111
Wolter, Helmut, 13-14, **14**, 39, 51-53,
   132, 135, 143, 212-13, 221, 227
Woronesch, Russia, 19

"You Are My Sunshine" (song), 124
Young Men's Christian Association
   (YMCA), War Prisoners Aid
   Committee, 61, 68, 71, 121, 125,
   133, 166

Zwilling, Christian, 203

About the Author

JEFFREY E. GEIGER is the retired chief civilian historian from Vandenberg Air Force Base, formerly Camp Cooke. He is the author of *Camp Cooke and Vandenberg Air Force Base, 1941-1966* and has published articles on historical topics in several magazines and newspapers.

www.ingramcontent.com/pod-product-compliance
Lightning Source LLC
Chambersburg PA
CBHW071701160426
43195CB00012B/1541